John Douglas S. Argyll

A Trip to the Tropics and Home Through America

John Douglas S. Argyll

A Trip to the Tropics and Home Through America

ISBN/EAN: 9783744754941

Printed in Europe, USA, Canada, Australia, Japan

Cover: Foto ©Andreas Hilbeck / pixelio.de

More available books at **www.hansebooks.com**

A TRIP TO THE TROPICS.

A TRIP
TO
THE TROPICS
AND
HOME THROUGH AMERICA.

DUTCH GAP CANAL AND GROUP OF SOLDIERS.

BY

THE MARQUIS OF LORNE.

LONDON:
HURST AND BLACKETT, PUBLISHERS,
SUCCESSORS TO HENRY COLBURN,
13, GREAT MARLBOROUGH STREET.
1867.

TO

MY FRIEND AND COMPANION

ARTHUR STRUTT,

THESE NOTES OF OUR JOURNEY

Are Affectionately Dedicated.

PREFACE.

These notes are extracts from letters written when I was travelling last year. I have hardly altered them, thinking they would, if I did so, lose whatever freshness they possess. They contain, of course, merely superficial views of the men, manners, and things that came under my notice; but as the countries they refer to have recently been the scenes of important events, I hope they may not be without some interest.

CONTENTS.

CHAPTER I.

Departure from Southampton—First Dinner at Sea—Terns in our Wake—German, French, and other Passengers—A Jamaica Planter's Opinion of Gordon—Indian Coolies—Revival Meetings in Jamaica—Ex-Emperor Soulouque and his Son-in-law—A Haytian's Account of Hayti—The Chiqua—Heavy Seas, but "no Danger"—Gulf-weed—Flying-fish—Underhill's Pamphlet—Quakers on Board—Beautiful Sunset—Distance by Land and Sea—Otan's Pamphlet "On Jamaica"—Barbadoes—Signs of Land—A Lawyer's Opinion on the Jamaica Question—St. Thomas's—The *Louisiana*—Polyglot Negroes—The Town, Fort, and Harbour—American Men-of-War—Santa Rosa's Residence—An Ice-house—Street Scenes in St. Thomas's—The Market—Visit to M. Rüsi's Collection of Natural Curiosities—Star-fish—Beautiful Spiny Spondylus—Intense Civility of the Blacks—Dark-coloured Pelican—On Board the *Tyne*—Intercolonial Boats—Port-au-Prince—Porto Rico—Opening of the Jamaica Commission

pp. 1—22

CHAPTER II.

Our First Night in Niggerdom—Haytian Functionaries—Native Soldiers—A Black Lady's Salutation—Negro Laziness—Fishing in the Lagoon—Hiring Horses and Mules—Port-au-Prince—Its Streets, Shops, and Houses—Sharks—English Methodist Chapel—Mr. Webbly—Character of the People—Squatting—Prosperity of Barbadoes—Triumphal Arch—Sleepy Negro Guide—A Treasure of a Man—Vaudou Religion—Story of Haytian Cannibalism—French Patois—Grande Rivière of Jacmel—Costume and Customs of the Negroes—Forest Scenery—Birds and Flowers—Returned Exile—The Gros Morne—Bay of Port-au-Prince—General Fauberg Petion—Plans for the Improvement of his Property thwarted—Manufacture of Sugar by Negroes—Conversation with an English Engineer—President Geffrard—Sahnave—Siege of the Cape—Interference of the *Bulldog*—Explosion of a Shell . . . . pp. 23—49

CHAPTER III.

Port-au-Prince—Scenery near the Town—Names of Streets—Inhabitants of the Town—The Military—Street Scenes—The Wharfs—The Market-place—Provisions—Pottery—Tirailleurs—Beautiful View—Haytian National Emblem—Motto adopted by the Blacks—Policy of the Government towards Strangers—Population and Trade—Town and Country Schools—Standing Army and Despotism—Sail among the Coral Islands—Our Boatman—Destructive Effect of an Armstrong Shell—Visit to our Consul—Refuge in Foreign Consulates—Troublesome *Protégés*—Taflia Fires in Port-au-Prince—Fenced Clearings—Rapid Growth in Hayti—Country Houses—Party at Dinner—Probable Fate of Hayti—English Niggers—Visit to the Presidential Palace—Interview with Geffrard—Relations of White and Black in the Negro Republic—Fishing Sharks—Geffrard's Opinion—Commerce of Hayti . . . . pp. 50—71

CHAPTER IV.

Jamaica in Sight—Morant Bay—The Court-House—The Palisades—Port Royal—On Board the *Duncan*—Model Community—Public Estimation of Gordon—The Wire "Cats"—Negro Evidence—The Coloured Class—American Buggies—Complaint as to the Administration of Justice—Burned Houses—Bath—A Survivor of the Massacre at Morant Bay—Rencounter with an Indignant Negro—Maroons on Duty—Hire's House—Hire's Defence, and Massacre of Inmates—State of Feeling among the Planters—The Anti-Buckra Movement—Escape of Mr. Sinclair and his Wife—An Obedient Idol—Folly of Negroes and Fears of the Planters—Scenery of Jamaica—Attack on Happy Grove—Dispute about a Mule—Our Footing with the Maroons—Their Manner of Fighting—Massacre and Burning by the Troops.—Account of Riots by a Coloured Schoolmaster—Merciless Conduct of Black Troops . . . . pp. 72—98

CHAPTER V.

Port Antonio—Negro Method of firing Houses—Prosperous Negroes near Port Antonio—Mr. Orgill's Opinion regarding the Cultivation of Sugar—Lovely Bays—Mr. Anderson, an old Scotch Gentleman—Complaints as to the Want of Labour—Negro Objection to Contracts—Co-operative System for the Manufacture of Sugar—Immorality and Education—Immigration—A Bastard Law—A Maroon Officer—Their Mode of Fighting—Captain M'Farlane—His Defence of the

Maroons—Dinner with the Maroons—A Sentiment received with Great Applause—Measures proposed for the Inauguration of a Better Order of Things—Reform of Elective Bodies—Of Vestries—Of the Present Magistracy—Appointment of Stipendiary Magistrates—Government System of Industrial Schools—An Education Tax—Fine Scenery—The Rio Grande—Forest-Trees—The Cotton-Tree—Undergrowth and Creepers in the Woods—Birds seen in Jamaica—Immense Butterfly—Botanic Garden at Bath—Court-House at Morant Bay—The Volunteers—The Massacre—Gordon's Grave—The Charge against him—Mr. Eyre—Martial Law—The late Governor's Policy—Site of Mr. Eyre's House, and View from it—Important Document—Evidence as to the Proceedings and Designs of the People—Illegal Drilling—Curious Document . . . . pp. 99—124

CHAPTER VI.

Flamstead—Cowardly Acts of Intimidation—Visit to Hill, the Naturalist—Sharks—The Political Prospects of Jamaica—Probable Disappointment of the Furious Supporters of the Ex-Governor—Substitution of English for Spanish Names of Places—The Road to Moreland—Mangrove Belts—Cultivation of Sugar Estates—The Cotton-Tree—From Moreland to St. Jago—Guinea Fowl—Ants—Want of Doctors—Humming-birds—Mandeville—Black Freeholders—A Negro's Necessaries and Burdens in Jamaica—A Negro Dodge—Attorneys for Estates—Laziness and Caprice of the Negroes—Stoppage of Wages—The Question between Overseers and Negroes—Domestic Servants—Price of Food—Position of the Black Freeholder—Precedence of Races—Abolition of the House of Assembly—Extravagant Application of Public Money—Neglect of Popular Education—Ignorance with respect to Contracts—Negro Interpretation of a Public Proclamation—Visit to a Large School—Congo Boys—Drunkenness among the Negroes—Jamaica as a Place for Emigrants—A Negro's Opinion of the Rioters . . . . pp. 125—151

CHAPTER VII.

Cuba—A Midshipman—Santiago de Cuba—Country in the Neighbourhood—Spanish Volante Carriage—Reckless Negro Postilion—Our Hotel—Strict Regulations—Adventure of a German in Hayti—The Theatre—The Church—The Service and the Preacher—Music in the Public Square—A Paradise for Smokers—A Volante Drive into the Country—Bound Blacks and Slaves—Conversation with an American Engineer—The "Fah Kee"—Feelings in the Torrid and Temperate Zones

—Swell in the Caribbean Sea—Our Captain—His Opinion regarding the *Trent* Business—Slavery in the South—Story of a Negro voluntarily returning to Bondage—Approach to New York—A Fog at Sea—Fort Lafayette—The Narrows—Brooklyn—View of New York—Steam Ferry-boat—General Aspect of the City—Broadway—Tramways—Barnum's Museum . . . . pp. 152—174

CHAPTER VIII.

Activity of the People—Question of the Fishery—The Civil Rights Bill—The Fenians—Reports circulated by the *New York Herald*—Fenianism among Waiters—Devotion of the Lower Irish to the Cause—The Roberts and O'Mahoney Sections—Civil Rights and Freedmen's Bureau Bill—Policy of the President—Trial of Davis—Visit to the *Dunderberg*—Construction of the Vessel—American Workmanship—Iron-clads sent round to the Pacific—Proposal of a Patriotic Member of Congress—Wounded Soldiers—Germans in New York—Excitement caused by the Arrival of a Pest-ship—American Railway Travelling—Appearance of the Passengers—Railway Literature—Raymond and the *Herald*—Extent of New York—The Rocks near the City—Small Towns and Wooden Houses—Boston—Made a Member of the Union Club—The Somerset—Longfellow's Bridge over the River Charles—Cambridge University—Our Cordial Reception by American Students—Boat Races on the River—The Powellian Club—Agassiz—Debate at the State House—View from the Balcony—The Massachusetts Regiment—Longfellow—A Lecture by Emerson . . pp. 175—196

CHAPTER IX.

A Ride to Winchester—Moveable Family Mansion—American Robin—Snapping Turtle—Amusement at the Fremont—A Fenian Waiter—The States and their Soldiers—State of the South—Visit to Lowell—Absorption of the Military—Peaceful Tendency of the Nation—Americanisms—A Yankee Steamer—Agreeable Recollections of Boston—Political Spirit and Sentiment—Return to New York—The Theatre—Negro Minstrels—Country beyond New York and Washington—Crossing Wide Rivers with the Train—Earthworks—View of the Capitol—The Streets of Washington—Public Buildings—Conversation with a Virginian Gentleman—Effect of the passing of the Civil Rights Bill—Hopes for the Future of America—Mr. Sumner—Military Commissions and the Trial of Davis—Mr. St. Leger Grenfell—Reconstruction of the Union—Policy of the Radicals—An American Gentleman's Opinion of Affairs in Mexico . . . . pp. 197—221

CHAPTER X.

White Labour in the South—Dying out of the Negroes—Would the South have armed the Slaves?—Confederate Forces at the End of the War—Davis's Flight from Richmond—The Capitol—Admission of Colorado into the Union—Committee of Reconstruction—Conduct of Business in the Senate—House of Representatives—Energy of the Speakers—Feeling in Congress against the President—Federal and State Authority—Southern Representatives—The Treasury—Ride into Virginia—National Monument—The Long Bridge—Vestiges of the War—General Lee's House—Interview with the President—The White House—Mortality among the Blacks in the South—Navy Yard—Monitors—French Occupation of Mexico—Visit to Mr. Seward—The Attack made on him last Year—Attack on Frederick Seward
pp. 222—243

CHAPTER XI.

Conversation with a Supporter of the President—A Freedmen's Village—White Labour in the South—Education of the People—Negro Enfranchisement—Feeling against the President—Politicians in Social Life—The Proposed Paris Exhibition—Indian Troubles—Grant's Respect for Lee—State Rights and the Union—General Grant on some of the Operations of the War—Sherman and Hood—Education of the Negroes—Cultivation of Land by the Blacks—Negro Village at Arlington—Good done by the Freedmen's Bureau—Intelligence of the Negroes—Gradual Disappearance of the Antipathy between White and Black—Military Courts—Report of the Reconstruction Committee—Journey to Richmond—Banks of the Potomac—Acquia Creek—Fredericksburg—Richmond—State of Feeling among the Inhabitants—State Sovereignty—White and Coloured—Communicativeness of the Negroes—Devotion to Kind Masters manifested by them . . . pp. 244—267

CHAPTER XII.

Situation of Richmond—The Capitol—Governor Pierpont—The Burnt District—The Tredegar Ironworks—The Two Prisons—Treatment of Prisoners of War—Sufferings of the Southern States—Loafing Negroes—Blacks in Mixed Uniform—Defences of Richmond—M'Clellan's Advance against Richmond—The Chickahominy—Agricultural Operations—Soldiers' Graves—Federal Cemetery—Antipathy of the South to the North—Galling Treatment of Federal Officers by Southern Ladies—View of Richmond from the James River—Butler's Lines—His Attempt to cut through the Dutch Gap—Farms on the James—City Point—Idle Negroes—Rail to Petersburg—Position of that Town—Murderous Contests in its Neighbourhood—Nothing to do with Yankees—Virginian Bitterness—The Natural Position of the African—Parallel between English and American Parties. . pp. 268—287

CHAPTER XIII.

Virginian Country Life—Birds of Virginia—Our Host—Conduct of his Sons in the War—Sufferings from the Presence of invading Armies—A Negro Traitor—One Generous Action of Butler's—Union as understood in the South—Objectionable Provision of the Civil Rights Bill—Farming Quarters, Clothing, and Nourishment of the Slaves—Admiration of England—Federal and Confederate Government—Names and Manners of the Darkies—Reverence for Age in the South—New York *Gamins*—A Go-ahead Youngster at the Theatre—A Freedman at Bermuda Hundred—Germans in Richmond—German Troops in the Federal Army—A Scotch Farmer—Charlotteville—Anniversary of "Stonewall" Jackson's Death—University of Virginia—A Virginian Secessionist and "Rebel"—Caution to the Radicals—A Better Time coming for South and West—Commemoration of General Jackson and the Conservative Dead—University Professors and Students in the Southern Army—Mr. Black's Schemes—Yankee Troops in the University—A Freedmen's School—Passengers in the Cars to Lynchburg—Campbell Court-House—Host and Hostess at the Inn—Talk with Niggers—Lynchburg to Staunton by Canal—Recruits for England in the South—Desertions from the Confederate Army—Administration of Justice by the Agent of the Bureau. . . . . . . pp. 288—318

CHAPTER XIV.

Lexington—Cadets of the Military College—Virginian Scenery—Natural Bridge—White and Coloured Men on Farms—Negroes eager to visit England—Education—Confederate Officers—Parties in the South and North—Injurious Effect of the Course pursued by the Radicals—Language of Thaddeus Stephens in the House of Representatives—Weakness of State Governments—Discomfort suffered by Ladies Travelling in America—Mode of serving up Dinner—A German Innkeeper—Remarkable Cave—Curious Bill—The Affairs of Virginia—Working of the Freedmen's Bureau—False Prognostications of the Southerners—Mixed Labour—Derision of Northern Fears—Baltimore—Enthusiasm excited by Confederate War Songs—Coloured Men in the Railway Cars—Action of the Civil Rights Bill—Decisions of the Judges respecting the State Courts—Niagara in a Mist—Night View of the Falls—Toronto—Sensible Irishmen—Kingston—Ottawa—Canadian Houses of Parliament—The Ottawa—Inconvenient Position of the new Canadian Capital—The Sawmills—The Fenian Invasion—Reports at Kingston—Skirmish at Fort Erie—Conduct of the American Government—American Sympathy with Fenianism.

pp. 319—355

A TRIP TO THE TROPICS:

NOTES FROM NEGRO LANDS.

CHAPTER I.

Departure from Southampton — First Dinner at Sea — Terns in our Wake—German, French, and other Passengers—A Jamaica Planter's Opinion of Gordon — Indian Coolies —Revival Meetings in Jamaica — Ex-Emperor Soulouque and his Son-in-law — A Haytian's Account of Hayti—The Chiqua—Heavy Seas, but "no Danger"—Gulf-Weed—Flying-Fish — Underhill's Pamphlet—Quakers on Board—Beautiful Sunset—Distance by Land and Sea—Otan's Pamphlet "On Jamaica"—Barbadoes—Signs of Land—A Lawyer's Opinion on the Jamaica Question—St. Thomas's—The *Louisiana*—Polyglot Negroes—The Town, Fort, and Harbour—American Men-of-War—Santa Rosa's Residence—An Ice-house—Street Scenes in St. Thomas's—The Market—Visit to M. Rüsi's Collection of Natural Curiosities—Star-Fish—Beautiful Spiny Spondylus—Intense Civility of the Blacks—Dark-coloured Pelican—On Board the *Tyne*—Intercolonial Boats—Port-au-Prince—Porto Rico—Opening of the Jamaica Commission.

WE left Southampton early in January, 1866, but it was not till the fifth day of our voyage that I was able to jot down a few notes respecting our progress, with by no means a calm sea to help one to sit

B

still or to write plainly. Even when sea-sickness, as I believed, was completely over, I did not feel quite so happy during our long *table d'hôte* as I ought to have been, and was sometimes much inclined to use bad language when a particularly distasteful dish was offered, or when an unusually long time intervened between the courses. The vessel in which we sailed was the *La Plata*, one of the best in this line, and our company, to judge from the number of officers' names we saw on the luggage as it was being hoisted in before we left Southampton waters, promised to be pleasant.

Our first dinner at sea began as we were steaming past the fort guarding the entrance to Southampton harbour. We fell to with great appetite, and remained comfortably at work for some time; but when near the Isle of Wight the rolling began, and there was a general exodus from the saloon, hardly any one appearing anxious to stay except some naval officers, who, feeling themselves as comfortable at sea as on land, kept their seats. I must confess I was also compelled to make my exit, though I did so very slowly, grinning as if nothing were the matter. Directly I was outside, however, I bolted like a rabbit to a porthole, and, in company with most of the passengers, went to bed as soon as we had seen the last lights of the English coast die out in the darkness. Of the thirty hours that followed the less said the better.

When I next went on deck I found only the officers of the watch there. A heavy wind was driving the spray in showers along the deck, and the vessel was pitching heavily over great dark rollers that dashed up against the bows in sheets of foam. That night our jib-boom was carried away, an event which made nervous people recall the similar accident that befell the *London* a few hours before she went down, some days ago, with nearly all hands, just about the place in which we then were.

The next day the sun came out, and though the pitching of the sea was as bad as ever, walking on deck was quite possible, and sometimes even pleasant. The great waves we had as yet seen in grey shade when they darted past our cabin porthole, darkening the little room for a moment, were now glittering hillocks of amethyst, that came rolling with a force that appeared irresistible against our advancing prow, before which they bowed as we steadily pursued our way through them, or dashed them back in showers of spray. One or two sharp-winged Terns kept following in our wake, moving along, with the strong wind under their wings, with hardly a flap, darting down to the water, or skimming past us with beautiful ease and power of flight.

We had an odd mixture of people on board—officers, some of whom were concerned in the suppression of the Jamaica riots; emissaries of the Anti-Slavery Society and of the Quakers, who were going out with the worst possible impression of the conduct of these officers; and lawyers sent to help the blacks—for there was a notion that the natives would not come forward to give evidence unless they were pressed to do so, or had legal assistance at their side.

There is also a German Yankee-looking gentleman, accompanied by about a dozen children, who walks about the covered decks below, trying to soothe their exasperating tempers, and to hush the horrid shrieks by which they disturb every one near them. The other day, when there was a practice drill for fire on board, and all the crew were pumping and manning the boats, and a good many passengers looking on, this German rushed up with a large plate, on which was a half-devoured chicken, and flew about with it from group to group, thrusting it into every one's face, and shouting, "Smell this; smell this; they would give rotten food to my children—to my children!"

You may imagine the expression with which most Englishmen on deck witnessed such a demonstration of paternal feeling.

There are a good many Spaniards among us on their way to Cuba, few of whom seem desirable acquaintances. The Frenchmen, of whom there are several aboard, seem to shake down into their places more slowly than the representatives of any other nation. Most of them have a chronic sickly look at sea. One of them was heard asking in a plaintive tone for "one very leetle piece of very meagre chicken," a *morceau* which I am afraid did him very little good, for it soon reappeared.

There are Jamaica planters going out to look after their estates. They express great surprise at the insurrection, and say they would as soon have expected one in Derbyshire. Some stories they tell of atrocities perpetrated by the blacks are very horrible. Of Gordon they have a very bad opinion. The officers speak confidently of the production of good evidence of the intended insurrection. The existence of papers that will astonish the friends of the negroes is mysteriously hinted at. The statement that the white women were to be distributed among the blacks is repeated with the most perfect conviction of its truth. Coolies are well spoken of as reliable workers in case of a black strike.

A Haytian on board, who was going back to his place near Port-au-Prince, told me that it was well known in August of last year that the so-called revival meetings taking place in the houses of Haytian exiles in Jamaica were gatherings of would-be insurgents. The son-in-law of the ex-Emperor Soulouque, named Villoumin, and his three sons, were also known to be chief instigators of the rebellious projects that had been hatching for some time. Soulouque and his son-in-law are now at St. Thomas's, and as Santa Anna also lives there, the place must be a museum of mummy potentates.

The account of the scenery of Hayti was so tempting that we thought we should very probably try to see something of it. Our informant said that travelling was perfectly safe, and advised us to stay a short time in the island. His description of its peasantry is very favourable. Hospitality is universal, and President Geffrard is very friendly to strangers. There is a Cuban merchant whose account of the slaves in the interior of his island is bad enough. "Many planters live only in Havana, and never look after their estates, or concern themselves about the welfare of their people, who are entirely neglected. The quarters of the poor blacks are allowed to go half to ruin, and their children suffer much from the attacks of the chiqua, a little insect that eats into the flesh under the nails, causing their hands and feet to swell, and which cannot be got out."

Sunday was the first day on which we really felt that we had left the Northern seas behind us. The sun was hot on deck, and the ladies and children, all looking pale and unwell, were able for the first time to stay comfortably on the quarter-deck. Two days ago the sea was very heavy; and the night before last hardly anybody slept, the ship rolling in such a way that every timber creaked so loudly and incessantly that it was impossible to enjoy a moment's rest. About two in the morning some heavy seas broke on deck, carrying away one or two spars and the ladder. Some of the water found its way downstairs, and the ladies, discovering a little of it in their berths, jumped out and rushed into the passage, all cackling in shrill tones, and by declarations that it was all right, and that they were not the least afraid, trying to reassure each other. With every lurch there was a great clatter of plates, forms, and tables overhead, accompanied by the constant chorus of agonized females, who were for ever reiterating that they were not the least afraid.

Another lurch, and an officer comes down the stairs.

"Oh, sir, what is the matter?" exclaim the ladies.

"Oh, nothing at all—glass is rising, and wind going down."

"Oh! there's no danger?" chimes in the chorus, with a tone of interrogation.

"No danger whatever, ma'am."

Some hereupon giggle hysterically, while one again asks whether there is really no danger, and says she never can believe officers, because they never will speak the truth.

Splash comes a sea over the deck, and a little cataract flows down the stairs, followed by general shrieks, in the midst of which the ladies were assured by the stewardess that she had never seen passengers behave so well. Meanwhile stewards came to swab up the counters, and from their conversation we learned that they agreed in thinking it was "d—d weather." One of them said—

"Dear me! if we go down now, what will become of poor Poy?"

We wondered why Poy should be particularly

pitied, and, on inquiry, found that, as he was engaged at the time in putting on shoes and stockings, he could not be considered, in case of such a catastrophe, quite so ready to meet it as the rest of his brethren on board.

To-day we had service in the cabin. A little beardless Missionary read the prayers in a voice that could scarcely be heard three feet off. I have been standing at the bow, watching the wonderfully blue sea, and the lumps of yellow gulf-weed floating past, the homes of little crabs of so exactly the same colour as the weed, that they are not distinctly visible, except when they leave their resting-place for a moment, at the approach of the vessel, to sidle quickly across the intervening water to another swimming islet. Flying-fish, too, now made their appearance. I had no idea that their flight was such a prolonged affair as it is. One I saw must have flown fifty or sixty yards. Their flight is heavy, the little animals' tails, as they skim along, sometimes touching the tops of the waves. When in the air they appear to one looking from above like heavy dragon-flies.

I have been reading Underhill's West Indian book, and his last pamphlet. It is curious how flatly planters and missionaries contradict each other. Underhill's book is full of accounts respecting the irregular payments on plantations to labourers, statements which M. flatly denies, at least with regard to such plantations as he knows, and they are many. He declares that whenever labour is forthcoming, it is always punctually paid for. I have finished an American account of Toussaint l'Ouverture—badly written, but very complete.

If all went well, the captain expected to sight Sombrero, the outermost of the Virgin Islands, on Friday morning; and then St. Thomas's is only eighty miles further on. The hope of seeing land again was a great relief, as we had seen none since leaving England. The evening we passed the Azores was hazy, and we could only tell that Terceira was not far off by the unusually thick bank of cloud that rested on the horizon where the island lay. One of the group, named Pico, a high mountain, we passed when night had already fallen. The weather was on the whole delicious, and so hot that we had an awning on the deck. The sea was perfectly calm, only rippled by a breeze strong enough to make it glitter in the bright sun-light, while large shoals of porpoises were seen leaping in our wake.

After dinner everybody usually came on the

quarter-deck to see the sunset, which sometimes was very fine; the west being lit up with a fiery copper, while great bands of dark cloud with gold-tipped edges hung across the sky. The twilight is very short, but the moon, at this time nearly full, cast a pillar of silver light in the water that reminded me of Dunrobin. All on board, about a hundred and fifty people, were walking about, as there was to be a dance under the awning, to the music of a fiddle, concertina, and a pair of castanets and cymbals.

On January 30th we finished another long run, this time of two hundred and ninety-two miles, in spite of a slight head wind; and another of equal length would bring us to the tropics. The thermometer stood at 75°, and the sun was very powerful when it showed itself, which was not always, as heavy clouds were drifting over us. The warm weather is the only thing that tells that England is far away. A land journey gives a great idea of distance, from the number of objects passed *en route*. At sea one has few opportunities of realizing by such means the distance traversed. On this route we have hardly met any ships, only three having as yet been seen.

I read on board one of the plentiful crop of pamphlets that have sprouted on the Jamaica question. This was one by Mr. ——, who had lived thirty years in the island, and ought to know something about it. They say he is crotchety. His main point is the advocacy of leases for sugar or other estates, and he holds that labour should be contracted for by the year. The representatives of the plantocracy on board said they would have no objection to the annual contracts for labour, but they ask how such an engagement can be entered into. The negro thinks anything binding him to work for a longer time than he chooses a species of slavery, and will not consent to be bound by any such contract, except for wages which it would be ruinous to give. As to leases, the planters say, "There are not capitalists in the island, and the people who would be willing to be lessees would raise a handsome sum from the land, and then skedaddle. America is too near to trust lessees. Leases have in a few cases been tried, but have come generally to grief, though in some places negroes have taken small properties on lease, and are paying regular fixed rents. These farms, however, are only for coffee; sugar-growing would require capital, which they have not got. But things may get better, now that the Legislative Chambers have been replaced by a Council." In the opinion of the planters, an "enlightened despotism" is what is wanted in Jamaica. They say, "All we want is to be left alone, with life and property secured." What one hears of the prosperous islands makes one wish to visit them. The accounts of Barbadoes especially were refreshing, after the lamentations that come from the mouths of Jamaicans.

When we got fairly into the tropics, Panama hats and white waistcoats, trousers and coats, came into requisition. Only a fortnight after we left England, how great was the change from the cold and drizzling rain, and the grey, dull, winter seas of the Channel! I was never tired of watching the wonderful blue of the water, in colour like that of the Rhone.

Flying-fish continued to be observed in great numbers, skimming over the waves, scared by the approach of our great black hull. None, however, were caught, or flew on board. They say their flesh is like herring, but not so rich. As we came near to the termination of our voyage, the luggage was taken out of the hold, and we began packing our carpet-bag for our Hayti travels. Our plan was to land at Jacmel, and ride over the mountains, a distance of eighty miles, to Port-au-Prince. Mr. S. was to go with us. We had an opportunity of sending letters to England by the boat by which we came, which left St. Thomas's about a fortnight after, on her return voyage.

The first sign of land we saw was a dark bird, which flew round and round the ship one afternoon. The only other living thing that showed itself was a large fish, nine or ten feet in length, which we saw a few hundred yards astern, leaping continually out of the water, its sides gleaming in the sun. The men thought it was a Thresher.

We expected to see the island of Sombrero on the 1st of February, about twelve at night, and to be at St. Thomas's at eight or nine the following morning. The Quakers' friend whom we had on board I found to be a lawyer, going out on his own hook to collect evidence about Eyre's administration, and the causes of negro discontent. In his opinion the island legislation had been abominable, and the Colonial Office was equally responsible with the governor if it allowed bills oppressive to the negroes to become law after passing the Colonial Legislature. The main points that seemed to require explanation were the large taxes imposed on single beasts of burden kept by small freeholders, while planters' stock was very

cheaply rated, and the enormous sum of 45,000*l.*
devoted to Church-of-England purposes, while only a
very small proportion of the population, and that the
richest, belonged to her communion.

We safely anchored at St. Thomas's on February 2nd,
the ship lying motionless in the little land-locked
harbour. The long-continued beat of the engines
stopped for the first time since leaving Southampton.
I had stayed upon deck the previous night for the first
glimpse of Sombrero. Great rippled rivers of cloud
hung over our heads, and the horizon was sharp and
clear. "There's the island," somebody said; and one
could just make out a dim, blue, low ledge, which was
my first sight of the New World. I tumbled down
to my berth, and, on ascending next morning, found
we were passing along through a group of small
islands. In the distance was Santa Cruz, and nearer
to us St. Thomas's. Every spy-glass was directed to
a large steamer, the chief object of observation, which
was running into the harbour ahead of us. She
turned out to be the *Louisiana*, a French steamer,
that started two days before us. She and we steamed
in abreast, and cast anchors almost at the same time.
We got slowly warped alongside of two other

steamers—one going to Jamaica, the other to Trinidad—to transfer the luggage and passengers.

After breakfast we all went on shore, although the place did not look very inviting. Some moderately high hills, covered with short scrubby trees, send down their spurs to the harbour, in which there was a great number of vessels, chiefly belonging to the company that owned our steamer. The little town is a thickly-built collection of small Dutch houses, looking very neat and clean from a distance, and extending some way up the hill buttresses. On a little bit of a fort, a few hundred yards from us, floated the Dannebrog. We were besieged by numbers of small boats, filled with varnished-looking negroes in large straw hats, jabbering to every passenger they saw in Danish, German, English, Spanish, and French—all spoken à la Nigger.

St. Thomas's harbour, which used to be considered a very deadly place, is now much more healthy, owing to a cut they have made through one of its arms to the sea on the other side, by which much of the pestilential garbage is led away, and got rid of.

We were told our new boat did not start till four,

and after arranging for the transference of luggage, we scrambled into one of the negroes' boats, and were rowed ashore. Our two negroes pointed out to us the different ships—" Da, massa, dem's two Yankee menof-wa'a"—and we rowed across their bows. One was a nice screw vessel, the other a clumsy-looking paddle, with a beam engine on deck, and an exposed rudder, a specimen of the class of indifferent hulks got ready in great haste during the war. Under an awning stretched on the paddle-boxes paced a Federal marine, rifle in hand. The uniform looked well: white trousers and blue tunic, with a belt and a *képi*. Next to these lay a Spanish steamer, with the red and goldbarred flag flaunting at the peak.

"Where does Santa Anna live?"

"Da, massa; dat's him in de large red house, round the corner," pointing to a red ochre-coloured house, on the top of one of the little clumps of Dutch buildings.

Soulouque was gone, but, for a wonder, of his own accord, to Curaçoa, with his daughter, the Princess Olive.

We landed at a little brick-built pier, and walked to the post-office through a crowd of cotton-clad negroes, who looked intensely lazy, and chattered unceasingly. The heat was so great that we put up our umbrellas, and felt as if we should like to lie down in the dust, and eat lollipops like the negroes.

The ice-house was the first attraction. We sat for some time looking at the strange scene before us. A small boy, with a guitar, was singing Italian songs, with a refrain of "Garibaldi e Libertà!" A number of small darkies crowded the door, looking at us new-comers. The ice-shop opened into the one long street of the town that runs along the shore. The houses on each side were generally two-storied, and always tinted, which gives them rather a neat look. The dusty road was full of people, nearly all blacks, or at least coloured, most of them carrying a bundle of sugar-canes, and with a piece of one sticking out from between their thick lips. The walk of the women is wonderfully upright, from always carrying everything on their heads. Several had nothing but a small saucer; but whatever it is, small cup or big package, it is carried at the top. The hands dangle loosely, or swing, breast high, backwards and forwards. The stores seem to be kept chiefly by men of colour, and occupy the whole of the lower part of the house, opening with high doors to the street. We went to the market, but there was not much to be seen there. It was a small square, planted round with trees, under which old negresses squatted, with a collection of oranges, bananas, cocoa-nuts, and yams, which look like enormous long black potatoes, before them.

After purchasing light coats, and white stuff to put round our hats, we went with Mr. M. to see M. Rüsi, a Dane, who has a beautiful collection of the natural history of the island. Some of the star-fish of the place were curious, delicate, and long in the arm. Several had bodies not bigger than two pins' heads, but with thread-like arms, an inch or two in length. There was one beautiful spiny spondylus, that would have brought a large price in the London market, and a fine collection of land shells. Several of the shells M. Rüsi had found recently, and one he has not yet described. Considering that the thermometer was 84° in the shade, the trouble he took to show us everything was wonderful.

The intense civility of the blacks to each other is amusing.

"How are you to-day, madame?"

"Quite well dis morning, thank you, sar."

This was the morning greeting between a lady with nothing on but some blue gauze and a scarlet handkerchief, and a shoeless fellow with a battered straw hat about two yards round.

As we rowed back to our ship, a dark-coloured Pelican flew over our heads—a hideous bird, not the least like its Asiatic cousin, except in form. Left at five in the evening, not badly pleased with St. Thomas's, probably because we had heard it painted much blacker than it really is, and because we enjoyed on it our first stroll on shore after the long knocking about on the Atlantic.

Next day we found ourselves on board the *Tyne*, at sea, between Porto Rico and St. Domingo. We had on board one or two of the officers of the *La Plata*, which did not leave the West Indies to return to Southampton for another fortnight. The Steam Packet Company has hardly officers enough for all its vessels, and has to shift them about from one to another.

"Well, Doctor, you and I are in for a long stay, and for one of the Intercolonials," I heard a young officer say, with a sigh, and an attempt to look bright which was a failure.

The Intercolonial boats ply only between the islands, and their officers have, of course, more chance of catching the "Yellow Jack" than those on the other routes. These ships are now, however, worked almost entirely by black men, the officers only being white.

We heard that all was pretty quiet at present at Hayti. The insurgent Salnave was still at a small town in the Spanish part of the island, where he was taken by an American man-of-war, after being forced to leave the Cape, and he was now reported to be raising troops for another attempt to get it back. The island is shaped like a lobster's claw. The main part is Spanish; the two pincers and a strip of the rest are French. Our ride took us across the lower pincer.

On the 4th we sailed along in sight of the shore of Porto Rico, a long mountainous land, but too distant from us to see much of it, except with powerful glasses. Two beautiful birds, called Boatswains, which looked like a species of Tern, white in the body, with some black in the wing, followed us all day.

We had news of the opening of the Jamaica Commission, and heard reporters were to be present. A Jamaica letter says: "I always said we should go from King Log to King Stork; and, as Sir Henry is come, I suppose I may consider myself a prophet."

CHAPTER II.

Our First Night in Niggerdom—Haytian Functionaries—Native Soldiers—A Black Lady's Salutation—Negro Laziness—Fishing in the Lagoon—Hiring Horses and Mules—Port-au-Prince—Its Streets, Shops and Houses—Sharks—English Methodist Chapel—Mr. Webbly—Character of the People—Squatting—Prosperity of Barbadoes—Triumphal Arch—Sleepy Negro Guide—A Treasure of a Man—Vaudou Religion—Story of Haytian Cannibalism—French Patois—Grande Rivière of Jacmel—Costume and Customs of the Negroes—Forest Scenery—Birds and Flowers—Returned Exile—The Gros Morne—Bay of Port-au-Prince—General Fauberg Petion—Plans for the Improvement of his Property thwarted—Manufacture of Sugar by Negroes—Conversation with an English Engineer—President Geffrard—Salnave—Siege of the Cape—Interference of the *Bulldog*—Explosion of a Shell.

WE arrived in Hayti on the 5th February, and spent our first night in Niggerdom very comfortably, in spite of the prophecies of our friends in the steamer. One of them asked if we had insured our lives; a second, how many revolvers there were among our party; another hoped satirically that we should enjoy Jacmel; and Captain C. gave a solemn promise that, in case we were taken by bandits or imprisoned by the authorities, he would come with the *Wolverine* to set us free. It is curious how people imagine all sorts of horrors about a place, simply because they know nothing of it, and it is out of the beaten track.

We did not get into the offing till about eleven o'clock at night—an inconvenient hour, as all the town had gone to bed. We had been in sight of the coast since two P.M., and kept steaming along, looking out for the lighthouse. At one turn we thought we saw it, but the light was only from a vessel. It turned out that the people on shore had, as usual, not taken the trouble to show a light at all. We went on till within about a mile from the shore, sending up a rocket and firing a gun. The mail agent very kindly offered to take some of our party ashore in his boat, the first which was to be had. The swell made a good deal of surf on the shore, and there was only an indifferent jetty to land at. As the waves swung us up near to the tumble-down timbers, each man by turns scrambled on to them, and the mail bags were flung after us.

We walked down a deserted street to the post-office, a wooden building, like all others in the town, roofed with shingle, and having a verandah and raised rough-tile flooring. We were directed to an hotel with three rooms, pretty large, with wooden floor, walls, and ceiling. Every room had large open windows, through which came the shrill, monotonous chirp of the cicada. Our luggage could not be got the previous night, having been confiscated by the douanier as soon as we landed. Even coats and umbrellas had to remain. Almost at daybreak the douanier came to look at our passports. He was very civil, talked very good French, made very good bows, and wore a very good French-made coat, with brass buttons, and laurel sprigs in gold on the collar—a much better equipped man than other Haytian functionaries we saw this morning and yesterday evening.

Upon landing, we were stopped by two ragamuffin negroes, with bad wide-awakes, and trousers that came down no further than the calves of their legs. Though they wore no uniform, these were native soldiers. Each had an old musket, which he rested against the ground, holding it slantindicularly, so that the bayonets of the two formidable weapons crossed. They waited till we came close up to them, when each sprang to a rigid attitude of attention, and let us pass.

The douanier has been about our house ever since we entered. We gave him a glass of sherry, which put him into such good-humour, that he condescended to tell a freckled German clerk in the verandah "what beasts his countrymen were, and how they talked from the bottom of their stomachs!"

Doors and windows being always wide open, many visitors, chiefly Hayti gentlemen with very black faces and very white waistcoats, walked freely in and out. Just now a black lady came in with a triumphant stride, her chin in the air and arms akimbo, and regarded me kindly for several minutes as I sat writing. I remained still, not taking any notice of her till I was startled by a change in her attitude, which drew my attention to her. She had assumed a magnificent pose. Her breast thrown out, her arm extended, and her shiny face glowing with satisfaction, she said, "You is Englis; I know you is. Me said last night, when you was in Massa Tansen's store, you was Englis. They said you was French, but you is Englis! Ha!" With which climax she marched out with a stride no less stately than that which had given so much dignity to her entrance.

Though we were to start in a few hours for Port-au-Prince, there was time, before our departure, for a hot walk through part of the town and down to the sea. We visited an old black merchant, who was very civil. The space in front of his house was piled with logwood, for which he said he got 2*l.* a ton. This wood and coffee are the only products that are much exported. Sugar is hardly cultivated at all, except for home use. Whether it is that its cultivation is associated in the minds of the people with old slavery times, or whether it be for no other reason than want of energy, I do not know; but a more favourable climate or soil for sugar plantations it is not possible to find, even in Cuba. The truth is that there is no work done here. People talk of going to work, and dawdle, and smoke a few cigars, and that is nearly all their *travail* comes to. Of course there are exceptions, but laziness is the rule.

The wooden houses of the town are topped in all directions with the great tufted heads of the cocoa-palm, the green fruit hanging in enormous masses at the top of the long thin stem. The walk to the shore, only a short distance, was agreeable enough. The ground was covered with thick vegetation. Low acacia plants and numberless short tropical shrubs formed a thick undergrowth, while the palm stems rose in numbers above, waving their green bayonet-fringed branches in the sea breeze; and the great almond tree, with its deep green leaves, gave a delicious shade. Numbers of birds—one of them called

the Mocking-bird, though it was not the true one—
and small insect-eaters were flitting from branch to
branch. Every stick and leaf was new to me, and the
variety and quantity of animal life seemed wonderful.
Lizards were darting about under foot in every direction. Large butterflies were flapping their bright red
and gold and black-barred wings on every flower; and
in one place, poised in the air at the mouth of a large
yellow cactus blossom, I saw a Humming-bird. It
was one of the larger sort—black, with dark green
breast.

A little further on was a fisherman throwing a cast
net into the shallow lagoon waters, under a grove of
palm. Nothing but very small fish came up in the
net. One like a dace was the most common, but
there were many large craw-fish, which, he said, were
very good *pour les malades.*

We had dinner *en famille* with our young host,
Mr. F——, who, if not a white, was very near being
one, and we were shortly afterwards to start for a long
ride.

What a people this is! Such energy in gesticula-
tion, in talking, and in laughing, and how little in
acting! We expected to get away from Jacmel at
four in the afternoon of the 5th at latest. Horses,

we were told, it was difficult to get. It was the season that they were out on the mountains, and not many were left in the town; but we were promised enough for our party, especially as the two T.'s had resolved to remain another day, and to come on after. Three of us found horses easily, but there were violent disputes as to where mules were to be procured. The gesticulations made by the blacks in determining the price we were to pay for the mules and horses, when got, were perfectly frantic. One would have thought they were going to tear each other to pieces. They loafed about the verandah of our little inn, and talked till tired, when they went and slept at the back of the house.

In about four hours after the time we were to have started, all the necessary beasts—three horses and three mules—were actually collected in the yard. One of the horses was Mr. S.'s own, a bony white; the other two were sturdy, ill-fed ponies. But although horses were ready, there were no saddles, and it was late at night before they were procured. Then all was dark, and we were told we must wait till the rising of the moon. F—— asked us meanwhile to take a walk and see some of the town with him. To pass the time, therefore, we made a long round, stumbling over the ill-paved streets, the most wretched thoroughfares I ever saw, in which there was no attempt at levelling. The French, at the beginning of the century, left the whole place tolerably well paved. Nothing has been done since, and, of course, most of the stones have disappeared. The wonder is that any are left still.

Nothing has been done to light the town, even with oil-lamps. The only light to be had on a cloudy night comes from the open doors of the wooden houses. These looked comfortable enough; and the little shops seemed generally neatly kept. No glass was to be seen, for even one pane would occasion a sensation of heat and closeness in this climate. The only window covering is the folding wooden shutter, which is rarely closed. Every shanty looks thirsty for air; and fortunately, in these islands, there is generally a pleasant land or sea breeze, without which one would stifle. The least walking makes one long for a bath; and the long surf rolling on the beach in the clear moonlight looks so deliciously tempting, that one would at once plunge in were it not for the sharks, of which, however, the negroes say one need not be much afraid except in deep water. Even then they do not rise to gulp you

down, unless they happen to be particularly hungry.
They would rather take a snap at something that
does not move and splash, as they are horrible
cowards. A man told me the other day, that having
waded out some way along a coral reef, with a
black servant behind him, to fish, he had got on a
jutting piece of coral, and was busy fishing, when
he saw three large sharks near him, watching him
intently, their heads all turned towards him, and
their tails gently moving to keep themselves in position.
As they were between him and the shore, there was
no avoiding them. He took the gaff the negro carried,
and began at once to retreat; the sharks, as they got
into deeper water, approaching uncomfortably close.
As he waded back with his servant in dreadful alarm,
the negro suddenly missed his footing, and fell with a
splash into the deep water—a calamity by which his
companion had no doubt the sharks would know how
to profit; but what was his astonishment when
he discovered that they had been so alarmed by
the noise that they had considered it prudent to
skedaddle!

F—— spoke badly of the Roman Catholic priests,
asserting that they did nothing, or very little, to stem
the enormous amount of immorality in the place, and

that several of them were as bad as any of the people. The English Methodists' chapel, and the house of Mr. Webbly, the minister, were pointed out to us, the house with verandah above, and the chapel below. The congregation only numbered about a hundred, although Mr. Webbly has been twenty years in the place. He speaks enthusiastically of the capabilities of the blacks.

The old merchant we saw to-day was a fair specimen of good ability and moderate energy; but such examples of the capacity of the negro make their general inferiority only more deplorable. Here the race has had full scope, assisted by the men of colour, to make a respectable community. They have had a great deal in their favour. The French left tolerable roads, and taught them the proper method of making the most of their land, by availing themselves of the best means of cultivation. It is true they also left their demoralization; but victory over their former masters ought to have inspired them with a self-respect which would have raised them above the childish vanity which is now their most marked characteristic. They imitate the white man's dress and ape his manners with great satisfaction to themselves; but even in imitation they are destitute of the power of continuous application. Now that the lash is no longer to be seen, they give themselves up to enjoyment. Poverty is unknown ; but, except with a few, there is no ambition to push their way. If there was only a little more white blood in the island, one might hope for an energetic race of half-breeds, but there is no hope of such a desirable consummation. The black population is infinitely the largest ; and few in number as the whites are, in all probability they will be still fewer in future ; and as the possessors of white blood disappear, it is to be feared that all trace of white spirit will also depart from the island.

Throughout the West Indies the prosperity of the country has, till within the last few years, when immigration has somewhat altered matters, been in proportion to the amount of land the negro population has been able to secure for squatting. A great amount of squatting is sure to involve a great want of labour. Barbadoes has had very little land to spare for the negroes to occupy ; and every square foot of that island is under cultivation. The price of land is enormous, the labour market is full, and the island thrives amazingly. Many of its people emigrate, chiefly to Trinidad and Demerara ; and some find employment as seamen in steamers, in which they work well, and are well paid. In Hayti land is easily got, and the people will only work for a very high profit in any business.

In the immediate neighbourhood of towns there is a good deal of rough cultivation, and for some time after riding out of Jacmel we passed between rough clearings in the woods where coffee and bananas were growing. By law every owner must keep his property fenced about, or, in course of time, it is claimed as common. Rude palings of bamboo are, therefore, kept up. The end of the town is marked by a triumphal arch, with a small flagstaff on the top. This magnificent erection is ten feet high, and would take an English carpenter about two hours to put up. There is an inscription on it, and close by a Haytian soldier sleeps at his post beside a charcoal fire.

For some time the road we took was so darkened by trees that we could not see much of the country we were passing. We were an odd procession. First came a little mule, heavily laden on each side with luggage, on the top of which snoozed an enormous negro, who was to act as our guide. He was one of those who had been most furious in gesticulating all day, and was so tired, that unless we had knocked him up, and almost pulled the ugly moustached animal out of bed, we should not have started till morning had dawned. This original wore an enormous brown wide-awake, a light cotton jacket, all torn, in which there was a hole that showed a great bronze bit of his shoulder, and the usual short white cotton trousers. He was always asleep, now leaning on one side, then on the other, of the patient little animal, which proceeded with a steady pace, as if unconscious of the fact that it was carrying a weight nearly equal to its own. We had to shout, and shake him at least a dozen times on the road, when he would stretch himself, repeat what was said to him in a lazy drawl, give some blows and bad language to the mule, and relapse into sleep again.

After him came another mule, fortunate in having nothing but heavy baggage to carry. This little beast was a capital guide, always knowing the way, and taking it quite independently of the sleeping negro and less intelligent beast in front. He was followed by a third mule, and by a black—one of three brothers in Mr. S.'s employment—a perfect treasure of a man, very quiet and steady, acting both as that gentleman's gardener at his villa, and as his travelling servant, and always ready and willing to do anything required.

A story of Haytian cannibalism that appeared in English newspapers some time ago, it may be remembered, caused some sensation. A child, the son of a brother of this man, was the victim. The mother of the boy belonged to a religion which it is supposed is of African origin, and is here called the Vaudou. Little is known of its mysterious ceremonies and observances, but it seems to be the worship of a serpent. The subject is one on which it is scarcely prudent to speak aloud in this country, as, though the religion is prohibited by Government, many of the people are supposed to belong to it, who would certainly resent any remarks depreciatory of their faith. Geffrard has done all he can to put it down; and all who were concerned in the eating of this child were shot at Port-au-Prince.

It is difficult to understand the French patois spoken here. They clip and round off their words in a very odd way. Instead of saying "*jusqu'il fait jour,*" they say "*jouk li fait.*" Instead of saying "*droit,*" they say "*drcnat net,*" for straight on.

Half an hour's walk brought us to the banks of the Grande Rivière of Jacmel. The bed of the torrent is fully two hundred yards wide, a little wilderness of rolled white stones, through one strip of which the river, shallow at this time of the year, flowed as if ashamed of the devastation it had caused during the rainy season. At that time the streams come down in furious torrents, sweeping over and covering with gravel everything in their way. Our course for the first few hours led up this river bed, and we crossed it more than a hundred times. The banks and country far and near were covered with forest. At first the hills were far off, but as we rode up they closed more and more upon us. It was too dark to see either them or the foliage of the trees very distinctly; but as we rode on, now crossing the white river bed, and then plunging for a time into the gloom of the bordering forests, we came upon scenes of wonderful beauty. The river, shut in by steep banks that rose precipitately on each side, was overshadowed by gigantic vegetation, and crept along, now in moonlight, now in shadow,— now forming delicious pools deep shaded by overhanging boughs, now again winding round the great limestone rocks that it had hollowed into a thousand fantastic shapes. The light, feathery foliage, so different from the solid clothing of English timber, hung down from the drooping trees. Here and there the straight stem of a tall palm gleamed in sharp relief, or the huge black mass of the great almond or bread-fruit towered like an old castle high above the path. To me it was like a scene of enchantment, and I was almost sorry when, by the pearly grey that gradually succeeded the darkness, we knew that the sun would soon rise and disperse the gloom that rendered these novel objects so fantastic in our eyes. Before it was quite light, we passed a tall rock, on the face of which have been observed traces of curious ancient carvings, supposed to have been executed by the aboriginal Indians. We could, however, see nothing except the sharply-defined horizontal strata.

Our guides here stopped suddenly without condescending to tell us why. On inquiry, however, we found it was to give themselves and us, if we liked, some coffee, which they got ready in a wicker hovel where they had lighted a fire. We sat for some time sipping it with the negroes, who were immensely jolly, laughing at anything and everything. One man, who took my long black gaiters for Wellington boots, called me "Grosses Bottes," thus creating roars of laughter. These men are, however, really very civil in manner. Every countryman whom we passed bowed a polite French bow, and wished us *bon jour*. I think courtesy sits well upon them, and that we shall miss it among the Jamaica negroes. How any one can talk as if this country were unsafe for travellers I cannot imagine. Provided the stranger is civil to those about him, everybody is civil to him, and a request for a cigar is the only form of begging that is met with. They dress quite in the style of the French labourer. The blouse seems very common, though it is often discarded for a white tunic. The large straw hat is, however, peculiar.

By the time our coffee was done the sun was up, and the full glory of the landscape was revealed. No word-painting can describe the charm of the scene, but its great peculiarity was the universality of the luxuriant tree-growth with which, from summit to base, the mountains were covered. Compared with English woods, in which every branch would be waving in the wind, the stillness here was remarkable, every spray being motionless.

We rode on, always near the river, which now wound along through deep glens. The rocks were covered with magnificent aloes, whose long stems bore round yellow blossoms. The red flower of the arrowroot was almost the only one I knew, except the convolvulus that covered a great many of the low shrubs. Orange-trees were growing everywhere, their fruit often covering the ground beneath them. The wild orange is so sour that one cannot eat it with any satisfaction. The absence of large ferns struck me. There were several small sorts, but nothing that could compare with our own bracken. The trees were covered with parasitical plants—plants that sometimes grew well alone. The choking fig, for instance, grew straight and tall, but it was more common to see it clasped to an acacia, or any other rough-barked tree. The smooth-stemmed cocoa scarcely seems capable of supporting these parasites. The height of the bamboo was, in some cases, immense. They rose together in clumps, each stem after a time bending outwards, and looking like a gigantic ostrich plume. On branches above the stream were great grey Kingfishers, with white faces, sitting watching the water, occasionally darting down like lightning, to rise again with a small fish in their beak. At one place there was a curious little brown Heron, and further on some lovely insectivorous birds, among which the "green robin" (the *Todus viridis*) was common.

The ascent of the hills was steep, but we still rode on through the tangled woods. A Haytian gentleman who had before passed us, and who had been a passenger from St. Thomas's, here joined us. He was

an exile whose pardon had just been procured from
the President. When we stopped to rest our horses
and eat some bread, the Haytian gentleman sat down
and ate some pills. Numbers of mules laden with
coffee bags and attended by a few men passed on their
way down to Jacmel.

As we got higher up we had extensive views of the
country through which we had passed. We were now
on volcanic rock-trap, alternated with what looked
like disintegrated lava, which, when washed down, as
it was by the rain, in some places formed a rich soil.
The high summits of the hills seemed to be all composed
of this material. The sharp gullies that swept
down to the lower glens were probably formed by the
rain washing the lighter lava down. Sharp-ridged
spurs were left between them, and all was covered
with forest.

We stopped at the top of the first hill, beneath the
shade of a thick mango, and looked long from under
half-closed eyelids at the gorgeous scene below us.
Ridge rose on ridge till far in the distance we could
see the heights above Jacmel. Down in the valleys
the sun shone on the glittering cocoas and
bananas, while on little cleared spaces were neat white-
painted cottages covered with heavy grass thatch.

The people held in their hands, or wore suspended from their waists, a long straight knife they call a manchette—a formidable weapon. This they use for mowing grass, for hewing a way in the woods, or for procuring their food.

The bridle path was sometimes so steep, and the clay covering it so slippery, that it was all the horses could do to struggle up. When we arrived at the top, we were on the Gros Morne, and at a height of about 3,900 feet above the sea. This was the highest point we had to cross. Before us, forty miles off, further than the northern slopes of the hills, beyond the great plain at their foot, was the Bay of Port-au-Prince, stretching right and left as far as the eye could reach, and in the centre of the panorama, rising from the sea, the mountains on the island of Gonaive.

Night came upon us as we rode down, and for the next few hours we had no lights but the stars and the fireflies. Of these there were myriads flitting from bush to bush. We crossed swampy lands where the frogs were croaking an extraordinary croak. It was a snore, kept up at a pace and with a continuity that no one could imitate, and at a high pressure that made sleep within reach of it impossible. There were sixteen miles to get to Port-au-Prince after we had arrived at Mommense, which we did at 10.30.

We had expected to find General Fauberg Petion there, a very distinguished Haytian, grandson of two presidents, and almost the only soldier in the country who, having been in Europe, had really studied military affairs. We were much disappointed when, after trotting through thick enclosures, planted with bananas, we found that he had left the day before for the capital. To his *officier d'ordonnance*, Mr. Borjelat, who was in charge of the house, we hinted that the horses were tired, and that we should like rest for them, and something to eat for ourselves, on which he immediately asked us most cordially to stop, and entertained us very hospitably.

We found an English engineer, a Liverpool man, who had been working for some time in Glasgow, and had been sent out by a company, whom the general had asked for assistance in setting up machinery for the pressing and refining of sugar. The general is bent on turning his property, which is very extensive, into sugar estates, on the plan of those in Demerara and Barbadoes. A few other proprietors—two or three in his neighbourhood—are going to follow his example. His plans have been thwarted for the present by a flooding of the river Mommense, which we had already crossed. The machinery had been almost all put up, and the sugar-pressing was in full operation, when suddenly the river rose, and in one night swept over the ground occupied by the machinery, destroying and burying everything three or four feet deep in the ground.

The Englishman offered to show us the works, and took us to the pressing-house, a circular, tiled building, raised some height above the surrounding gravel levels. Around were heaps of crushed sugar-cane, which they use here for fuel. The great wheel, put in motion by water, was driving the crushing roller, which revolved at the bottom of a large trough. Men, women, and boys were sitting near, chattering and laughing as we stopped to see what they were doing, which was little enough. A boy now and then supplied the crusher with a scanty bundle of canes, which he thrust in, pressed down, and passed beneath the roller, without taking the trouble to untie the grass or reed fastenings. Much grass must have passed into the juice in this manner.

We went also to the adjoining boiling-houses. The sugar runs into large vats that were steaming with the heat of lime-fed ovens beneath. They say here that the General's works can only be expensive toys, which can never pay. The engineer informed us that the arrangement is that the workpeople should have one-half the profits. The clearing of the gravel, he said, would probably cost 4000*l.* or 5000*l.* at least.

"Do the people work well?" I asked.

"No, no, sir; I cannot get them to do as I tell them, especially as I have to speak through an interpreter, and he has been long on the estates, and is one of themselves like. They wont attend to what he has to say, and are always a-laughing at him."

The workmen are people of the place, bound to give the General so many days' work when he wants it.

"Have you begun to dig for the machinery?"

"Yes; but I can't noways get anything done regular. I can't get on with the people at all; they try to shirk work and lie down whenever your back is turned."

"But it's their own interest to get the gravel away."

"Yes, if they get it cleared, and everything set going, they know they would get half the produce; but you see, sir, they wont. In the morning perhaps no one comes at the appointed time, and I have to send round, and by the time they come it is too hot for me to stay, and the work has to be laid over till the evening, and so little is done."

"Can you get any skilled workmen to help in building?"

"No; leastways, it's very scarce; and a fellow I got to put up a little bit of wall not more than ten feet high, and not long, why, he took a week to put up a thing a good workman would have put up in a day; and then when I wanted to put them 'ere iron plates up on that frame, why, there was two down, and two up above, and some of the plates were on end and some not, and the time it took to make those fellows place a plate was something awful. The two above kept jumping like so many *Cures*, saying that it was too hot for their feet, and those below kept laughing, till I did not know what to make of them."

If this is the way they go on when it is so manifestly their immediate interest to work, what can be done?

I should like to have seen the place by day. This first experiment of sugar-growing and manufacturing is quite new to this country since the French days, when thousands of hogsheads used to be exported.

They expect to get seven hogsheads a day from this place. Almost all the sugar used here, except by quite the poorer people, is imported, and is usually French beet-root sugar! Was there ever such a case of carrying coals to Newcastle?

Mr. Borjelat talked of the recent war at the Cape. He was there when the *Bulldog* came in and knocked about the insurgent batteries. I do not think the Haytians, not even those on the President's side, liked that interference in their domestic quarrel. The truth seems to be that Geffrard is not popular. The people are tired of him, and already want a change. They think he has had his good time, and that it is the turn for others. Salnave was very popular. Now, however, that his cause is lost and he has retired to St. Domingo, he is forgotten; but if he had succeeded, he would have been received with open arms.

The siege of the Cape lasted from May till November. The interference of the *Bulldog*, and afterwards of the *Galatea*, was the turning-point of the war. If it had not been for Captain Wake's shot and shell, Salnave would have been probably by this time at Port-au-Prince. The *Voldrogue*, the vessel that was sunk by one of the *Bulldog's* hundred-pound shells, was a wretched affair, bought in England, and made, although quite unfit for it, to carry a few guns. Her iron sides were as thin as possible; so much so, indeed, that they got bulged in whenever a heavy sea struck them. One time, when the guns were first put into her, and the Haytian crew wanted to fire a salute, they forgot altogether that a gun when fired would recoil; so they fastened up the piece, loaded it, pushed it through the porthole, and banged. Back went the gun, and knocked a great hole in the other side of the vessel. One of the *Bulldog's* large conical shells sent her, of course, to the bottom.

By-the-bye, one of those shells—they are conical percussion shells—flew over a fort it had been aimed at, and buried itself, without bursting, somewhere in the country beyond. Some Haytians had observed or found out where the shell lodged, and four of them went to dig it out. They had never seen anything of the sort before, and to satisfy their curiosity, one of them lifted a hammer, and struck a blow on the conical end. Of course the shell exploded, and with the most disastrous effects, for of the poor Haytians nothing but a few fragments was ever seen afterwards.

We slept three hours at Mommense, and then went on, our poor horses going very slowly over the muddy roads; indeed, it was all a nasty swamp for some miles. Most of the way led us along near the sea, which crept in lazily, bathing the roots of a broad belt of logwood and mangrove that grew along its margin. Day broke long before we got into the town.

CHAPTER III.

Port-au-Prince — Scenery near the Town—Names of Streets—Inhabitants of the Town—The Military—Street Scenes—The Wharfs — The Market-place — Provisions — Pottery — Tirailleurs — Beautiful View — Haytian National Emblem — Motto adopted by the Blacks—Policy of the Government towards Strangers—Population and Trade—Town and Country Schools—Standing Army and Despotism — Sail among the Coral Islands—Our Boatman—Destructive Effect of an Armstrong Shell—Visit to our Consul—Refuge in Foreign Consulates—Troublesome *Protégés*—Taffia Fires in Port-au-Prince—Fenced Clearings—Rapid Growth in Hayti—Country Houses—Party at Dinner—Probable Fate of Hayti—English Niggers—Visit to the Presidential Palace—Interview with Geffrard—Relations of White and Black in the Negro Republic—Fishing Sharks—Geffrard's Opinion—Commerce of Hayti.

MR. S. offered us the use of his house, as we rode into Port-au-Prince dusty and hot, and our horses so tired that we could only get a league an hour out of them. As the hotel was very bad, the offer was most acceptable, and we were comfortably lodged. The house, which is in the principal street, is one of the best in the town for coolness, which is here another word for comfort. The first floor, which is the goods store, is of brick, and the rooms are provided with broad verandahs above. Nearly every house belongs to one of the foreign merchants, many of whom are Germans, a smaller number French, and only about nine or ten English. The foreigners in the island do not exceed two hundred and fifty, and that in a population, black and coloured, supposed to exceed three hundred thousand. The estimate is far from certain, for all attempts to take a census have ended in failure.

The last portion of our journey we rode along the foot of high hills, with the wide bay on our left. Across it we could see the highlands of the northern coast; and at its head, extending some way along the bay, was Port-au-Prince. There were several low and small islands in the bay, with thick-growing mangroves overhanging the water. Between them were anchored merchant vessels, on a few of which—one of them a steamer, the *Galatea*—was the Haytian red and blue flag.

At the back of the town, which was laid out by the French in right-angled streets, the land rises gradually, and then sinks into a level plain, called the Cul-de-sac. At the barriers, as they are called, though there is little to justify the name, there is a mouldy fort. The walls are half fallen into decay, and on the ill-kept ramparts are two guns, which look as if they must infallibly burst on the first attempt to fire them.

We turned down an approach called a street. At first there was nothing but mango and bread-fruit trees to be seen on each side, then a few shanties, and a large building that had been erected by the French as a hospital, but was now falling into ruins from neglect and age. The houses that followed were very comfortable and well adapted for the climate. The state of the streets would disgrace any capital. They do not smell so badly as those of Cologne, and they are not narrow; but they are not properly levelled, and are crossed with wide mud-filled ditches, into which, if a passer-by fell, he would be unendurable even to himself for weeks. These gutters run under the houses on both sides of the street, and into them a great deal of the house sewage is thrown. The odour from them by day is insupportable, and at night they are the resort of numbers of the croaking frogs already described. They are crossed by little wooden bridges, stretching across them from the verandah platform of each house.

The names of the streets are very democratic—Rue du Peuple, Rue Républicaine. Ours is called Rue des Miracles, and certainly the people seen riding and walking in it are perfect miracles to a European. If one of them were introduced on an English stage, he would be called an absurd exaggeration. Now and then some gorgeous general of the Etat-Major passes, in a uniform bran new from Paris—a light blue coat and faultless magenta trousers. Then comes an aide-de-camp on a nag about half the size of an English charger. His hat, perhaps a cocked one, or a *képi*, or a shako, is ornamented with an enormous plume to show it off. His trousers do not descend more than half-way below the knees, and his spurs are tied by a piece of cord to naked brown heels.

The soldiers are the most tag, rag, and bobtail man ever saw. No two of them seem to be dressed alike. Each uniform is, apparently, the worn-out property of some sixth-rate theatre. But the men themselves are often fine fellows, well made, very muscular, and if clothed in some sensible way, would make a very good show.

Carts are driven about by stick-beating, sturdy blacks, with teams of donkeys, often four or five abreast. Women walk with stately gait, in long gowns without crinoline, bearing enormous bundles on their heads. Small boys drive donkeys almost hid beneath the load of Guinea-grass and bananas. This is the commonest fruit here; and, when fried, it is excellent—a mixture of pancake and good omelette. The guava is common, but disappointing. In the jelly we get the quintessence of the fruit, but there is a want of taste in it when eaten raw.

On the 18th we had a walk all over the town; first to the wharfs, where there was a busy scene. Piles of mahogany, fustic, and logwood were lying about, with here and there heaps of coffee-bags ready for shipment. There is a great want of good jetties. In some places the boats could not get close to the shore, and the bags and packages had to be carried some way into the water before they could be hoisted in. Everything was done by manual labour. No cranes were in use. No levers were used, even in rolling heavy logs, which were shoved along by numbers of men. The place has quite a commercial look. I did not expect to see so much life in it. There are about twenty ships in harbour. Work might be found for two hundred.

The market-place was full of people, with fruits and wares, under wooden coverings. Bread, bananas, and coarse pottery were the chief commodities. Bananas are very cheap. A *régime*, or crop, from a single tree is sold by the grower at two shillings. Bananas and mangoes alone would furnish sufficient provision for this people, were a famine to come from disease in beasts or vegetables. Bread, though much eaten, is not a necessary. The last war has made it double as dear as it was before. I bought a large piece of bread, which one could hardly have eaten unassisted, for one dollar; that is, a Haytian dollar, which just now is worth threepence, having, once upon a time, been worth four shillings. The currency is frightfully depreciated, and has become more so of late years.

The pottery is good of its sort. Capital bottles are made from a red clay found near the coast at Jacmel. The richer people only seem to use them, however, the common class having calabashes, or old iron vessels, for carrying water, often with holes in them, which they seldom take the trouble to repair, and through which half the water escapes before it is carried to its destination.

In an open place behind the town we fell in with a fellow from Guadaloupe, who is military instructor to the troops. Many of the soldiers came up to receive orders—all fine men, and many of them very intelligent looking. They belonged to the tirailleurs, of whom there are five thousand, the cream of the army. They are better dressed than the other soldiers, and

are all clothed alike, which is more than one can say
of any other Haytian regiment. They are armed
with rifles, and make a fair show at drill. Their pay
is fourteen gourds, or dollars (three shillings and sixpence), a month.

We rode to Mr. S.'s country-house, a charming place,
with a little garden and avenue of cabbage-palm and
cocoa. The first of these trees, with the addition of a
cap of Liberty on the spike, forms the Haytian national
emblem. The view of the bay and opposite hills is
beautiful, and would bear comparison with that of
Naples. S. is much disgusted with the country, finding, he says, bad faith everywhere. "*Voler le blanc
n'est pas voler*" is a black motto constantly acted
upon.

This country place, and others like it, are held by
foreigners under the name of a third person, a
Haytian. There are strict laws against foreigners
holding any land in the country, but, like a good
many other Haytian laws, they are frequently relaxed
or evaded.

The general policy of the Government is very
hostile to foreigners. They have to pay forty per
cent. on imports, instead of the thirty-six per cent. paid
by Haytians. Natives marrying foreigners cannot

succeed to any property. The coffee-sellers, who, having cleared a patch of ground, procure with little trouble a small crop, cannot sell it at once to the foreign merchants, but must dispose of it first to Haytians. Land is very cheap, and can be procured easily.

As we rode home, we met long files of people going into the town with little bundles or bags of coffee, carried on the head, or on donkeys' backs. Foreigners can buy it by the sack, containing 240 lbs., which now costs 3*l*. The average coffee crop of the Republic may be set down at 60,000,000. Auguste Eley, the Minister of Foreign Affairs, says the amount of goods exported is annually increasing, a circumstance which, as he truly remarks, shows that either the wealth or the population of the country is also on the increase. The population is certainly not decreasing, in spite of the general promiscuous intercourse in which the people live. Government has established very fair schools in the towns and in the different arrondissements. There is a large school in Port-au-Prince, with about 250 children; but these town schools can hardly be said to be within reach of the country-people in the mountainous interior—that is, the large mass of the negro population, who are in a state

of happy savagery. According to the account of
an American, who has commenced sugar cultivation
and refining in the plains not far from Port-au-
Prince, the number of small freeholders does not
interfere with the plentiful supply of labour. One of
the worst proceedings of the Government, virtually a
coloured one, is the maintenance of a large standing
army. The rowdy portion of the people are thus
encouraged to put on their shabby uniforms, flourish
a sword or a musket, and kick up a disturbance whenever anything happens to put them out of humour.
This is a military despotism which is neither good
for the ruler, whose generals are likely to turn against
him, nor for civilians, who are not encouraged in any
little inclination they may have to work their land
steadily, or to acquire or invest in property, which the
next petty revolution may snatch from their hands.
One may be expecting too much, but it is disagreeable
to see a country progressing only at a jog-trot, when,
with its favourable position and the fertility of its
soil, it ought to drive at a gallop to prosperity. It is
a community that lives comfortably itself when not
disturbed by wars, but it is one that might help
others to live a hundredfold more than it does at
present.

In the evening we took a boat, and rowed about the quiet waters of the harbour. We visited the little coral islands that rise in groups from the shallow bottom. Mounds of the coral, which is fished out in blocks, lie about the wharfs ready for burning as lime. It is generally coarse, but here and there one comes upon a fine piece of mæandrina.

Our boatman was a marine on board one of the two Haytian corvettes that had been engaged in the siege of the Cape. Although he was in Geffrard's service, he talked quite openly of his admiration for Salnave, and his belief that that general would be president at the end of three months. "Ugh! au bout de trois mois—ugh! Oh!—ugh! vous verrez, vous Anglais. Geffrard ne restera pas—ugh!"

Another story is told of the Armstrong shells. One flew wide of the forts, and descended on a house three long miles away in the interior of the country, where a party of men were playing at cards. One of them rose to go, and had scarcely left the room where his companions were when he was arrested by the shock of a fearful explosion, and, on looking round, he beheld them all lying dead, he alone having escaped.

Paid a visit to Mr. St. John, our Consul, and found him with Mr. Byrone, his Vice-Consul, and Don Alvarez, the Spanish Chargé d'Affaires. Mr. St. John had been very busy lately collecting evidence in explanation of recent events at the Cape for our Government. What an extraordinary custom it is that political offenders should be allowed to take refuge in foreign consulates!—but it is a system which is objected to by none of the rival aspirants to power, as each of them in his turn may have to seek safety for himself! But was there ever a more convenient method of getting embroiled in a country's domestic quarrels than thus giving protection to any hunted black politician who is compelled to fly for his life? The Chargés d'Affaires alone have the right at present; but can one expect a furious mob to stand venting their rage at a consul's door when the object of their fury has just found refuge under his roof? Of course not. The mob will enter, consul or no consul, if their blood is up, and the scent is hot; and then, forsooth, our flag is violated, our honour is insulted, and we must run the risk of losing men and ships in useless bombarding of rotten fortifications. The consul at the Cape, from whose house the refugees were taken, had strictly no right to shelter them, as he was not a Chargé d'Affaires;

but whether Chargé, &c., or not, why should we protect such troublesome *protégés?* The custom could only exist in a weak country. Our ability to protect must be limited by the power of the Government with which we deal. Even here, where the weakness is so conspicuous, we have seen how much we may lose by meddling. Surely the sooner such troublesome Quixotism is abandoned the better.

Taffia is the chief liquor drunk here. Of all the shops, the spirit shops, here as elsewhere, thrive the best. Vermouth and taffia are always at hand.

Our party having got horses, we rode through the town, and then up to a country-house at the foot of the hills. A part of the upper portion of the town is being rebuilt, after the great fire that took place last year. Many of the houses are chiefly of wood, sent out from the States in portions ready for building. A fire is a great opportunity for pillage and savage frolic to the roughs of Port-au-Prince, where there are no firemen, and is joyfully hailed accordingly. Some of the merchants have pumps for their own use. These are placed at the disposal of Government in an emergency, and although in such cases they are generally utterly spoilt, no money is paid as compensation. At the time of this last fire the mob ran up to the reservoirs and stopped the supply of water, hoping for the extension of the fire, and the opportunity to plunder.

Mr. B., who has lived in the country for many years, takes a gloomy view of the state of things, thinking that everything is going from bad to worse, that bad government and bad habits are increasing, and that there is at present no prospect of a change.

The path we followed led us through the bush, which was in many places cleared away for cultivation, and for the erection of the wooden villas of well-to-do people in town. Clearings were always fenced, the palings being generally composed of tall sticks cut from trees, and stuck close together. These were sprouting again, from the wonderfully fertile soil, as willow sticks do in England. But here the growth is much more rapid. A brown, leafless, lopped-branch paling will, in a short time, be a row of flourishing young trees. Inside these palings the bush has been cleared, and the ground has been swept of plants; but the stumps of the larger bushes have been left sticking out of the soil to a height of two or three feet as supporters for beans, various kinds of which are eaten by the negroes, and go a long way to give the curved line of beauty their bodies exhibit to the stranger. Between these stumps the cane or Guinea-grass grows. Lime-kilns are frequent. The lime is good, and much used for the purifying of sugar.

The country-houses are charming, though there is, of course, no good lawn or turf. They are more in the style of the *campagnes* near Geneva, if one could fancy one of them with palms and mangoes instead of elms and walnuts. From Mr. St. John's verandah we had a splendid but rather too bird's-eyeish view of the town and bay. A great charm of these *campagnes* is the quantity of water brought round the houses in aqueducts and tanks. There is generally a plunging-bath, too, well shaded, where one can take a short swim at early morning or in the evening.

The party at dinner was the same as at the consul's. There we were—representatives of France, Spain, and Britain, in a land that each of our nations had coveted, for which each had intrigued and fought, and yet where nothing now belongs to them but the ships that lie far out on the blue sea, waiting for cargoes of coffee from the descendants of their slaves;—where now we cannot hold a foot of ground except under a false name, and by the connivance of a government of that race which ours had enslaved, and abused, and worked for selfish profit alone. The only marks of powerful foreign dominion now to be seen are the broken aqueducts, the ruined plantation walls, and the dogs at the door, which have evidently yet some trace of the bloodhound. The present state of things is certainly strange, and I cannot but think will prove transitory, unless, indeed, the blacks are able to rise to a higher state of civilization and energy. Their power does not seem destined to last; and I much doubt whether, after all, it would not be for the best that America should in time possess and develop this garden of the western tropics, from which she could get more abundant crops than can its present possessors, and with whom she could foster a larger trade. She has men who could endure the climate well enough, such as those from Louisiana and Florida, who are particularly healthy here. The yellow fever hardly ever attacks Creoles; and even if a larger white population could not permanently settle on the island, wiser laws, and better men to administer them, might yet make Hayti one of the richest spots in the world. One can only wish for the absolute independence of her people if they prove themselves worthy of it. None should be allowed to possess such an island who do not use every exertion to make the most of its wonderful capabilities.

St. John called early on the 12th to take us to the palace. He had with him a very good black servant, a Canadian, who hates Hayti, as is generally the case with negro immigrants, especially if they come from Jamaica, or any other English colony. They are called English niggers, and are looked upon suspiciously by the Haytians.

But to return to our presidential visit. We passed through gates which are not imposing, with red brick pillars, and rusty cannon-balls as ornaments at the top. The palace is a long building of one story, originally built for an English general. In front, stone steps lead to a raised verandah that runs along the whole of the building. There is a large open court before the house, and on each side are offices and stables. An orderly showed us into a handsomely-furnished room, the paper of which was of the French imperial pattern and colours—golden bees on a green ground. On this imperial background hung a three-quarter length oil-painting of the President and his wife, and a print of "Old Abe." Eley, the minister, who has now three portfolios, but the salary

F

of only one office, received us. He is a coloured man, and has a very good head. His talk was chiefly of the trees, plants, and birds of the country.

After we had waited some time Geffrard came in. He was dressed in black, with white necktie, and began to talk immediately. His manners are charming, quite those of a polished French gentleman, and he is evidently more accustomed to speak than to be spoken to. He is of about middle height, his figure rather spare, but well knit. The white wool is brushed back from a high but not broad forehead. His eyes are very black, and quick in their expression, and the mouth and jaw seem to show decision and firmness. He has white blood, but is so dark that no one unless practised in the various shades by which the distinctions of race are marked would say so. He and his Government are quite looked upon as representing the coloured, not the black class. He has been elected President for life, but I doubt if he will be in his present position many more years, unless aided by foreign power. They say here that Seward offered to send him a gunboat for protection. If so, it is in contradiction to the policy of Captain Walker, the commander of the Federal man-of-war the *De Sota*. This officer, it is almost known, had entered into correspondence with Salnave, who had held out hopes that, in case of assistance being given him, he would do his best to give the Americans a large island off the north coast of Hayti.

We told the President we had come from Jacmel, and were going to leave by this day's steamer. "Messieurs," said he, "I am afraid you have had a rough journey, and over bad roads." We could, of course, not deny that the roads were bad, but praised the scenery and the politeness of the people. He said, " Yes, they are a polite and good people. Great crimes are unknown; one never hears of a murder. A man may travel alone with large sums of money, and be perfectly secure. Arms are carried, not for defence or to hurt others, but because it is the custom of the people. It originated in the number of wars in which they were engaged. Larceny and small offences are the only crimes."

We told him of the town school we had seen, and asked if the education system was carried on under Government alone. "Yes, messieurs; nearly all the schools are under Government. There are only a few that are '*particulier*.'" Eley talked of the exertions of the President to further education. "Oh yes!" the President said, "but we are quite ashamed of the poverty of our institutions, when they are seen by foreigners. Remember that we had everything to do; that this is a new state which we had to build from the ground." After much in the same strain, he said he wished we would come in another twenty years to see the progress they would make in that time. We spoke of the imperfection of schools even in England. "Yes; you are not so far advanced as they are in Switzerland. We have now 15,000 children in our schools, but most of them are in the towns, where are chiefly the coloured men. We have schools also in the country, but there the children are so scattered, and there is such a distance to be travelled, that it makes teaching very difficult. In this arrondissement of Port-au-Prince we have one-tenth of the whole population of the Republic" (this is put down at 28,000, which gives 280,000 as the total population).

Referring to the soldiers, he said there was no sickness to speak of among them, and that, as there were no large barracks, they always lived in the neighbourhood or in the town. We asked him about the laws against the settling of strangers, which made him speak a good deal on that subject. "Yes," he said, "we do not allow strangers to hold landed properties. Our laws are against it. They are not the class of people we want as immigrants. But several of your countrymen do occupy land; there is Mr. William Lloyd, for instance, but others hold the title. Strangers are allowed to be *fermiers*, not proprietors. This is the difference, and the unwillingness to have foreigners is owing to political reasons. If they were allowed to have land as they liked, their influence might soon be dominant, and their presence might excite stern feelings of enmity, leading to war, that I am so anxious to avoid. You have the same laws in England against foreigners possessing land. I got the chambers to strike out the word *white* in their laws, and substitute for it the word *stranger*. The animosity between the white and the black is much decreased here, and our people will receive and satisfy your demands with even greater alacrity than they will ours. This is especially the case with Englishmen, whose country was the first to acknowledge the equality of the human race, and to recognise that the colour of the skin alone should not cause such a separation. I wish for fusion, not only of blood, but of sentiment."

We spoke of the abolition of slavery in America, and asked him about Seward. He said the Secretary had come to the palace to visit him, and seemed to suffer much still from his wound, in consequence of which it was difficult to hear him speak. "It was the case with me; my tongue is too large for my jaw. When I was young I used to stamp my feet with rage at the difficulty I experienced in expressing myself." After staying for about half an hour, he rose to take leave; but when out of the door, we were recalled with the exclamation, "Ah, messieurs, quelle impolitesse!" and, on re-entering, he gave us some sherry, apologizing that the wine was not of the best, and again saying he hoped we would return twenty years hence—a long invitation, which we accepted. I wonder if the old President or we shall be alive at that time! He is as likely to be in England as we in Hayti.

We left the island on board of one of the fine Glasgow transatlantic boats, which was taking out troops to Jamaica. We found the officers engaged in attempting to catch three large sharks that were swimming about under the stern; one was hooked, but got off almost immediately. The officers wont land, not expecting to find anything to their taste in a negro republic. "Haw—where have you been? Devilish long ride. What's to be seen? Nothing,

I'm sure, in such a d—d hole. Fancy a black republic! Haw—haw! I wouldn't land for anything. I always feel inclined to knock a nigger down when he's impudent; and what they must be when they're free, like that, I don't know," were some of the sensible remarks addressed to us. We remembered the courtesy and refinement of President Geffrard's conversation, and we made our own reflections.

I forgot to say that Geffrard remarked, as if convinced of its truth, that the commerce of the Haytians and the quantity of goods exported were enormous for the size of the country and the number of people. This was almost the only subject on which he spoke with satisfaction of anything in the land he governs. It is a magnificent country, and one cannot help wishing it a happier and a more industrious future.

CHAPTER IV.

Jamaica in Sight—Morant Bay—The Court-House—The Palisades—Port Royal—On Board the *Duncan*—Model Community—Public Estimation of Gordon—The Wire "Cats"—Negro Evidence—The Coloured Class—American Buggies—Complaint as to the Administration of Justice—Burned Houses—Bath—A Survivor of the Massacre at Morant Bay—Rencounter with an Indignant Negro—Maroons on Duty—Hire's House—Hire's Defence, and Massacre of Inmates—State of Feeling among the Planters—The Anti-Buckra Movement—Escape of Mr. Sinclair and his Wife—An Obedient Idol—Folly of Negroes and Fears of the Planters — Scenery of Jamaica—Attack on Happy Grove—Dispute about a Mule—Our Footing with the Maroons—Their Manner of Fighting—Massacre and Burning by the Troops—Account of Riots by a Coloured Schoolmaster — Merciless Conduct of Black Troops.

ABOUT three in the afternoon, on the 14th of February, I was roused from my cabin by the news that Jamaica was in sight. Grand cloud-capped mountains, wood-covered, and trending down to the sea-coast in sharp spurs, formed a fine background to the lower hills near the shore, where were broad fields of sugar-cane. Port Morant was first passed, where we could make out a gunboat lying, her awnings stretched over the deck, and about half-a-dozen wind-sails up. Morant Bay then opened out—a wide-stretching expanse of water. The houses scattered about seemed pleasantly surrounded with wood. Close by the sea was the town—a little cluster of houses; and near the town was a square, large-windowed building that looked ruined. This was the Courthouse, where the first massacre took place. Another gunboat was keeping watch below the town walls. Gunboats, indeed, were everywhere. What a force to bring against some riotous negroes! There must be more than a dozen vessels round the coast. Each bay is guarded by a ship, and more troops were expected. The 3rd West India regiment is to be here in a few days.

We got in here before dark, after running along the narrow strip of land and islands that forms Kingston harbour, and are called the "Palisades." At the end of this spit, and five miles from Kingston, is Port Royal. The ground is so low that the houses look as if they were built on the water. A duller place to be quartered at I cannot conceive. Thousands of sand-crabs swarm in the Palisades, and feed on the buried corpses of the garrison. The coffins have to be held down to prevent the water that oozes through the sand from lifting them before they are decently covered over. Thick mangroves make it an impossible task to walk along this spit.

Next day we paid a visit to H. on board the *Duncan*, and were royally entertained by him in the gun-room. He has got leave to make an expedition to Morant Bay and the eastern end of the island with us. He is, of course, a violent pro-naval and military man, and swears that it will be a "horrid shame if anything is done to the Governor."

Many people called on us the morning after my arrival. It was amusing to hear each man who came abuse the man who last went out. "Have you seen A.?" says B.; "because you really know you must accept that man's word with caution." "I saw B. here with your lordship, I think, just now. A most untruthful man," says C.; and C. declares that D. has been kicked out of some office for peculation. All seem at loggerheads in this model community.

One thing only do they all concur in—that is, the rascality of Gordon. However opinions may vary respecting the justice of the trial and execution, a bad impression of Gordon's character seemed to be general.

On all but this subject public opinion seems divided. The planters say that the outbreak was a generally-organized conspiracy and rebellion, that it was most dangerous, and that Gordon was the leader of it. The coloured inhabitants, for the most part, do not believe that the disaffection was so general as it is represented to have been; and though, in the majority of cases, they do not stand up for Gordon's political morality, they yet think he had nothing to do with the outbreak at Morant Bay. The blacks believe that the Queen is angry, and that all the officials who, in the suppression of the riots, treated them with so much severity, will be hanged. Most of the military and naval people only damn the negroes.

Much excitement and some surprise was caused by the evidence given before the Commission. As to the wire "cats," the officials and military say they know nothing of them, and do not believe the evidence respecting them. Many, indeed, deride the evidence wholesale, and say that it is impossible to get anything but a lie from a negro, and that no testimony given by them can be believed. In saying this, they seem to forget that many of those hanged during martial law were condemned on the evidence of black men, and some of it very meagre in its nature. I do not say much here regarding the evidence before the Commission—first, because I was not often present; and secondly, because full reports of it may be found in any English or Jamaica paper. The best idea I could form of the state of feeling in the island at this time was gathered from the accounts of the people themselves. They told me, no doubt, much that was contradictory, but with a little care and patience it will be found possible to pick the grain from the chaff. The class I most desired to see was the coloured one. They hold a middle position, and from these *mezzotintos* one may expect to gather *mezzo-tinto* opinions, which are probably the best.

We got a buggy with some difficulty, and proceeded to Lyssons, near Morant Bay, where we did not arrive till past dark. We passed through the town of Morant, but saw nothing of it. The American buggy is the universal carriage here, and the most abominably uncomfortable thing. It is a light gig with a hood, and has two pair of large wheels, whose axletrees project a long way beyond the sides of the body of the machine. These wheels are so large that unless one is supernaturally thin it is difficult to get past them to the seat. With ladies the business of getting fairly housed is dreadful. The buggy has to be brought forward and half turned, so that the hind and front wheels shall not be in the same line, an operation which renders the breach a little more accessible. Shawls being then placed over each wheel, a gentleman mounts, holds out his hand, and hauls, while another behind shoves and compresses crinolines, &c., till the cargo is fairly aboard. Once inside, there is a low iron bar to make one's back uncomfortable.

We engaged one of these buggies to go round the east end of the island as far as Port Antonio. The road led us across the streams, through which our chariot went splashing up to the axle-trees. We were very lucky in falling in with P. Ramsay, the inspector of police for the parishes of Portland and St. Thomas-in-the-East, and brother of Gordon Ramsay, of whose intemperateness so much has been said. He was most kind to us, putting horses and men at our disposal. It is curious to hear from these planters the same complaints of the administration of justice of which the blacks also speak. The larceny of the negroes they are very bitter against. The blacks go upon the idea that stealing from massa's property is no theft, for do they not work for the estate, and what harm can there be in taking a little wood, &c.? Planters, equally with negroes, complain that justice cannot be had, the verdict, as they say, always going against the oppressed whites. "Why, only lately, a lot of niggers stole a quantity of wood from my property. They cut it down bit by bit when your back is turned, and you cannot get justice in the courts. I have known the negroes carry down logwood bit by bit until they had a ton or two collected to sell. I have known them take nails one after another, and conceal them. I knew a man take some every day, concealed in the wool of his head, till the loss was considerable. The nigger rules this country, sir."

On leaving Port Morant, the road turns aside from the sea and enters the valleys, where the scenery is most beautiful. We saw some burnt houses, but not many—not more than five or six—along the road. They had been wretched erections of lath and plaster, and it would not take their disconsolate inhabitants more than a fortnight's good work to put them up again. One or two small wood-built chapels were pointed out as places in which Gordon had been in the habit of holding forth.

At Bath, which must have been a pleasant place in old times, but looks now terribly tumble-down and neglected, we stopped for some time, and had a good deal of talk with Dr. M., one of the survivors of the massacre. He had concealed himself in an aloe hedge at the back of the Court-house, and was found and dragged out by the rioters. They were going to put him to death, when he told them he was a medical man, and asked to be led to Bogle, who spared him. He corroborated the general testimony I have heard against Gordon's character. He had been under the impression that Gordon was a friend of his, but was amazed to learn that among Gordon's letters to Laurence was one which said that M.'s conduct was such as to class him with those who must be swept away. In his opinion the planters had not used the negroes well, the treatment of the latter having been more like that of dogs than of men. The blacks had much to complain of, especially of the magistrates, in whom there was no confidence. Hire had been one of the greatest gentlemen among the planters.

At a spot on the road near Gordon's old estate

(the Rhine), we passed a tall black man, who looked uncommonly sulky. Ramsay's silver lace caught his eye.

"Ah!" cried he, "ah! you d——d brute! where you go? Where the hell you go, you d——d brute?"

"Ha! what's that you are saying?" said Ramsay; and we stopped the carriage.

"Ah, you d——d brute!" said the man again, as Ramsay went up to him.

"What's your name?" he asked; but received no answer, either from the man or from some people who stood near. The negro kept his ground, looking savage. Ramsay, who was apparently unarmed, as the revolver was hidden under his coat, went still closer to him. The negro carried a large yam and the usual cutlass. As Ramsay got near, the negro stuck the yam under his left arm, and lifted the cutlass.

"Ah!" said Ramsay, producing his revolver, and tapping it; "see that, my friend—see that!"

"Come away, come away," said the negro, and moved off a few paces.

A herd-boy then came up and offered to give us the fellow's name, which was taken down.

A little further on we met two Maroons.

"Maroons," said Ramsay, "I wish you had been

here just now. A fellow insulted us on the public road. Just ride on and take him into custody, and leave him at Bath."

The faces of the Maroons lighted up with satisfaction, and they spurred on their mules with a hearty good-will, exclaiming—

"Yes, massa; we'll take him."

This was the only open insolence we met with on our way. One or two other fellows looked sulky, but said nothing, or only muttered, "D——d brute!"

We stayed a day or two with Mr. Harrison, who made so narrow an escape from the rioters. Almost all his people—all with the exception of one or two—did what they could for him; and it was owing to them that the rebels were bamboozled into believing that the ladies were hiding in another trash-house from that in which they were. Much is said of the increased laziness of the people since the Commission. Harrison's people work well enough, and so do Wallace's and Lysson's.

We rode out one day to poor Hire's house. It is prettily situated on the top of one of the hills belonging to the range that bounds the plain of Plantain Garden river, and is not more than a musket shot distant. We rode through the level cane-fields, and then ascended the hill, from which there is an excellent view of all the estates which the bands that left Morant Bay, after the burning of the Court-house, visited and pillaged. In the distance was Golden Grove, nearer Duckenfield, Winchester, Hordley, and one or two other estates, all with neat-looking steadings, surrounded by the green level sea of cane crops, which are beautifully laid out and cultivated. To the left, beyond other fields, is the sea, and winding along through the plain towards it is the Plantain Garden river, the course of which, though we could not see its water, was marked by the long lines of bamboo tufts.

Hire's house remained as the rioters left it, after they had done their worst to its furniture and inmates; the latter consisting of the two Hires, father and son, the last of whom still survives; a visitor, Mr. Crichton; Mr. Jackson, who was left for dead; and Dr. Crowder, who, as well as other medical men, was spared on that fatal October evening. Most of the party were in bed. Hire himself did not expect danger. He had been friendly with Gordon, and both from him and from his men thought he might expect forbearance, if not protection. Though that day he had sworn in a few constables, chiefly men of his own about the place, he was not prepared for the dreadful scenes that were enacted.

When the shouts of the advancing mob and the smashing of the door were heard, his arms were not within reach, and he went out to meet the rioters with only a sword. A letter Harrison had sent him, after hearing reports of the Morant Bay massacre, had reached him. Gordon had been a friend; and if the affair had been a carefully-organized rebellion, Gordon's friends would have been safe, but the outbreak was premature. The rebels were not under the chiefs who had incited them to action. Under the influence of the liquors which they had got on the estates they had already broken into, they were in no mood to spare man, woman, or child.

Hire rushed out into the passage, and though, being a good swordsman, he was able to keep his assailants at bay for some time, he must have been at length severely wounded, for near the door the floor is dark with blood stains, which we could trace also in the passage and in the bedrooms. One account says that he was not disabled till some blacks had broken in at the windows of another room, and one of them succeeded in wounding his sword arm with a blow from a matchet. All were killed or left for dead. Hire lived for some time in agony, and, when dead, was dragged feet foremost, his battered head knocking against, and leaving bloody marks on each step, down to the sward in front of the house, and buried in a shallow grave close by.

Each room was a scene of perfect chaos. Letters, papers, books, magazines from England, and newspapers lay about torn and soiled. Marks of blood were everywhere—on the flooring, and on the beds; on clubs left by the murderers, and on articles of clothing. Mattresses were scorched by fire, or blackened by smoke. Not a bit of furniture was left; and every piece of glass or crockery had been broken to atoms, and even ground to powder.

We examined many of the letters, and found among them one from Gordon, and also Harrison's letter of warning. On a slip of paper, dated 12th October, the morning of the murder, I read the names of some special constables who had been sworn in by Hire on that day. Gordon's other letters to him must have been already taken. The houses on most of the other estates in the valley had already been refitted; and except where a bedpost or door panel had been staved in or cut, bore little trace of the riots. All the furniture, however, has not been replaced, and the poor ladies must, in many cases, be living in a state of great discomfort.

There is a general feeling among the planters in this district that, if the verdict of the Commissioners should be favourable to the late Governor, a fresh rising will take place. The consequence, of course, is, that the planters are unwilling to refurnish their houses in the same expensive style as before. Knowing that the soldiers will probably be withdrawn in a few months, they not unreasonably fear the recurrence of spectacles which it is dreadful enough to have witnessed once in a life.

A considerable quantity of furniture was carried away, and as it has not been recovered, it is probably concealed somewhere in the bush. Plate that has once disappeared has rarely been seen again. The reception by the common people of goods taken by the rioters from the planters' houses was one of the worst signs of the state of the country. The excuse advanced for them—a very feeble one—was that they considered they had a right to receive something from the estates for which they had worked so long. This circumstance shows that, on the part of the people, acquiescence in the rebellious proceedings of the rioters was much more general than many are disposed to admit. I do not imagine that the whole peasantry was actually in favour of the Anti-Buckra movement, but I fear there is sufficient evidence to prove that there was no such thing as an *active* pro-white party in the island. The most that could have been hoped for was, that the mass of the people would have waited quietly to see which side got the better, and would have attached themselves to it.

At Duckenfield Mr. Sinclair told us that he and his wife escaped to Manchioneal, driving the whole way along the road in advance of the band of rioters. None of the men they met on the road showed any inclination to stop them. Only in one case was there any indication of an attempt at violence, which the miscreant relinquished as soon as he saw that the party was prepared to resist. If there had been anything like regular organization among the negroes in that district, it would, in all probability, have been manifested by much greater decision in their conduct.

We drove on through the waving cane-fields of the rich plain to Golden Grove, the first plantation to which the band we have been referring to came. The overseers, flying into the cane, escaped the fate with which they were threatened. Mr. Chisholm, who was in Hire's house just before it was entered, escaped by crawling away in the darkness of night.

A Maroon sergeant of police brought us an Obeah idol, which H. immediately seized upon, vowing he would carry it off to the *Duncan*. We took it with us, but whether it will escape the tender mercies of the *Duncan's* gunnery room, and ever arrive in England, I do not know. It is a hideous idol of wood, with eyes ingeniously made of brass nails, and square-cut hair and whiskers.

The negroes are said to have shown a great difference in their bearing since the Commissioners came out, and the most unfounded ideas are prevalent amongst them. They will not work so readily, because they believe the land is to be theirs. The Queen, they are convinced, has sent them money, and the old buckras are to be packed off. A proclamation by the Governor has had a little effect in quieting them, but none seem to believe that the population will continue loyal for many months. I do not believe that after the thorough check they have experienced they will be foolish enough to rise again;

but the folly they have already shown almost justifies the planters' fears. What could be more ridiculous than their imagining that the Queen would approve of their sweeping away the white race, and that the blacks would be allowed to work the estates, and to send to England the produce got from the property of the murdered men?

The houses were all left standing, and the works and machinery were in no instance injured, being reserved, as they hoped, for their own use. All that I heard in this part of the country, which bore the whole fury of the outbreak, confirms my conviction that there was nothing like a regular organization among the people, though some may have known of the plans of the leaders, and officers may have been appointed in each parish. The country-people, indeed, were kept in a state of discontent and ferment, that when the time for action came they might be disposed to join the bands by whom the work was to be begun. The evidence before the Commission leaves us no room to doubt that the outbreak was premature. The right time was to have been either at Christmas, or when the magistrates were all assembled in session at Bath, when in all probability they would have been better prepared to act in concert under any leader capable of conducting them. The band by whom Hire was murdered was a half-drunken rabble, utterly contemptible as a military force, and only capable of damaging furniture and assaulting unarmed whites.

Our course to Boston, in the parish of Portland, took us along the line of destruction. Crossing over the last ridges of the Blue Mountains near the sea, we kept northward along the shore—a beautiful drive. The roads were bad in comparison with those we travelled over near Kingston, and in crossing some streams the wheels of the buggy were severely tried. Most of the road is grass-grown, and in some parts was merely a track across smooth savannahs belonging to breeding-pens, where herds of cattle browsed, and the turf was as green and close-cropped as that on an English common. The day was overcast, and great waves were rolling in on sandy reaches, or broke in high columns of foam on the rocks of lovely inlets and promontories, thick-grown with tangled bush and palms, which grew so near the water that the fronds and cocoas were wet with the sea-spray. Inland were those long ridges of mountains that form the backbone of the island, wooded to the peaks, except when some precipice rose abruptly, too steep for anything but the aloe to cling to. Matted masses of convolvulus hung on each rock. The country looked a perfect paradise, and only the ruins of the old sugar plantations made one remember what a tumble-down paradise it was.

As we rode along we were all eyes and ears for traces of the rioters; for though the planters are very anxious they should be called rebels, they were nothing more, nor did the so-called rebellion exceed the dimensions of a riot. " What, sir, what! you won't call this a riot now? It was a rebellion—a rebellion that would have given Jamaica to the niggers if it had not been for Governor Eyre. You don't call a disturbance a riot that spread like this?" It is useless to remind them that the Chartist disturbances extended over a much larger surface, and involved far greater interests, and yet were never called anything but riots. They will have it that the outbreak of the negroes was a rebellion, and one can only get peace by allowing that, if the designs attributed to the blacks had been carried out, the men belonging to these bands would have been not only murderous rioters, but revolutionists.

We stopped at a place called Happy Grove, and went up to the house, the banisters, doors, and windows of which were all "mashed," as they call it. Inside there was nothing but black emptiness. Outside a negro was attending to some trays of arrowroot that were lying in the sun. This man had been in the house when the mob came, but ran and hid in the bush close by, where he heard the noise made by the rioters shouting for him as they broke the furniture. I asked him about the conduct of the people of the place. "Well, sar, many of them went down and jined as soon as they saw the large body of men; and they were not compelled, but they formed themselves into a small separate body, and marched along with the rest. Many others ran away into the woods with me. They had been in service with white, and fear they have heads cut off."

A complaint was made to the inspector about a rebel having come and removed a mule that the soldiers had taken with them, and which this man had bought.

"He rebel, sar, dat came. It was he horse. His mother say, 'Kill d——d Dr. Jones.' He one of rebels. Now he come two days ago with his cutlass, and take mule away."

"Oho!" says the inspector, and makes a note of

this evidence. The man, who had vowed he was no rebel, got off with a flogging. Now he will be hunted down, and the forcible capture of the mule will be another item of accusation against him.

We went on to Dr. Jones's. He was not at home, but his son received us. The latter escaped in a boat before the mob came, and had a tremendously long row right round the east end of the island till picked up by the *Wolverine*. We sat down on rickety chairs—all that was left of the furniture—and listened to some more of the people's complaints. This time two men came, and said that their beasts had been carried away.

"Who took them?"

"De soldiers, sar."

"Who has them now?"

"A Maroon, sar, who will not give them up."

"Ah, then I cannot do anything for you—I can't touch those people."

Here was a pretty statement, which shows a little the footing we are on with our mountain allies, the Maroons, a brave and intelligent race, who live perched up upon the hills, secure from attack in their almost unapproachable fastnesses. They utterly despise the niggers, as they themselves call the blacks of the plain, from whom they are hardly distinguishable in colour. They are devotedly loyal, and can always be depended upon as faithful subjects of the Queen. But what do they expect for this? To have their own way in things which, however commendable they may appear to them, can scarcely be considered justifiable by us, and to be permitted to take and plunder the lowland blacks exactly as it may suit them. On this last occasion they secured lots of loot, among which were many Sambo girls, for the restitution of whom no one dares to ask them. If a lowland black ventured to go up to their mountain on such an errand, it would be scarcely short of a miracle if he were permitted to return alive. We do not ask them for anything, because we know it would be difficult to get it; and what is more, we could not enforce our demand, at least not without a serious war, in which, even though we should prove victorious, we should be the greatest losers. We have been at war once with them, and we know what it cost us to reduce them. After they had bid us defiance for three years, they were at last brought to terms only by means of bloodhounds, a species of "dogs of war" whose employment is not considered desirable by us. The Maroons are our necessary allies. Without their assistance we could not long hold Jamaica, and they are quite aware of it. They know their position, and take advantage of it. It would be Quixotism to refuse their alliance, even though, in order to maintain it, it is difficult to avoid sacrificing to some extent principle to policy.

The Maroons are commanded by some English gentlemen, but I doubt if any of the officers by whom they are led would care to appear in Exeter Hall, and give an account of the doings of their followers to negroes at a time like that of the late outbreak. They fight capitally in the bush, covering themselves all over with leaves, so as to be almost invisible, and use spear and rifle well.

At Manchioneal, a little collection of scattered huts buried under palm-trees, and close to the sea, R. had to pay some police. S. and I rode up a wood path, and came upon several burnt cottages, on which a notice had been posted up that Mr. Lewis would come down to collect evidence; and I suppose we were taken for his party, as many people flocked to us with their stories of wrong and suffering. If they are to be believed, the burning and shooting inflicted by the troops must have been most promiscuous. One man, whose name was Lindsay, gave this dismal account of his case:—

"This house" (pointing to a blackened timber or two and a mud wall) "is mine."

"Who burned it?"

"The soldiers burnt it—burnt it all."

"Why did they?"

"Dunno, massa—dunno. Dey came up, and looked round, and lay fire to my house."

"Well, they must have found some stolen things."

"No, no, massa, house have no stolen ting; me no rebel."

"Were you standing by at the time, or did you run away?"

"No, massa, me present the whole time."

The next man we met was a sharp-looking mulatto, with whom the following conversation was held:—

"Is that your house?"

"Yes, sir."

"The soldiers did not lay fire to it?"

"No; they did not burn my house, but they burned my father's for nothing. There was nothing stolen in it; and the poor old man was put out, and his house burned; and he has since died from distress of mind."

"Who was the officer in charge of the troops?"*

"There was no officer with them then: he had gone on. I saw a man shot down because some one said he was a rebel. He had no trial. He was pointed at, and began to speak; but the soldier fired, and he fell."

We must have seen at least six houses that were burnt. The greater number, however, were spared this calamity. A woman told us how she had begged the soldiers to spare hers, and had succeeded. The houses seemed to have been of a better sort than usual. There was a good deal of rough stone-work in them. Each had the thick bush on all sides, and the palms were drooping over them.

We entered a square-built old fortalice, used as a police-station, in an upper room of which we found a coloured man, Mr. Jardyne, teaching a school. He spoke freely of the riots. He had fled into the bush. The rebels had only burnt two houses; the troops, eight or nine. One woman, Amelia Scott, who had been burnt out, he spoke of particularly as being certainly innocent. We went down again to find her, passing two or three more ruins. She lived near the sea with her son, who was with her at the time, and

---

* These troops belonged to a West India regiment, whose men seem to have got beyond the control of their officers.

her brother. She described how, at a time when she was so ill with some foot disease, and her son from a sore, that neither could walk, two or three soldiers had come in—one a white doctor; and though she declared she had no stolen goods, the latter hastily bundled them out, his only reply to their pleading being, "No use, no use," and himself set fire to a corner of the thatch. Young Scott said that the people could not leave their houses for fear of being shot. One man, David Burke, was shot close by. A black soldier said to him, "You d——d rebel." He said, "Me no rebel. Me work for Mr. ——." The soldier shot him down directly. Another man, a special constable, said he saw eleven men shot down without trial, one of whom he was certain was not a rebel. This occurred, probably, when the rioters first met the troops, who drove them back from Port Antonio.

The troops that came down on this band from Long Bay had been sent round by Colonel Nelson from Morant Bay. Whatever the wisdom of after measures, their first movements were well conceived and properly executed.

We were most hospitably received here by Mr. Orgill, the English Church clergyman. After the gutted tenements we have seen, the house is a picture of comfort. Only one of Mr. Orgill's congregation was in the riots. We sat listening to stories of escapes from the rebels, while the cool air was blowing up from the sea some hundreds of feet below us, and the fireflies were lighting up the woodlands by thousands.

CHAPTER V.

Port Antonio — Negro Method of firing Houses — Prosperous Negroes near Port Antonio—Mr. Orgill's Opinion regarding the Cultivation of Sugar—Lovely Bays—Mr. Anderson, an old Scotch Gentleman—Complaints as to the Want of Labour—Negro Objection to Contracts—Co-operative System for the Manufacture of Sugar—Immorality and Education—Immigration—A Bastard Law—A Maroon Officer—Their Mode of Fighting—Captain M'Farlane—His Defence of the Maroons—Dinner with the Maroons—A Sentiment received with Great Applause—Measures proposed for the Inauguration of a Better Order of Things—Reform of Elective Bodies—Of Vestries—Of the Present Magistracy—Appointment of Stipendiary Magistrates—Government System of Industrial Schools—An Education Tax—Fine Scenery—The Rio Grande—Forest-Trees—The Cotton-Tree—Undergrowth and Creepers in the Woods—Birds seen in Jamaica—Immense Butterfly—Botanic Garden at Bath — Court-House at Morant Bay—The Volunteers—The Massacre—Gordon's Grave — The Charge against him—Mr. Eyre — Martial Law—The late Governor's Policy—Site of Mr. Eyre's House, and View from it—Important Document—Evidence as to the Proceedings and Designs of the People—Illegal Drilling—Curious Document.

PORT ANTONIO, at which we arrived on February 21st, is only a few hours from Boston, so we took our long journey easily, not starting till after breakfast—an excellent one—and till we had made an inspection of Mr. Orgill's little garden, which is really charming. I expressed surprise that the family was not there, and was told that only two days ago an incendiary attempt had been made on the house of a neighbour, and as the residence could only be thought secure with ready revolvers and barking dogs, they preferred to have the ladies in the town at present. The plan of the negroes for firing houses is excellent in its way. A bamboo is split at the end into fine shreds, which burn furiously. A hole is then made in the shingles, into which the bamboo is introduced, and it is not long before the whole roof comes down.

Much was said in favour of some negroes living near Port Antonio. Many of them have freeholds on which they work hard, and for which they have paid a good deal of money: 100*l*. was paid lately by one for ten acres of land. Another paid 270*l*. for some land. These men were quite opposed to the recent disaffection, and were loud in their declarations that they would fight for the Queen—a manifestation of loyalty, however, which is hardly peculiar to them, as the rioters seem not only to have had a great respect for Her Majesty, but even to have imagined that she would quite approve of their doings in sweeping away the Buckras whom they dislike. They carry provisions for the town from Kingston in boats, many of which are built by themselves.

Mr. Orgill's place is a cattle-pen, and he declares that the land hereabouts ought to be used for little else. In his opinion sugar takes too much out of the land. People, he also informs me, were only induced to plant cane in this quarter by French war prices. On our way here, our spare horse—a wretched brute—was perpetually breaking a rotten rope that tied him to our buggy, on which occasions he always made off, giving us hot chases in the sun to get him back again. Guava fruits consoled us a little, but H. was so anxious to bathe, that it was almost impossible to prevent him from stopping and jumping into every tempting bay we passed. I never saw a more lovely spot than one of these bays, called the Blue Hole. It was a round sheet of the bluest water, surrounded by high wooded banks, and was hardly disturbed by the sea-swell outside, which could only come in through a small channel.

While in this part of the island I stayed with Mr. Anderson, a fine old Scotch gentleman, who has lived long in the island. Our talk was more of Jeffrey, Scott, and the old Edinburgh set, all of whom he had often seen, than of Jamaica hubbubs. Two middies from a gunboat lying in the bay, whom we had at dinner, spoke touchingly of their sufferings from mosquitoes. Much was said against the reasonableness of the complaints made by the planters as to the want of labour. "One disadvantage is that the people are often widely scattered, and in many districts men have to go fourteen or fifteen miles to the nearest sugar estate. It would undoubtedly be very beneficial if they were encouraged to form villages in the immediate neighbourhood of the works, but this is not done. In what part of England would you always be sure, in a district where population is scant, of getting one, two, or three hundred hands whenever you wanted them? Sometimes, when it is not crop time, so many are not wanted, and when there is no work on the estate, provision grounds must be set apart to supply them with food. These grounds occasionally require looking after at a time when every hand may be wanted on the estate. Such is the only arrangement that can be made when there is no settlement near the works, and no contracts are made for labour. At present the negroes are such fools that they look upon a contract as temporary slavery, and will not enter into any engagement of the kind. Mills in the centre of the small cane grounds would be an advantage. A mill might manufacture sugar from the cane brought by the proprietors of the small cane grounds around, and the miller get every third hogshead. Shares should be apportioned by weight—so many hogsheads for so many tons of cane —and the whole business could be carried on by a co-operative system by the negroes themselves. A better price might thus be obtained for the products of their fields than is now got from the imperfectly manufactured stuff which they produce. Not more than thirty thousand at present obtain work out of a population of half a million.

"The immorality prevalent among the people is dreadful; and what between the state of the law and the natural disposition of the negroes, there is little inclination to exert themselves. A man may have fifty children, and be obliged to support neither woman nor child, for there is no bastardy law. Ignorance is the rule. An educational tax of three-pence a week might easily be paid, but it would be difficult to collect it. A little paring away of the 45,000*l.* given to the English Church would be very serviceable in the establishment of schools. In this parish, where the English Church has more members than in any other, there have been only two or three marriages in the last six months, a fact which shows how little even the best clerical supervision has been able to effect in the improvement of morals. There is a cry for immigration. The immigrant might live on the higher grounds, and cultivate provisions or sugar. If there had been as much practical ability, as much active exertion, here, as there has been talk, things would have looked different by this time." Our heads soon became heavy with port and politics, and we went to bed.

On the 22nd we stopped at Millbank, in the mountains, because we were told we could not get on further, owing to the badness of the bridle-path on which we had been riding since morning. Our object in coming up these hills was to see the Maroons. We were not fairly off till ten, as Ramsay had to pay some police-stations further up the coast, and was not back till nine. On leaving the town (which is poor, but has some chance of mending, as soldiers are to be kept there, and others will stay in consequence), we struck up the valley, at whose head we now are. It is one of the cols of the Blue Mountains. The way was a mere path across streams and mud, and rock and bush. A handful of men could, in any part of it, have stopped a large force. Nothing more would be necessary than to fell across the path some of the gigantic bamboos that grow in towering groups on each side. We were met about half-way up by the commanding officer of the Maroons under Colonel Fyfe, a negro, who appeared duly caparisoned in blue serge, a red ribbon in his cap, a silver *plaque* with George III.'s head on his breast, and a pair of enormous gold epaulettes on his shoulders. He rode in front of us up a narrow path, and soon some of his men appeared, one or two with guns. These fellows, as they went along, tore down some of the creepers and bushes, and wound them round their bodies, so as to look like moving shrubs. Their mode of fighting is to stand motionless with this invisible costume among the trees, and to shoot the enemy when he has passed. The town which they inhabit is a scattered collection of neatly-thatched huts, each with its inclosure and provision ground, where cane, cocoa, and bananas are roughly cultivated. We were received by a Captain M'Farlane, a fine, stalwart, long-eyebrowed Maroon, and conducted to his hut, which was scrupulously clean, with neatly-polished boards for floor, and a large four-post bedstead in a little room hardly bigger than itself. A crowd of men and women pressed round the cottage, and watched us closely through the windows, till M'Farlane went and told them confidentially that such "conduct was not manners." He made many small orations to us, chiefly in praise of his own people, some of which, as I have mentioned the reports spread against them, I ought to repeat.

"Yes, I am a Maroon," he said, drawing himself up to his full height, "and I *am* proud of it; and you, sirs, who have come from England, may now see what kind of people the Maroons are. They tell you that Maroon is savage, and cruel, and uncivilized. You go home, and say you have seen Maroons, and all dat untrue. Yes, sir, all untrue. Tom write, Bill write, Sam write; but they all tell untruth. Maroon not cruel. In St. Thomas rebel fire eight, nine volley before Maroon fire a shot. Dey not cruel; but rebel could not stand loyal Maroon," &c., &c.

He introduced to us one young man who had been wounded in the encounter with the rebels. He wore a large bandage over one eye, swore that his wound was as bad as ever, and looked very well pleased with himself. A tall man, a good specimen of his race, and said to be a great warrior, was also presented to us; after him an old man, who said, "He old man, and no walk; but against rebel he run, he twist, he

turn, and make them go;" and finally a clerk, of whom
M'Farlane said, "He write beautiful, he can," an
accomplishment which for himself he modestly disclaimed, saying, "I no write—not me; I write with
my tongue."

Our dinner was ring-tail pigeon and smoked wild
pig, caught by the Maroons. Both were excellent,
as was the cocoa we drank. On our departure,
M'Farlane made another speech in a stentorian
voice to the crowd at the door, telling them what we
had come for, and what a good report we should give
to England about the Maroons, to which S. added, in
going, that he should also tell them what pretty girls
the Maroons had—a sentiment which was received
with immense satisfaction and applause, and by the
young ladies themselves with a great deal of smirking and giggling. One of them was, indeed, dragged
forward by her laughing companions to S., whose
horse's paces were quickened at the amorous demonstration. In accordance with the Maroons' advice, we
had another good ring-tail dinner here, with an addition of fresh-water periwinkles from the river, the Rio
Grande, that flows by the house.

After having been now round the district which was
the focus of the so-called rebellion, my impression is

this:—In a limited district around Morant Bay and Port Morant, disaffection had long existed, arising from well-known and reasonable causes; and this disaffection had been fostered by designing men, by whom preparations for a rising had been made. The people in the neighbouring parishes do not appear to have known exactly what was to happen, but had heard vague rumours. The movement was begun by certain turbulent blacks, the number of whom would no doubt have very speedily increased, had not the outbreak been at once vigorously suppressed. Having been prematurely hurried on by Bogle, the insurrectionary movement was under no real control. The bands of rioters seem to have been so contemptible as a military force, that if the volunteer corps had been kept up, small as it was, it would have held the mob at bay, especially as there was nothing worthy of the name of organization among the blacks. It was, on the whole, fortunate that with so many reasons for discontent, they were not better prepared to act in concert. The state of affairs in these parishes, where the riots broke out, was such as no Englishman could have stood for a week; the inhabitants having no faith in the justice of the magistrates by whom the law was, or ought to have been, administered.

Among the measures which have been proposed with the view of inaugurating a better order of things, the following are the principal. First, as to the elective bodies, and especially the vestries, these have not only to do with Church matters, but are boards of management for the parish divisions of the country. By the boundaries of the parish, or several parishes, the police have their department framed. The larger divisions of counties one hardly ever hears of. A planter at Plantain Garden River would be spoken of as Mr. ——, of St. Thomas-in-the-Vale, not as Mr. ——, in Surrey. The vestry has the management of the parish. The right to vote for a member is held by a 6l. property qualification. Two churchwardens in each parish sit *ex officio*, and thus get involved in political disputes. There are, I think, three magistrates on the vestry-board, and five others. All expenses of the district pass through their hands. Every act is subject to their supervision, and they can *veto* payments, and are responsible to the Governor and to the House of Legislature (when there is one) alone. These vestries, as they exist, ought to be abolished. They have been a constant source of dispute and trouble, from the struggles and animosities engendered by attempts to get on the board, and by the decisions of the body. All appointments in a community like this ought to come from above, not from below; from the Government, not from the people.

The next great requisite, if it does not stand first, is the abolition of the present magistracy. It is impossible that the common people should have confidence in these men. They are either shopkeepers anxious to keep their custom, or planters who are almost unavoidably influenced by their feelings as masters, and cannot be expected to look with an impartial eye on the claims of servants. It was principally owing to the want of confidence among the people in the magistracy that Gordon was able to foster that disloyalty which ended so disastrously last year.

Stipendiary magistrates are an absolute necessity. Mr. Harrison thinks that they should be itinerant, none staying in any place so long as to be influenced by local feelings. To this official all parish disputes ought to be referred for decision.

A Government system of *industrial schools*, with competent masters, and a Government inspector to look after them, would be highly desirable. Every child ought to be obliged, as they are in some parts of

Germany, to attend one of these schools. Education, to be useful among these people, must be compulsory, otherwise the child will be sent to school for a short time only, will learn to read and write a little, and will then be taken away before he has acquired much to benefit him, to become afterwards, probably, an infinitely more disagreeable member of society than he would otherwise have been. Nowhere is it more true that a little knowledge is a dangerous thing than it is here. Compulsory teaching would take a few hands from the crops, but the communication of sound knowledge to the rising generation would more than compensate for the evil thus inflicted.

A clergyman of the Church of England to whom I spoke the other day believes that the people might be made to pay threepence a week as an education tax. The difficulty is to levy it at present. The only thing that reaches them is the tax on donkeys—three shillings and sixpence each. If little can be got, the bishop's salary ought to be appropriated for the purpose, the Church-of-England revenues being so ample as to admit of being shorn a little. A bastardy law would be of immense benefit. At present there is no stimulus to work for wife and child, or rather for mistress and children. A law of this nature would drive many hands to the labour market, and would probably prove more effective than preaching in preventing that immorality which is confessedly too prevalent at present among the blacks. The House of Assembly could never be persuaded to impose any such tax either on itself or others; and though attempts have been made to legislate on this subject, no law of the kind has ever been passed.

The finest bit of scenery we have met with in the tropics was the range of country between Millbank and Bath. No one thinks of walking here. If a man wants to go to a place to which his legs would carry him in five minutes he always mounts a horse, or is carried in a buggy. Personal exertion is eschewed here even by the most healthy.

After an excellent breakfast of fresh-water periwinkles, ring-tail pigeons, and some coarse brown sugar and coffee, we mounted and rode on through the glades to the head of the col. We crossed the Rio Grande before descending—a very pretty stream, winding along between the large boulders with which it has strewn its course, and the high wooded hills on each side. The charm of the forest is somehow rather spoiled to me, since I have heard that the chief trees— the cocoa, the mango, bread-fruit, and pimento, none of which attain a great girth or height—have only recently been introduced. In the size of the trees the woods of Jamaica are said to be very inferior to those of South America. The cotton-tree is the only one that attains any great height; and when seen on the high hills it is not to be compared in beauty with a beech or an elm. The stem is straight and round, the bark of a glistening white, and the branches are thrown out at a formal right angle. The foliage is very scanty, and in no proportion to the immense size of the trunk. The chief beauty in these woods is the undergrowth and creepers, and on a lower zone the palms, which are not seen high up on the mountains. A remarkable plant, called the long thatch, sprouts from the ground in great palm-like branches, thirty or forty feet in length, without a stem. The tree ferns, of which there are several varieties, give, with their lace-like fronds, the greatest beauty to the undergrowth.

On our ride the handsome Banana-bird was common, and a species of Humming-bird, with a long tail and white breast, green head and back, many of which allowed us to get quite close to them. Flocks of parrots of a large species, green, with a blush red round the neck, fled screaming from the top branches of the trees, apparently very wild. A peculiar kind of butterfly appeared, with orange wings edged with black, and of an immense size. There are no blue ones here, the species being, I believe, confined to the Brazils.

Sometimes the creepers and parasites rather mar than add to the beauty of the woods. In one place we passed they looked like a green pall flung over the trees, whose tops were only marked by a swell in their covering. There is a botanic garden at Bath. The plants are all foreign to the country, but every sort of tropical tree flourishes without need of care.

We slept at night at Lysson's, and met Mr. Gurney going down to Bath to take evidence of the people thereabouts. The following day we drove to Morant Bay, and stayed for some time examining the ruins of the Court-house. The square in front of the building is a space quite capable of containing a considerable mob. It is full of stones, none of them, however, very large, which the rioters brought with them on October 11th, and some of them so rounded that they look as if they had been taken from the neighbouring river. I do not know whether any of the numerous accounts of the scrimmage and massacre published in England have particularly noticed the mistaken clemency of poor Baron Kettlehold. He was standing with others on the steps to the right, the volunteers drawn up below between the two stairs that led to the upper floor, and extended some feet beyond the front of the house. As the mob advanced, throwing large stones at the volunteers, which they were allowed to do till within six feet of the line, Hitchens shouted to the Baron, "Shall we fire?" The latter took no notice, but went on hurriedly reading the Riot Act, which ought to have been read as soon as the mob entered the square. "Shall we fire?" again asked Hitchens, but still without receiving any answer. "Three paces step back," was then the order given by the volunteer leader to his men, but still the mob advanced. Again Hitchens ordered the volunteers to retire three paces, after which they could retreat no further, their heels being against the masonry in front of the house. The mob had now come so near that they were able to seize some of the muskets, on seeing which Hitchens ordered the volunteers "to present," and the little band fired, killing several of the rioters in front, but leaving themselves defenceless. Those behind immediately closed in, and all the volunteers who could escape sought for safety in the Court-house.

In the meantime the school-house adjoining had been fired, and the flames spreading to the Court-house, those who had sought refuge within leaped from the windows only to meet death in Price's house close by, where they were massacred. If Kettlehold had only had the presence of mind to tell the mob that, if they came within a hundred yards of the volunteers they would be fired at, this lamentable sacrifice of life might have been spared. The fault was not that the volunteers fired, but that they did not fire sooner. It was from the central blackened window of the Court-house that Gordon was afterwards hanged, with the men who had been concerned in these murders. His grave, as well as that of many more who were buried with him, is in a trench behind the Court-house, in front of a battery built on a rise above the sea. How much has been spoken and written about that man, who, after all, was nothing more than a paltry demagogue! I do not think that any evidence I have seen is sufficient to prove that Gordon prepared plans for rebellion. His great object seems rather to have been that others should rebel than that he himself should be exposed to the charge of being a rebel. His part was to counsel rather than to act. He might have been prosecuted, perhaps, for sedition; but no jury would have given a verdict against him if he had been

arraigned for high treason in a court of common law.
Meanwhile, lawyers may be justly dissatisfied about
his death, for there were no legal grounds for conviction.

On our way to Kingston, we met —— and ——,
who were going to visit the Rhine to hear what Gordon's
labourers say of their late employer. There is an
evident disposition, on the part of these gentlemen,
to take only negro evidence, which is eagerly swallowed,
while that of whites is jealously tested and sifted
before it is accepted.

On the 25th we dined with S. C. B——, W——,
H——, P——, and some ladies. They were anxious
to excuse S. W. Gordon; and it was observed, as some
proof that he was not dishonest, at least in mercantile
transactions, that no actions had been brought against
him. He was considered, however, a "man of straw,"
and an action to get money would not have been of
much use.

On the 26th we came up here to Mr. Eyre's country-
house. He had sent an invitation to us as soon as
we landed, but it arrived too late, as we had already
gone away on our trip to the eastern end. He seemed
as firm as ever as to the absolute necessity for the
long continuance of martial law. He judged, from

what he knew of the state of the island, that common law would not have been strong enough to punish offenders so promptly as to strike necessary terror into the minds of the people, who, he is persuaded, would have joined the rebels on the slightest pretence. This persuasion was the result of the almost unanimous expressions of fear of an outbreak and warnings sent by numbers of the white inhabitants of the island. No one will, I apprehend, blame him for having, at the first, proclaimed martial law; and although civil law was not restored after the riots had been put down by military force, yet full consideration ought to be given to the difficulty the Governor experienced in putting an end to a state of things by which alone, owing to the unreliability of the civil law, he thought the disaffected could be kept well in hand. We ought to remember that while martial law was kept on for, perhaps, twenty days after resistance had ceased in Jamaica, civil law has been suspended in the Southern States of the Union for a full twelvemonth after the last Confederate regiment surrendered to Grant and Sherman.

I differ from Mr. Eyre in the policy of acting without law in Gordon's arrest; but no one can help being very sorry for him. He did what he thought his duty, and has avoided no responsibility, but, on the contrary, has declared himself to be the only person to whom blame, if blame there be, ought to be attached. It is a cruel thing for a man who has acted and worked as he has for what he thought the good of the community to be branded as a murderer. He was, and is, thoroughly convinced that the crisis required the measures he adopted. There is reason for his belief in the slowness and uncertainty of justice as administered by Kingston courts of law. His policy was severe, for he believed it to be the most merciful; but I do not think the English public will be inclined to agree with him that the crisis required such steps as the illegal transfer of Gordon to Morant Bay, or the continuation of martial law when resistance had ceased.

The situation of the house is delightful. It is four thousand feet above the sea, and the harbour of Kingston and fifty miles of coast lie spread beneath us. The climate is quite English. I have slept with blankets on my bed for the first time since I have been in the West Indies. One has to ride up the hill, as the carriage road only goes to its foot. It is curious to feel the change of temperature as one mounts from the blaze of the plains to the cool and mist of these hills. The house is guarded by sentries, as much threatening talk has been heard about taking the Governor's life. He walks about unarmed, which is hardly wise.

Mr. Eyre was so good as to show us a long despatch. It was his report and analysis of a number of documents furnished him by custodes, clergymen, attorneys, and others, to whom he had appealed for evidence regarding the events that had happened, and their experience as to the state of feeling in various parishes. In his opinion the report clearly shows that, if there was not an organized combination throughout the different parishes, there was at least in most of them a disaffected and seditious spirit—a disposition to rebel, which any trifling circumstance might unexpectedly have stimulated into open revolt, drawing the whole of the black population into the ranks of the insurgents.

In looking over these papers, their contents left it impossible for me to entertain any doubt as to the sincerity of the conviction, on the part of the whites, that Eyre was the saviour of the colony, of their lives and property. A certain amount of preparation for insurrection appears to have been made, and as to the intentions of the people in Morant Bay district, no doubt has ever been entertained. The testimony of some men, too, in Trelawney and elsewhere seems to make it but too apparent that the people had been anticipating some serious crisis in which it was their determination to take an active part.

E. G. S. Mitchell, Trelawney, stated that, shortly before the time of the riots, he knew illegal drilling was going on among the people. W. Coley, a deserter from the 1st West Indian regiment, was aware that meetings had been held before and after the riots at St. Elizabeth, and was asked to join the rebels as a drill-sergeant. "I heard the meeting told," he said, "that they must arm and burn the house of a Mr. Coke, and that Christmas would be the time for a successful rising." Mr. Hildebrand knew that illegal drilling had been going on at Manchester, as well as at the other places, all far distant from the Morant Bay district. The people appear, too, to have become very insolent in their manner, indulging in a great deal of nigger brag, talking of killing the whites wherever they could lay hands on them; and uttering menaces which must have been sufficiently alarming to the scanty number of Europeans living isolated on their properties, who knew that, in the event of an insurrection, their lives would not be worth a moment's purchase. The reason for all this ill-feeling on the part of the labourers is clearly expressed in the statement of Charles Maclean, of St. David's, who testifies that ill-feeling and dissatisfaction are daily increasing, that the decisions of courts of law are held in no respect, and that proclamations and messages from the Queen are treated with contempt, and called *lies, red lies.* Here the right nail is struck on the head. Believing that justice was not meted out to them, the negroes had come to the determination to sweep away the Government that administered the affairs of the island, because they did not believe it represented the Government of England.

The following is the copy of a document showing the want of faith the negroes had in the regular courts :—

"Letter Hilb. Memory of a Meeting held on July 11, 1863. Move by Mr. James Steen, and was unonimously carried—That Mr. W. C. Menknob be appointed State General. Move by Mr. D. Baily, seconded by Mr. W. Bowie—That the qualification Baristers and Lawyers be a Sartificate from the Judge, and he receiving a fee of 1*l.* Move by Mr. Lake, seconded by Mr. Baily—That the fees of the peace-office for each process be 1*l.* Move by Mr. Ford, seconded by Mr. W. C. McKnob—That two petty sessions be held, one on the 18th, and one on the 25th inst. Each court do commence at six o'clock in the afternoon, and that the Court of Arispagus be held on the 4th August, 1863. Resolve—That the Courts be held at the above-name place. Resolve—That all person or persons who shall wilfully misbehave themselves shall be committed for trial, and if won't submit, be disbands as unsivilize. Resolve—That 3d. be considered as 1l., and due deference be paid to the Chairman and his Sobadinates. Resolve by Mr. William Bogle, seconded by Mr. W. Bowie—That Mr. Paul Bogle be appointed Justice of the Peace. Resolve—That the Prevance Marshal General do stick up a list on the 25th inst. of the names of persons to serve on 4th August, inserving in the Court House, ledgable written for every omission 4l., and likewise every officer in the same for omission or neglect of duty."

In the "Memory of a Meeting" held, persons were elected for the office of Judge, Clerk of the Peace, "Prevance-Marshal," Inspector, and Sargent. One unfortunate was raised to the post of Privett; another was appointed Founder, whatever that may mean; and this assembly was broken up on a "move unonimously carried that this Meeting do objurn."

These papers are curious, showing as they do that the negroes were trying to get up courts of justice for themselves. I think the *Arispagus* delightful.

CHAPTER VI.

Flamstead—Cowardly Acts of Intimidation—Visit to Hill, the Naturalist—Sharks—The Political Prospects of Jamaica—Probable Disappointment of the Furious Supporters of the Ex-Governor—Substitution of English for Spanish Names of Places—The Road to Moreland—Mangrove Belts—Cultivation of Sugar Estates — The Cotton-Tree — From Moreland to St. Jago—Guinea Fowl—Ants—Want of Doctors — Humming-birds—Mandeville — Black Freeholders—A Negro's Necessaries and Burdens in Jamaica—A Negro Dodge—Attorneys for Estates—Laziness and Caprice of the Negroes—Stoppage of Wages—The Question between Overseers and Negroes—Domestic Servants—Price of Food—Position of the Black Freeholder—Precedence of Races—Abolition of the House of Assembly—Extravagant Application of Public Money—Neglect of Popular Education—Ignorance with respect to Contracts—Negro Interpretation of a Public Proclamation—Visit to a Large School—Congo Boys—Drunkenness among the Negroes — Jamaica as a Place for Emigrants—A Negro's Opinion of the Rioters.

OUR time at Flamstead was very pleasant. Mist and rain prevented our seeing much the first day, but the weather cleared up afterwards. Mr. B., a clergyman living in a house on the hill below the military station of Newcastle, asked us to stay a night with him, and we rode down from the Governor's with him and his wife—a lady who remained in this country-house all the time of the riots. At a village post-office in the glen, between the Governor's house and their own, they got a parcel of letters, one of which was directed to "Mrs. Dora B." Mr. B. knew that the island papers, in their report of Mrs. B.'s evidence given before the Commissioners, had printed her name as Dora instead of Laura. He therefore luckily opened the letter himself, thinking the address an odd one, and in it found a drawing of a woman in a night-shirt being hanged by two diabolical-looking negroes; and, to leave no doubt as to the person intended, the name "Dora" was written beneath.

Such cowardly acts of intimidation render whites extremely suspicious of the negroes generally, and therefore it is that so many, even clergymen, like to sleep with watch-dogs in their verandahs and revolvers near their beds.

After staying some time at Spanish Town to hear different persons examined before the Commission, we went on to Mr. M'Kinnon's, at Vere, twenty miles from Spanish Town. Sir James Hope and I went the other day to call on Mr. Hill, the naturalist, who gave us much information both on politics and natural history.

Hill is one of the few surviving stipendiary magistrates of the island, of which he is a native, and has lived in it all his life. As his collections and drawings were locked up in the upper rooms of the King's House, we did not see them, and all he had to show us was a skin of one of the long-tailed humming-birds.

He talked a good deal about sharks, and on Sir James telling him how a diver of the *Duncan*, while fishing for a wreck, had seen through the sunken funnel of a steamer a shark looking at him from the other end, said these brutes never take a man in mid-water, and that anybody who could dive would have them at his mercy. They can only feed off the ground, or from the surface, and a diver may let them snuff about him at pleasure. Hill had given up birds, and taken to insects.

He is hopeful about the future of Jamaica. The overflowing of the prisons with people convicted of larceny he attributes to a law passed by the Assembly, making the picking up and eating of sugar-canes (formerly a misdemeanour) a larceny. He is not in favour of stipendiary magistrates moving about from place to place, considering the prohibition of their possessing property a sufficient guarantee for their strict administration of justice.

After the cool impartiality of King's House, we found ourselves again among very furious supporters of Eyre. They will be terribly chagrined, I fear, their feeling in his favour being so decided, when the Commissioners' report is made public. At present they seem determined to expect that which they wish—viz., Mr. Eyre's reinstatement in the Government.

"You'll see if he wont be made a K.C.B. and reinstated. I believe the Commission to have done much harm; and about that d—d rascal, Gordon— why, was not his property in the martial-law district, and did not his sayings work so much mischief there? Why should he not be tried in the place where his offence was committed?" &c.

The following is some doggerel in which the woes of the planter are bewailed:—

A PLANTER'S LAMENT.

I.

Our estates are in ruins, and wearied, we try
To coax the dear niggers to work ere we die;
But the isle that was flowing with sugar and rum
Lies untilled and neglected, for scarce any come!
We're heartily tired of this tropical land,
Where rebellion is nursed by the Government's hand!
Why, who can we look to, to set us straight now,
But to the great thinker—good Chamerovzow?

II.

The sounds of the crunching and pressing of cane
We almost despair of e'er hearing again;
The boilers are empty; the still-house is dry;
There's little to sell, and there's no one to buy.
We offer good wages, and heartily pray
For the poor chance of getting some nigger to pay;
But they wont listen to us, for they've listened and bow
To the words and the wisdom of Chamerovzow!

III.

Our house, once well furnished, has tumbled to rot,
And we speak of what was, but what now is not.
An estate that is paying 's a *lusus naturæ*
So rare, that you ask if it really can true be.
From King Log to King Stork we have fallen, and still
No progress is seen, but the progress downhill.
We are poor, and are not what we were, but e'en now
We're "haughty and cruel!" says Chamerovzow.

IV.

The negro is lord of himself and his toil,
The run of the land and the fat of the soil.
He makes his own bargains for labour, and works
Whenever he pleases, and, when he likes, shirks.
He's a very good fellow, if but let alone,
But you've meddled and muddled, and mischief you've sown,
And 'tis you who have kicked up this troublesome row—
Yes, you, my philanthropist, Chamerovzow!

V.

It's all very well, when in Exeter Hall,
To measure out mercy; speak ill of the gall
We showed to those who, not content with their votes,
Had schemed to cut all our civilized throats!

It does seem most curious, unaccountably queer,
That England don't value the lives of us here!
If *he'd* been expecting a blow on *his* pow,
Would *he* still have been a calm Chamerovzow?

VI.

And as for the gents that have sat and have talked
Of the plans of the planters that ought to be balked,
Who've believed every word of each lie that was told,
Who've clasped their white hands, or their pig's eyes uprolled,
Who've still a Society for Slave Abolition,
When the slavery system has gone to perdition—
Why, every one's joined against slavery now,
And they fight against phantoms, great Chamerovzow!

Most of the Spanish names in this country have disappeared. Cromwell's Puritan soldiers did not like the appellations given by the former masters to streets and districts, especially as they were all named after saints; and consequently now, instead of the musical Spanish, we have the familiar English, the town itself being called "Spanish Town," instead, as of old, St. Jago della Vega, &c.

The road to Moreland is uninteresting, as it passes over the flat country covered with the short wood of the cashaw, a tree between a mimosa and an acacia, with a flat top and light green foliage. The sun was very hot, making the penguins growing by the road glitter like a hedge of bayonets. Every now and then we passed near the sea, but there was no open beach with yellow sand and white surf, but instead, an eternal belt of mangroves rising from the water, and extending into it their numberless forked roots, making a tangle of wood impenetrable to any creature but the alligators.

Old Zachary Macaulay, father of the historian, had estates hereabouts, but they are mostly in bush. It was a relief to come upon the magnificent cane-fields of this (Moreland) property. No crop is so handsome as that of the sugar cane. Most persons know what the cane itself is like; but in the fields one sees but little of it, as it is sheathed in the long, reed-like leaves, that cluster thickly at the top, and fall drooping downwards.

I rode over the estate with Mr. M., looking at the different operations, from the cutting of the cane to the stowing of the fine brown sugar in the enormous hogsheads. The teams of oxen employed are very large. Yoked to one plough I observed no fewer than fourteen oxen. The most picturesque part of the process of sugar-making is to be seen when the great vans, loaded with cane, come in drawn by the cattle to the pressing rollers. The negroes look like bronze statues when you have the advantage of seeing them half naked, each muscle standing out glossy in the sun, as they bear great loads to the roller, and stand around it while it sucks in and crushes the bundles, sending a white stream of sugar juice into the pipes that lead to the boilers.

These operations will now go on night and day for nearly three months, at the end of which the overseer hopes to have about three hundred and twenty hogsheads from each of his three estates. The houses for the manufactory are ugly, and the smell that comes into the verandah and bedrooms from the boiling house is very heavy. That from the still-house is even more disagreeable. It is a great relief when the sea breeze springs up and drives these odours away.

St. Jago, in the parish of Clarendon, is a most delightful place, at the foot of low wooded hills. The limestone mound on which it is built is grass-grown, and overlooks a wide park-like cattle-pen that lies between the house and the sugar works, about a mile off. In front of the house is a very fine cotton-tree, which looks so well that I think I must withdraw anything I have written in disparagement of these trees; for although I do not admire their growth on the hills, they are undoubtedly very fine in the plains. The trunks, which are immense, are made larger by the buttresses thrown out from the stem. The leaf, about the same size as that of the orange-tree, is of a lighter green and narrower.

Mr. M. and I rode the twenty-two miles between Moreland and St. Jago. The roads in some places were very bad, mere by-ways in fact, on which Government money is not now spent. Formerly, when money was given for all the roads in the country, they were in a very unsatisfactory condition. Now the high-ways alone are helped, and they are very good, while all others are much worse than before. Heavy rains had recently fallen and turned the roads into nasty mud, spoiling the planters' trash, or the crushed cane they use for fuel. S. has a fever in consequence of traversing some swamps by night.

The sand and loam plains we crossed were overgrown with green ebony and logwood, to which, in many places, hung the wild liquorice, whose scarlet seeds, with their black tops, are so common in Brighton boxes of shells. A purple Orchis, which was also in flower, appeared in great beauty in some places. Where the soil was poorest the tall dildo cactus threw its ugly green-ribbed shafts into the air. A Woodpecker, invisible to us, was making a hoarse chatter in the underwoods. As we continued our journey, the Jamaica Nightingale, a handsome grey bird the size of a thrush, with a long tail and a white bar on his wing, and a small bird they call the Greendow, were frequently seen. Near a river that we crossed was a very fine White Heron, and Pigeons were numerous; one of the latter—a ground bird—having a very melancholy note—a sepulchral coo, more melancholy even than the note of the solitaires that are to be heard in the Port Royal mountains. My gun was still, unfortunately, in the Kingston Custom-house, as I thought I should not require it, or I might have had some fair sport here.

Guinea-fowl are wild, and not uncommon in the hills. Those birds that feed on small insects, as several species here do, must, if they are not fastidious, find abundance to supply their utmost wants, especially if they care about ants, of which there appear to be millions. These insects are very particular, some kinds eating meat, and refusing to touch oil, while others like oil and will not touch meat. Each kind, in short, has its own particular taste. The most conspicuous species is a little yellow creature with a black head, that, on a paling or the upright branch of a tree, builds an enormous nest of brown mud, so large that it looks like some swelling or deformity in the tree itself. One sort never travels except by covered ways; and a long thin strip of mud, that runs twining up the bark, is found on examination to be an arched passage, along which an army of ants may pass unobserved.

On March 12th I rode up with Mr. Logan, Mr. M.'s overseer, to an estate belonging to Lord Dudley, who has two or three more in the West Indies. The estate, which is of small extent, not more than a mile and a half long, is very curiously situated, being evidently the bottom of an old lake in the hills, and is completely walled in on all sides. As the height is at least fourteen hundred feet above the level of the sea, and the road very steep, the labour of bringing up the heavy hogsheads of sugar must be troublesome. They are dragged on sledges, a few oxen going before, with a larger number yoked behind to prevent the sledge slipping down too fast. According to the local story, the place was discovered by a runaway slave, who, to propitiate his master, told him of its existence. The circular cattle-mill and water-wheel are still standing, as steam machinery has not yet been brought up. The conical roof of the old cattle-mill, which is still the chief power, makes it the prettiest building connected with sugar-making I have seen. The water is brought to the wheel by a long aqueduct, but the supply is so small that little can be done with it. These solitary sugar-fields enjoy the advantage of monopolizing all the labour in the vicinity, as there is no other estate for some miles to compete with them.

Nearly all the planters in this neighbourhood employ coolies. On Mr. Mitchell's estate in Vere there are a number of them. Their slender forms and long black mops of hair contrast strongly with the burliness and woolliness of the negro, who, when disposed to work, can do perhaps as much again. Few coolies can do more than their fifty cane holes, while a negro does his hundred if he works hard. Although M. has such a number of coolies, he is anxious for more, and talks of having Chinese. I wonder if the last could be procured from Cuba, into which a very great number have already been brought.

There is a great want of doctors here. We have had to send nine miles for one, and he charges a doubloon each visit. Medical advice is almost unattainable for the blacks, and the consequence is that they trust entirely to the bush doctors and the Obeah men. There is some talk now of establishing a Government school at Kingston for medicine, and of sending blacks out as doctors, allowing them to charge a dollar only for each consultation.

We sat some time in the porch reading. Flowering shrubs grew on each side, and Humming-birds were whirring about the blossoms close to our heads; they might easily have been caught with a hand net. One was lovely—emerald green, with a tail of two long feathers, each about six inches in length.

I should have much liked to have gone further to the west, to the great cattle-breeding and grazing pens at the end of the island, and to have seen the parishes of St. Anne's, St. Elizabeth, and Trelawney, districts I hear spoken of as more flourishing than any in the country. Mandeville itself, a place that looks in apple-pie order, appears prosperous. There are people about it, too, which is more than can be said of Spanish Town, where the streets look as deserted as— well, as some of the streets of Edinburgh during service time. The white inhabitants were looking cheerful, a detachment of troops having come and pitched their tents on a grass-plot in the middle of the settlement; and people like to be under the range of Enfield rifles even now. Bags of coffee were piled in front of many of the stores, ready to be sent down to Kingston.

This coffee is all grown by black freeholders, a class of people who, in this neighbourhood, are doing very well. Their condition, so far as regards corporeal wants, is as satisfactory as that of any peasantry I know. They have their own provision grounds, and are able, when the crop is coffee, if only moderately industrious, to make a good deal of money. Nor are they, nor the rest of the blacks, as far as I can learn, too heavily taxed. I think Dr. Underhill has made too much of this. They form by far the larger part of the community; and if taxes are not to reach them, little enough revenue can be gathered.

If a negro wishes to set up for himself, with a little land and a house, the articles he requires are very few, and the taxes he has to pay I do not think too heavy. In the following statement the things necessary to a black on settling are put in one column, and the taxes he has to pay on them in another. The allowance is certainly liberal, for few men want two full suits of clothes a year, or as much salt fish as I have supposed the negro to need:—

Negro's Wants, and Taxes on the Articles.

	£	s.	d.		s.	d.
Two Suits of Clothes, Osnaburgh	0	6	0	...	0	9
A Bill for Cutting Cane	0	2	6	...	0	3¾
A Hoe	0	2	0	...	0	6
A Cutlass	0	2	0	...	0	6
A Donkey			—	...	3	6
One Acre of Land	1	0	0	...	0	1

Two hundredweight of salt fish cost about six shillings. For a horse, which many of these people have for riding, they must pay ten shillings, as must planters for their saddle-horses; such an animal being a luxury in both cases. For stock, a planter pays very little, perhaps too little; but a heavier tax on cattle would make the working of an estate very difficult; and I think it of the first importance that the sugar estates should not fail. They give a great deal of regular employment, and are an immense boon to all classes of the population. The planter pays heavily for shingles for his roof, which the negro, who thatches his hovel or cottage, does not require. There are a few other things, perhaps, in addition to those I have mentioned, which, for convenience, might be thrown in: a hatchet, for instance, which would cost an additional three or five shillings; but hundreds of articles, which are more or less necessary to a European or Creole, are never wanted by the negroes. The calabash answers all the purposes of water-carrying. There is no house-tax.

The negroes often cheat the dues by calling their riding beasts brood mares, by which dodge they succeed in paying sixpence for them instead of eleven shillings. Much has been said about the drought from which they suffered in some districts; but it is useless to complain of such a misfortune, which occurs very rarely, probably once or twice in a lifetime, and which no man can help. There is more sense and reason in their complaints regarding the stoppage of wages by the overseers, a proceeding to which these gentlemen are too prone, as a punishment, perhaps, for some act of carelessness. At the same time, it ought to be remembered that it is the only mode of correcting the negro which is now left to them. In some cases they are too dishonest to pay at all systematically, even when work is regularly performed for them; but men of this stamp, far from being the rule, are very rare exceptions. Occasional instances of dishonesty are to be found in all places, and in all professions.

Some irregular wages-paying estates there will always be, and the battle must be fought out between labourers and owners; the latter, I have no doubt, being destined, in the long run, to have by far the best of the contest. The overseers are men who make a regular profession of the business of looking after estates. They begin as book-keepers, of whom there are generally two on each estate, and rise to be overseers, and sometimes also attorneys for the estates. An attorney has nothing to do with law business, as the name would imply with us, but is simply the manager, occupying very much the same position as a Scotch factor. Of course it is the overseer's interest to make as many hogsheads as possible to please the attorney and owner, and get the reputation of a good manager.

Driving goes on actively all day. The house is built near the works, so that the overseer, though not actually in the latter, can, at all events, see all that goes on from his verandah, from which he shouts out his orders to the people. His tongue is ever at work, calling, directing, and often abusing, or, as the overseer would prefer that it should be phrased, "loudly reproaching;" the language not being always such as one likes to hear from one man to another, however degraded and idle the inferior may be supposed to be. The overseer, indeed, will tell us that harsh language, or, if that should fail, the stoppage of wages, is the only way by which he can reach the understanding, and insure the obedience of the labourer.

The grounds for the stoppage of wages, though not always satisfactory, are sometimes reasonable enough. At one plantation I remember seeing one of the brick-built supporters of an aqueduct completely knocked down and destroyed. "Now look at that," said the overseer; "that's the way your property is destroyed. That column was knocked down the other day by a careless nigger, who drove his team of oxen and heavy waggon right up against it. That man's pay must be stopped." At another place, where the men belonging to a gang of teamsters would not come out on Saturday to their work, the manager was disconsolate at the position in which he found himself. "There they are," he said, "squatting in their houses, and doing nothing—in houses we have given them on the estate. They wont come out, simply because they say they want to have Saturday, besides Sunday, to themselves. All my other men come out, and are at work, and these fellows wont; and they throw everything out of joint. Don't you think now, sir, their pay ought to be stopped? I think I shall stop those men's pay for a week."

Such a question as that involved in this dispute

must be left to owners and labourers to fight out. The men have a perfect right to their Saturday if they please, and the overseer has equally a right to stop payment. The wages of the negro might be raised if he had the sense to organize regular strikes; but luckily for the estate he has not the brains, and in the meantime the overseer thinks he is terribly ill used because the idle black wants his Saturday to himself.

It is the same story with domestic servants at Kingston, where, also, complaints of irregular payment are rife. A man's wages are instantly stopped if the master's or mistress's ears are horrified by the sound of a falling teapot, and he never receives all the dollars which in his own opinion he has fairly worked for. He stays, in general, because he has probably changed before, and not found that improvement in his situation which he had anticipated. His position, however, is in many respects different from that of an English servant in similar circumstances, for all food is so marvellously cheap that the change, which would probably reduce the latter to starvation, makes no material difference in the condition of the former. Just look at the prices of the fruits and yams; and a yam is a thing that would take me an hour to eat and stow away properly.

		s.	d.
Yam, about a foot and a half long, and thicker than a man's fist, for		0	6
Bananas, a hand (12 pints), and a good lunch		0	3
Oranges, 1½ doz.		0	1½
Limes, 24		0	1½
Loaf of bread, 9 oz.		0	1½
Salt fish in boxes, prepared (good)		0	4½
Mangoes, 3 doz.		0	1½
Sugar Pine		0	6
Canes, length of 5 feet		0	1
Sugar, ½ pint		0	1½
Beer, 1 bottle		1	0
Rum, 1 quart		1	3
Young Pig		4	3

If a man choose, he can always earn eighteenpence before one o'clock. So satisfactory is the position of the black freehold coffee-grower in some districts, that I should not consider the island a failure if it could be peopled by such as the best of them in Manchester. The position of the black freeholder who cultivates cane is not nearly so satisfactory. He uses no manure, and the cane in a short time gets weedy, scarce, and poor. The land becomes rapidly worked out, and if he does not wish to impoverish the ground, he moves on. Coffee cannot be grown in the low grounds nearly as well as on the mountain sides; and it would be lamentable if the blacks were to get gradual possession of the plains (from the failure and abandonment of the large estates), and should cut them up into small, badly-cultivated properties.

Many of the whites say that the estates must be abandoned sooner or later, if things go on as badly as they have heretofore. Risings, too, they are convinced, will occur again, and discontent will take away the scanty labour which is all that many of them can command. This, however, I do not believe. Any fresh rising is not probable for the next forty years at least, and under a new form of government affairs may brighten rapidly. I do not anticipate, certainly, any rapid intellectual improvement in the people of Jamaica. Their progress in that respect will depend on the opportunities which are given them; but as long as the present race in Jamaica remains, *white*, *brown*, *black* must be the order of precedence. It will take, I fear, several generations to put the mass of the people on a higher level than that on which they stand at present. Now that the House of Assembly is gone, it is possible that their advancement may be more rapid. I look upon the abolition of that body, which acted as a clog on every good measure that was proposed, as a turning-point in the history of the colony. The inhabitants generally are delighted with the news that in future they are to be ruled after the manner of Trinidad, by a Government and Council only; and the only fear I have heard expressed is that the new Government may not be able to exercise despotic power enough. The abolition of the House will leave some salaries and Government payments to be dealt with in other ways, and I hope that a more liberal sum will henceforth be devoted to education.

There is much room for the better application of funds. I see among the officers of the old House a "Black Rod," who, I suppose, must be a useless functionary now. In the list of payments, the ecclesiastical expenditure is put down at 29,365*l.* Then the vestry boards, institutions I look upon as very mischievous, take 4398*l.* for their clerks. Turning, on the other hand, to education grants, one finds the noble sum of 3485*l.* set down as the total spent on what ought, as I think, to be the chief item of expenditure. 30,000*l.*, rather than 3000*l.*, should be given to schools.

It is almost inconceivable that so little should have been done in the way of teaching the people, who, it is no exaggeration to say, are lost in ignorance, hardly knowing their right hand from their left. Scarcely any of the black population can read or write. To make a contract for work is, in their eyes, to bind themselves to slavery. When we went round the east end of the island with the inspector of police, that functionary paid his men at several of the stations. In that select body of officers, the guardians of the law, chosen specially for their honesty and respectability, there was scarcely one who, when he signed the receipt acknowledging payment, was not under the necessity of affixing his mark, being unable to write his name.

It is a curious circumstance with regard to contracts, that the same idea as to the indignity supposed to be involved in the act of signing them prevails in Hayti. In that independent republic, the man who signed any obligation binding him to labour for another was supposed to subject himself temporarily to a state of slavery, and he was deprived of such political rights as he enjoyed.

The ignorance in Jamaica extends so far that, except when he is addressed in the nigger *patois*, the plainest language is not understood by the negro. When Sir Henry, the other day, issued a proclamation, with the intention of giving the people some idea of the plan of the new Government, and the object it had chiefly in view, a man was asked if he knew what the proclamation meant. "O yes," he said, "me know quite well. It means that the Queen beg we pardon."

The planters themselves, it must be acknowledged, do not seem to regard education as a panacea for the evils of Jamaica. When talking with them they will invariably tell you that the negroes who have some education are always the worst, and that extra knowledge breeds extra dishonesty. Such a result, however, we know can only be exceptional, the consequence of an imperfect system of tuition on an ignorant and distorted mind. All experience teaches us that a well-conducted system of education, however limited, tends invariably to elevate mankind, white or coloured.

I visited a large school at Kingston, the master of which, Mr. Gordon, seemed a very intelligent black. The boys were mostly blacks, but there were many coloured, and in the class I saw most of, only one white boy. Mr. Gordon declared that he always found the blacks fully as intelligent and quick as the others, and in a very large class which I heard examined in history, they certainly shouted out the answers as quickly as any of their schoolmates.

They always *act*. At Lyssons were some Congo

boys. They belonged to a set of negroes taken in a slave ship brought to land at Jamaica, and indentured to various estates. We made them talk a little in Congo, translating phrases we told them to repeat. They invariably gesticulated violently, often turning round and talking with laudable energy to an imaginary person.

Drunkenness one sees little of among the negroes. Religion, of an excited kind, is very popular among them. That they are really under its influence can hardly be said, seeing how little effect it has on their daily conduct. During all the psalm-singing of the revival meetings, many professedly pious negroes put no restraint on themselves in the pursuit of the less legitimate pleasures in which they are in the habit of indulging. Education, in my opinion, is the great want of Jamaica, and if a proper system were once established, I should not despair of the island. They are not a bad people, but they want a good Government, and that the House of Assembly has hitherto denied them. The more intelligent inhabitants of Jamaica are very anxious that Scotch and other emigrants should be induced to come out and take small mountain properties. They say, "Here in our mountains a man may do well and make money, while he and his children may be perfectly healthy. Our mists are as thick and damp, and the air is almost as cold as any in Scotland, and if they came out they would be the saving of us." But even if it were possible to persuade them, I do not think it would be advisable. Canada is so much nearer, and its climate is so much more like that at home, that I do not think there is any comparison between the two countries. I have no doubt that in Jamaica immigrants would do well, but in the western states the chances are that they would do far better; and they are there among their own kith and kin, and not in a tropical climate and in the midst of a degraded race.

I stayed only a short time at Mandeville, but was much pleased with what I saw of it. Mr. L. tells me that he calculates that a man possessing ten acres and a cottage is not taxed more than to the amount of two or four pounds a year, while he makes thirty, forty, or sometimes even fifty pounds from coffee alone.

During the time of the riots everybody in the district was quiet. Near St. Jago I asked one of the negroes to whom I spoke if he thought any of the people near the place he lived in would have joined the rioters.

"No, massa. no; me no tink so."

"You never heard talk about the rioters as if the people sympathized with them?"

"Gracious, no, massa; no one sympatize. Dem's wicked men, de rebels. Bery wicked indeed, dey is. People here very orderly, very orderly indeed," with an approving wag of the head.

"What would they have done if the rioters had come here?"

"Oh, dey all sartin run into bush, and wait to see."

"Do you think none would have stayed to resist?"

"No, dey would all hab run away. No fighting, massa—no, no."

"Well, but do you think they would not have defended their masters at all?"

"Oh, massa, what could they do? They could do nothing."

"But they had matchets, just as the rioters had."

"Oh, massa, me no tink they could do anything. No, brackman here are too great cowards. We'se great cowards, massa. We no lift up hand. De brack not like white pusson—he no spirit."

The man seemed quite happy under this conviction, and I should say his estimate of his own people, and what they would have done, is very accurate.

CHAPTER VII.

Cuba—A Midshipman—Santiago de Cuba—Country in the Neighbourhood—Spanish Volante Carriage—Reckless Negro Postilion—Our Hotel—Strict Regulations—Adventure of a German in Hayti—The Theatre—The Church—The Service and the Preacher—Music in the Public Square—A Paradise for Smokers—A Volante Drive into the Country—Bound Blacks and Slaves—Conversation with an American Engineer—The "Fah Kee"—Feelings in the Torrid and Temperate Zones—Swell in the Caribbean Sea—Our Captain—His Opinion regarding the *Treat* Business—Slavery in the South—Story of a Negro voluntarily returning to Bondage—Approach to New York—A Fog at Sea—Fort Lafayette—The Narrows—Brooklyn—View of New York—Steam Ferry-boat—General Aspect of the City—Broadway—Tramways—Barnum's Museum.

WE are now at last in Cuba, having started from Kingston in the French intercolonial steamer, the *Caraïbe*, a vessel that brought us here in a day and a night. H. C. came to Kingston, and spent the last evening with us. He was in great spirits, and very much amused by the account he had received of G.'s playing on the bagpipes. He is quite charming. I was very sorry to say good-bye to him at Port Royal. He came with us so far, when we stopped for a moment to let him get into a canoe that came alongside, and paddle off to the *Duncan*. The French officers looked surprised to see anybody so tiny in uniform. One of them came up to me, and pointing to the canoe, and at the small thing sitting in the stern, said inquiringly—

"He midship?"

"Yes, midshipman," I said.

"Oh, midship*man*," he repeated with a grin. It looked almost as if he had left out the "man" on purpose.

At daybreak we found ourselves steering up a long, narrow, and very tortuous inlet, at the head of which is the town of Santiago de Cuba, or Cuba, as it is often called; a large place, containing, I am told, forty thousand people, half of whom are Spanish, or Spanish Creoles, and the other half black. The proportion in the town of whites to blacks is about equal. In the country the blacks are the most numerous.

Three Spanish men-of-war, a paddle steamer and two screw corvettes, lying before the town, were firing their morning guns as we anchored, and the soldiers' bugles from the town were sounding the reveille. The houses, which are on the crest and slopes of a low hill, rise immediately above the harbour. The country in the immediate neighbourhood is flat, but soon rises abruptly into high hills, whose forms on one side of the water are very fine. The safety of the houses seems to be looked after with watchful, jealous care here. The large windows are protected by strong ironwork, in marked contrast to Jamaica, where everything is left open. The buildings are of brick, covered with stucco, which is usually painted a deep cobalt blue or red and yellow, keeping up a constant glare. The roof is always tiled, and looks picturesque, but heavy. Verandahs are not turned in general to the streets, which are much narrower than in the English West Indian towns; but here and there is an overhanging piazza. Almost every establishment has a court, and the large doors are left open as in Italy, giving one glimpses of high, cool-looking rooms within. The streets are simply villainous, very steep in many places, and anything but pleasant to the foot passenger, from the large shapeless blocks of stone with which they are paved. They have the advantage, however, over those of Kingston and Port-au-Prince, that they are gas-lit.

The Spanish volante carriage, which is always to be had for driving about, is indispensable here, for no other carriage could get over the rough streets, and take the daring leaps over ditches, &c., that this machine accomplishes. Much attention is evidently paid to the equipment of the postilion, who, besides long jack boots, wears a costume on which a great deal of finery is exhibited; and although the carriage itself is stuck with silver wherever it is possible, the ornamentation of its conductor evidently forms the main distinction between vehicles of this description belonging to different classes of society. The wheels, which are quite behind the little body of the carriage, are enormous, and so widely placed that an upset is almost an impossibility. This vehicle is drawn by two horses, one of which only is in the shafts, and bears the whole weight. The other, the near horse, which is attached to the carriage by traces, is on the outside, and ridden by the postilion, who holds its companion by a leading rein.

We hired one of these volantes to take a drive through the town. The postilion was a young black, without exception the most reckless rider I have ever had the pleasure of being driven by. We started at a tremendous pace when near the bottom of a hilly street, and drove furiously along the levels, and up the opposite hills. After nearly upsetting a dignified old nigger lady, who was sailing along chin in air, with her long skirts training behind her, and quite without a thought of the flying volante tearing along towards her, we came to a dead stop by the near horse falling with a crash, sending, at the same time, the rider some way over its head. The latter, who was soon on his feet, mounted again, and for some time we rode on at a more furious pace than ever. If the reckless postilion had determined to provoke a second disaster, he could not have taken more certain means to assure it; and accordingly the horse in the shafts came down in his turn, cutting his knees so severely, that it was impossible for him to go on. We therefore got out of the volante, leaving the negro to raise the poor brute, which he attempted to do by labouring it unmercifully with his whip, and walked home, resolving not to have a nigger to take us about next time.

Our hotel is a building of one story, with two courts. In the middle of the largest is an iron well, with a cross upon it. The dining-room fronts a steep street, leading down to the harbour. The waiting is done by a Spaniard, who seems to be much the most hard-working man in the house. There are slaves, who cook and grin, and do a little of the business of the establishment, but it does not seem to be much. The house is very noisy, and pervaded by smells

which are anything but inviting—garlic, of course,
being predominant. The cooking, in my opinion, is
abominable, as I suppose Spanish cooking generally
is to a stranger. A little girl (I am sorry to say, in
a complete state of nature) has made great friends
with me. She belongs to a woman who is boarding at
the house, and plays all day long with her companion,
a little black slave girl, in whose person decency is so
far respected that she has a dirty shirt to cover her.
I observe many of the negroes well dressed; they are
probably those who have bought their freedom. The
mass, who are not free, are not well dressed, but far
from looking unhappy. They are the same cheerful,
grinning race which one sees everywhere in these
islands.

I had a little difficulty with James, the coloured
servant I took from Jamaica. He was not mentioned
in the passports, and the Spaniards at once said that
he must not land. The poor man was therefore
compelled to remain in the vessel in the harbour.
The regulations are very strict. The landing and
carrying of arms are strictly prohibited. No boats
are allowed to run the harbour after eleven o'clock.
A pass is given on landing, which one must present
when demanded, or be subject to a fine of ten dollars,

or fifteen days' imprisonment, and so on. In fact, one jealous safeguard succeeds another.

Among the company in the hotel is a Louisianian, who talks more bitterly of the war than any other American who, in my hearing, has alluded to the subject. Another is a German, who tells me a story of a recent adventure of his in Hayti, that makes one moderate one's ideas about the safety of travelling alone in that country. He was on his way to Mexico, but falling ill with dysentery when near Jacmel, went ashore at that place for quiet—certainly an odd place to choose for such a purpose, and by no means the best for the restoration of health. When a little recovered, he set out for Port-au-Prince with only a guide, and when not two hours from Jacmel, was stopped by a party who were going to rob him, but hesitated on perceiving his menacing air, and finally went off on his producing a twelve-barrelled revolver, and declaring he would certainly use it if they offered to touch him.

We went yesterday to the theatre. It is a large building—larger than any theatre in London—with capacious galleries, painted white, and supported by posts of solid mahogany, beautifully polished. In the upper gallery were whites and blacks, soldiers

and free negroes, mixed indiscriminately together.
The women were on the opposite side; for these
people assume the semblance of great delicacy—a
quality, however, which, if rumour does not belie
them, they exhibit only in some of its outward and
superficial aspects. The stalls, which extend to the
lower gallery, were filled by men only, the women
being in a gallery corresponding to our dress circle,
and in boxes at the sides. Some of these boxes had
gauze veils drawn in front, and were occupied by
people in mourning, who did not consider it *comme il
faut* to be seen at the theatre so soon after the death
of their relatives. As they were there, however, they
must doubtless have been very much bored by an
arrangement which not only prevented them from
bending forwards to get a good view of the stage, but
also rendered it impossible for them to see or be seen,
even with the aid of an opera-glass. The ladies in
the lower galleries, and in the uncovered boxes,
appeared to me pretty, though they had no colour in
the cheek, a feature of beauty which seems to be
peculiarly English; for, except in the very young, it
is rarely seen on this side of the Atlantic, and is by
no means common even in the other nations of
Europe. But the absence of one characteristic of

female beauty was amply compensated for by the presence of another—those dark Spanish eyes, so piercing and expressive. The Spanish beauties, however, looked very grave, as if in their opinion attendance at the theatre was more a matter of business than of pleasure.

The play had rather too much talking in it for me, as I could not make out what was said; but every now and then came a song, decently well sung, which brightened one up a little. It was, however, neither the beauty of the singing nor the excellence of the acting that kept me awake, but those tormentors, the mosquitoes, which were very troublesome. There was one amusing scene in a convent, when a music-master was introduced to give lessons; but as to me, it was all pantomime. I did not stay to the last.

The church is a large and very ugly building, on the top of the hill, and on one side of a pretty square, with trees, a shady walk, and a fountain or two. As the bells were clanging awfully, I walked in, and stood watching men and women, of all classes and of all colours, streaming in. Negroes and whites were standing about the doors, along the walls, and on the church floor, without any attempt at separation according to colour. The prayers were repeated with the usual muttered droning, the responses were chanted by the choristers, and there was all the bowing, crossing, and censer-swinging which accompanies the service in every Roman Catholic church. The pavement between the tall white-washed columns was soon covered with women. For the rich who were present, of whom there were very few, there were chairs, but by far the greater number knelt on the bare slabs. Some of the former had slaves, who stood behind them, helping their mistresses to keep their dresses in order when a more than usually strong breeze swept through the sacred edifice.

A priest then appeared, and mounting the pulpit-stairs, stood before the congregation. When he began to preach he put on a square-shaped cap, which he had previously carried in his hand. Sometimes, in the middle of the sermon, he paused, and, removing his cap, turned towards the altar, and prayed for a time, the whole congregation kneeling till the cap and preaching were resumed. He was a young man, with a fine voice, and I thought the language sounded very impressive as it came from his lips, the beauty of the Italian being in his tones apparently blended with the majesty of the Spanish,

M

which is, indeed, too fine a language for those who now use it.

In the evening there was music in the square, and we walked for some time among the crowds that kept lazily moving about. The women, of whom there were many, were generally in black, or with black lace shawls. The gentlemen were all smoking, and the air was full of the fumes of Havana tobacco. The musicians, belonging to the band of one of the Spanish line regiments, were short men, dressed in light-blue tunics with red facings, and coarse whity-brown trousers.

There never was such a paradise for smokers as Santiago. Cigars that one could not get under sixpence in London can be got here for a penny. I have bought five hundred, for which I paid only 2*l*. 10*s*. Everybody smokes, except the ladies. The negro women are hardly ever without a cigar between their pouting lips.

We had another volante drive—this time, as we had a Spanish driver, with no bad results to the horses. We drove some way into the country, along broad roads, unmacadamised, but very good as long as there is no rain to make them heavy. The usual hedge of penguin bordered the road-side, and there was a sugar-cane field every now and then; but we had no time to see the works. The cabbage-palm and fine mangoes were the only trees. Slavery, they say, may be considered practically extinct here. It is now two years and more since any slaves have been landed in the country, and, as they believe, no one would dare to renew the base traffic again. The last that were brought were indentured for a short term of years only: I think they said for not more than eight. This is the same term for which the Chinese coolie, of whom many are being imported, is bound to serve. The condition of the bound blacks is said to be worse than that of the slaves. The masters work them harder, knowing that they will have them for a shorter time. Chinese coolies are becoming unpopular. They are disliked for their temper, and their value is uncertain, seeing that, when sulky, they are too ready to hang themselves.

I had some talk with an American engineer, who has been for some time on a plantation twenty miles from this. The free negroes, who sometimes work on the plantation, he informs me, can earn two dollars a day. They do not work with the slaves, but in a separate gang, and at another piece of cane, cane-cutting being the work to which they generally take.

My informant further told me that he had seen very little flogging on the estate on which he was engaged—not more than half a dozen being so punished during the eight months of his residence on it. When they were flogged, however, it was laid on pretty tight; the lash, a long flaxen thong, being applied so vigorously that blood was drawn freely. Six hundred and forty hogsheads were made on the estate, and about forty negroes were employed on it.

I noticed a bit of copper ore on the road to-day, and find there are fine mines within sight of the town. Black vultures are very common, and there are many guinea-fowls, black, grey, and white; the white being often tame, and the grey in general wild.

We have determined to proceed at once to America, having learned that the journey to Cape Fuegos is very disagreeable. The latter place, we are informed, is a very bad one, and the steamer takes six days to perform the voyage, as she stops at no end of small ports to take in sugar, &c., rendering the passage under a hot sun very tedious. Finding a good American steamer, the *Fah Kee*, proceeding to New York almost immediately, we shall go by her. The voyage to New York is only six days, and after we have been there, we intend, perhaps, to take our course down the Mississippi, and up to Virginia through the Southern States.

I was sorry to miss Havana, and the chance of seeing a little of the slavery here. I regretted, above all, that it was out of my power to see the grave of Columbus, but it could not be helped.

In the evening we started for the cold seas of the Northern States. What a blessing we felt it would be to get another whiff of a good cold north-easter! One is sensible of one's energy slowly oozing out at the finger-ends in this torrid region—indeed, to be comfortable in it one must possess some of the qualities of the salamander. During the last few days I sometimes felt as if I should have liked to be packed up in ice, as the salmon are when sent to Australia. It was difficult to realize that we should be in wintry weather again in five days.

We were longer, however, on the voyage than we expected, the weather was so abominable. We left Santiago on the evening of the 19th. The moon rose as we got clear of the narrow entrance, when we were challenged by sentries below the old fort on the hill, and steamed out into the Caribbean Sea, in which there was a heavy swell, causing us to pitch a good deal. The sky, however, was clear, and we flattered ourselves that we should have good weather; but, alas! the promise held good only for a day and a half, after which we were constantly knocked about in a very nasty sea. The vessel was luckily a good sea-boat, having been built for the China trade. During the war she was taken up by the government, and turned into a gun-boat, in which capacity she lay off Charleston and other Southern ports on the look-out for blockade-runners, her big guns being ranged all along the space where the cabins now are. How they ever expected to catch a blockade-runner I do not know. I should not the least mind having her in chase of me·if I wanted to get into Charleston. She never made more than eight knots on the voyage, and often, when we were tossing about, only two or three. Our worst day was when we passed out of the blue waters of the gulf-stream into that part of the sea whose green colour showed that we were in soundings off Cape Hatteras. The current running up against a wind at the rate of eight knots, kicks up a heavy sea along the borders of the great stream.

The difference of temperature was very great. In winter the water hereabouts is often at 40° Fahr., while in the stream it is at 72°. Our vessel was guided from a steering-box near the bow, instead of at the stern. We were laden with hogsheads of sugar, and a disagreeable sugar " reek " came up from the hold when there was no wind to blow it astern. One could almost fancy himself in a boiling-house. We had, luckily, but few passengers, and were comfortable enough, the cold being very refreshing. A large right whale came up to look at us yesterday, but stayed only a short time, and we were alone most of the voyage. Only one or two ships were seen : one, with the union Jack flying, a barque, laden, as the captain supposed, with copper for Swansea. We looked through the telescope for her name, and, to my astonishment, it was the *Duchess of Sutherland*. I was so pleased that I blessed the ship loudly as she sailed away gracefully on her homeward voyage.

Our captain is a fine old man, a Creole from New Orleans, but has lived most of his life at sea, and a good deal in the North. About the war and slavery he was very impartial, taking the line of State rights, but saying that the South ought to have argued it out in Congress, and not on the battle-field. He is still sore about the *Trent* business, which one would have supposed he would have been able to get over by this time. He says that when once Seward had allowed Welles' dispatch, approving of Wilkes' conduct, to appear, the Southern commissioners ought to have been kept. "It was a national disgrace, that giving them up, sir. We were in the position of the man who wanted to sell his horse, and told another that he had a horse to sell, eighteen hands high. When the intending purchaser came to the market, he looked at the horse, and said, 'Why, you told me that horse was eighteen hands high.' 'No, I didn't,' says the other. 'Yes, you did, that's a fact.' 'Well, if I did say so, he is eighteen hands. Yes, sir, he is so.' That was our position. Having once said that it was right, we ought to have sworn that it was legal, and that kept they should be."

Talking of the slaves in the Southern States, he said, "After all, the people that treated them best were their masters; and many a slave loved his master too. There's one, I remember, ran away from an estate in the Carolinas. When he got safely to one of the free States, he stayed and lived there for some time. He made a little money too; but, after some years, he thought he'd like to go home again, and he sent and asked his master if he would flog him, supposing he returned. 'No,' said his master; and the man returned. He had been perfectly free, and he returned of his own accord into servitude. He worked well, and earned money by his labour in spare hours, and his master proposed that he should buy his freedom.

"'No, massa; not money 'nuff.'

"'Well, you have been a good man; suppose you pay half your price, and be half-owner of your labour?'

"The man did so, putting down, after a little hesitation, a good round sum. After some time passed in this peculiar relation to his master, the negro came back, saying he did not want this half-freedom, but would prefer to have his dollars with complete servitude. The money accordingly was returned, and the man became again, without reservation, his master's property. I saw him when my ship was at a port near the estate, and asked him why he who, I had heard, was such a good man, had worked so well since his return, and might no doubt have been soon able to purchase his entire freedom, had acted in a manner that seemed so unaccountable?

"'Well, massa,' he said, leaning confidentially towards me, and speaking low, with the air of a man expressing his opinion on some point important in a commercial sense to him, 'well, massa, dis de reason: nigger property d———d bad property, massa.'"

We touched at the Bahamas in coming up the coast, but did not land. The island we saw was so low, that it looked as if a high sea must wash over it. We expected to reach New York early the following morning.

A thick fog came on as we neared the entrance to New York Bay, and we were stopped at last in the most provoking way within five hours of the city. The fog lifted a little after we had been waiting for an hour or two, blowing hideous steam whistles, and making as much noise as possible, which was useless enough, as no other vessel was likely to run up the narrow channel in such a yellow darkness. We went on at last, however, steaming slowly up the muddy waters, every now and then catching a glimpse of the masts of some vessel that, more cautious than ourselves, preferred waiting for clear weather.

"There's Fort Lafayette," some one said; and we saw the Bastille of America looming through the haze, a lumpy, casemated fort, where a very few wretched Confederates remain imprisoned. We were now passing the Narrows, and if the fog had lifted, could have seen the frowning rows of the batteries on each side.

The view of New York from the sea we did not get; but the air was clear near the town, and we watched through a drizzling rain the villas, factories, and ship-yards of Brooklyn, the part of New York separated from the city by the east river, a piece of water as broad as the Thames at Greenwich.

The city, immediately opposite to us, is low-lying, and hidden behind a dense hedge of masts belonging to ships moored alongside the innumerable wharfs. Steam ferry-boats darted perpetually in and out of this hedge, carrying horses, carriages, and men. Our carriage was driven on board one of these boats, and secured in a high-covered passage in the middle, appropriated to such vehicles, there being another for carts and drays. The sides were occupied by ladies' and gentlemen's cabins. The whole machine is guided from a wheel-house on the top, and the passage is made with wonderful speed.

Really one feels as if one had leaped a century coming here from the tropics. Instead of the lazy, half-alive movements we had been accustomed to for a month or two, there was a frantic haste and hurry, a general movement and bustle, that told of an eager life and dollar-scramble refreshing to witness. The town is an odd mixture of all sorts of European towns, but unlike any one of them. The chief character of the houses is height, and a certain degree of stateliness, combined with all the vulgarity inseparable from large staring name-boards and advertisements. The prevailing colours are red and green. The houses are generally built of red brick, though a fine dark-red freestone is employed in the erection of the best dwellings, and the windows have green jalousies thrown open on each side, ready for the heats of summer. The general effect is to me very imposing. There are trees at the side of every street, and, as there have been no revolutions to cut them down for barricades, they have been allowed to grow higher than in Paris.

Broadway is certainly very handsome. The churches are generally fine buildings, and many of the hotels and houses belonging to large firms are splendid blocks, with tier upon tier of windows, to the height of five, and sometimes six stories. The pavements are very bad, generally made of round stones, like thé old French *chaussée*. There are no cabs, but tramway omnibuses traverse the city in every direction, even in the most out-of-the-way-looking streets, and the wheels of all other carriages are being perpetually dislocated by having to cross the tramways. I wonder that more do not suffer in the same way, considering

the very delicately-built gigs one sees in the streets.
Like an eight-oar race-boat, they seem built entirely
for speed, the wheels being so light that they look
like the work of spiders. Each spoke, however, is of
tough hickory, and they are said to last very well.

The most prominent establishment of any description in Broadway is, perhaps, Barnum's museum, which is rendered attractive by the immense flags floating before it, while the wonders which it contains are advertised in most shop-windows. It was the first show-place we went to in New York; but, as might have been expected, except a seal, a menagerie, and an albino, there was nothing of a very novel or surprising nature to see. The museum was pretty full of people, to whom some fierce prints of the battles fought during the recent revolutionary struggle seemed the chief attraction. In these works of art the stars and bars were always to be seen flying ignominiously in the right-hand corner of the picture, while in the left the stars and stripes were being borne in triumphantly over the bodies of Confederates, bayoneted by the victorious soldiers of the Union, a group of whose generals, in the centre, were represented twisting their necks into the most unnatural position, that the spectators might have a full view of their countenances. The museum is rather a humbug; but it is only just "reconstructed," as the first was burnt down. I was not sorry I went up, however, as we got a very good view of the town from one of the top windows. A gorgeous crimson sunset lit up the sky above Long Island, and bathed all the housetops in the city in a dazzling blaze of gold.

CHAPTER VIII.

Activity of the People—Question of the Fishery—The Civil Rights Bill—The Fenians—Reports circulated by the *New York Herald*—Fenianism among Waiters—Devotion of the Lower Irish to the Cause—The Roberts and O'Mahoney Sections—Civil Rights and Freedmen's Bureau Bill—Policy of the President—Trial of Davis—Visit to the *Dunderberg*—Construction of the Vessel—American Workmanship—Iron-clads sent round to the Pacific—Proposal of a Patriotic Member of Congress—Wounded Soldiers—Germans in New York—Excitement caused by the Arrival of a Pest-ship—American Railway Travelling—Appearance of the Passengers—Railway Literature—Raymond and the *Herald*—Extent of New York—The Rocks near the City—Small Towns and Wooden Houses—Boston—Made a Member of the Union Club—The Somerset—Longfellow's Bridge over the River Charles—Cambridge University—Our Cordial Reception by American Students—Boat Races on the River—The Powellian Club—Agassiz—Debate at the State House—View from the Balcony—The Massachusetts Regiment—Longfellow—A Lecture by Emerson.

THE weather was very cold, but the warmth with which we were received here by all whom we knew compensated for its severity in that respect. With the exception of senators, Congress, and their satellites, the town was at home, its entire population, with that active energy for which they are renowned, daily busy in the pursuit of wealth, pleasure, and excitement.

People here, whom I found a little anxious about the fisheries, seem to think that we should yield, and I am of opinion we ought to do so. I do not like that barring of the sea. There is to be a great row about the Civil Rights Bill.

The newspapers in New York were very busy discussing the proceedings, intentions, and prospects of the Fenians. The *Herald* was every day giving circulation to rumours more or less threatening, and encouraging them with predictions of certain success in whatever they should undertake. The previous week it had positively announced that an expedition of five thousand five hundred men had started for the Bermudas. The next day an island in the Bay of Fundy was said to be their destination, and from all parts of the land came accounts of mass meetings, in which there was no end of speechifying. and of big talk. The streets were placarded, " Revolution in Ireland," &c.; and Stephens, to whom a great reception was to be accorded, was anxiously looked for every day. The more rational Americans laughed at the whole affair, many of them being of opinion that after O'Mahoney had collected all the money he could get, nothing would be done, and the whole affair would be allowed to end in smoke. I feared, however, they would attempt something, if only to justify their words, and be able to go on agitating. There was a report one day that a band had gone to Eastport. The enterprise they had in view was most likely a foolish incursion into some unprotected corner of Canada.

The earnestness of a great number could not be doubted. One heard of women and poor men giving almost all they had towards the Fenian funds. They had collected a great deal of money, and were said to have enough to fit up privateers that might be very troublesome to our shipping. All the waiters who were Irishmen (and most of them in New York are Paddies), in this hotel were Fenians. An English waiter discoursed eloquently to me of the way in which, however poor they might be, they always paid their subscription to the funds. These men belonged to the Roberts side. I do not know that the division of the Fenians into the Roberts and O'Mahoney sections will be productive of any advantage to us. It is rather likely to cause a spirit of rivalry between the two sections, a contest not only as to who shall get most money, but who shall strike the quickest blow. After all their vapouring they are "bound to do something;" and if it be only to break their heads against Canadian fortifications, I think they will make the attempt.

We heard, while in New York, that in spite of the President's veto, the Civil Rights Bill, which gives all privileges, except the suffrage, to the freedmen, had passed. I do not see anything in the bill to justify the violent talk against its provisions that one reads in the ultra anti-Radical newspapers. Johnson's dislike of assuming unconstitutional power, and of the over-centralization of the Government, does him all honour. The protection the North wishes to give the freedmen is, in my opinion, only the fulfilment of a sacred duty, to which it was doubly bound by its conduct in giving immediate emancipation to the blacks, and by the help the blacks afforded it in preserving the Union. The President had expressed his opinion that the Freedmen's Bureau Bill, as it then stood, was sufficient for the protection of the blacks, and in the veto of the Civil Rights Bill showed his hostility to the spirit, only too evidently evinced by many in the North, to favour the freedmen at the expense, or even abasement, of the Southerners. "Give Quashie his rights" is, no doubt, an amiable cry; but when one finds that this new-born zeal for the negro is merely a pretext by which they seek to cover their determination to humble their prostrate enemies, our admiration of the patriotism displayed by the North must be very much qualified.

The policy of the President I considered one calculated to reconcile the South, and induce its population to join him hand and heart in the reconstruction of the country. There was a strong feeling in his favour, and public opinion was sure, ere long, to back him up in his wish to see the States of the South again represented at Washington. All accounts from the Secession States agreed in their statements that the people were willing to do what they could in their desire to promote the common good. Their fortunes were gone, and they were manfully trying to recover the position which they had lost. Semmes was to go his ways—a fresh proof of the clemency that does such honour to the President's policy. They still talked of the trial of Davis; but no one seemed to know when it was to be, and they said that he was to be allowed more liberty. The longer action is delayed, the more unlikely is it that anything will be done against him.

Communication was much broken up while we were in New York, owing to the state of the railways.

Although the post from New Orleans ought to reach New York in four or five days, it took eight or nine. The Mississippi steam-boats were said to be abominable, all worn out, and not replaced since the war, when most of the good ones were burnt or used up.

Sir Edward Cunard called, and we went with him to see the *Dunderberg*, one of the new iron-clads building for the Government in a private ship-yard. All was quiet when we arrived. The place was deserted, and not a hammer was lifted on any of the ships in preparation. We found on inquiry that the men were on strike for eight instead of ten hours of work, to which they had lately been accustomed. I was not sorry that we were enabled to see all that was being done without having our ears stunned by that perpetual clang of hammers to which one must generally submit when one desires to witness the process of shipbuilding.

The *Dunderberg* was afloat in a dock, her stern projecting into the river. She was nearly completed, only a few plates yet requiring to be fixed. She is a hideous monster to look at. Imagine a long, low, raft-looking hull, only a few feet above the water, but rising gently near the bow, and then sloping steeply down again into a long, plough-shaped stern. This ugly nose is composed of fifty feet of solid metal. On the middle of the hull rises the armour protecting the battery—a long, low pent-house, about seven or eight feet high, that looks as if made of solid iron, pierced with narrow port-holes, eight or nine on each broadside, the walls sloping back at a sharp angle to throw off shot, and in the middle of the vessel forming a sharp angle with the sloping sides of the hull. At bow and stern the battery walls leave the side, and are rounded off, so that two or three port-holes look out upon the long, raft-like stern, and on the platform at the bow and the great ram. An immense smokestack and two masts on the pent-house show that the monster is meant for a ship. The plates on the hull are three and a half inches thick, and there are six or seven feet of timber behind.

The batteries consist of armour-plates five inches thick, set perpendicularly against the slanting oak and pine wall, which is three and seven feet thick. The plates, which extend from top to bottom of the wall, are thickly pierced with holes for rivets, and the joining is anything but neat. The plates seem to have been taken out of the mould, and clapped on the battery's walls without any attempt to smooth the sides so that they might fit closely. In some parts the chinks between the armour-plates are so wide that a man could almost stick his finger into them. There is an utter want of the polish that is so conspicuous about English work. All seems to be done on the rough-and-ready plan. Where we should finish up a bit of timber with a carefully-selected piece of oak, they put a piece of deal. It is the same with the engines. The extreme finish of fine work is wanting. The armament of the *Dunderberg*, which is to be very heavy, was not yet on board. She is steered from the battery, and the screw, completely concealed, is placed within some feet of the stern. The officers' cabins, which are in the low part of the hull aft, must be beneath the water line, but looked comfortable, and tolerably well lighted. The vessel would be an ugly customer, and although much larger than the monitors, she would be a small mark compared with the gigantic broadsides of England and France.

The Americans speak very well of the sea-going qualities of some of their iron-clads, one of which has gone to Rio Janeiro, and behaved very well on the passage; and they talk of sending a monitor, or one of the vessels of the *Dunderberg* or *Ironsides* class, round the Pacific. Much amusement has been caused by the proposal of some patriotic member of Congress that an American iron-clad should be sent over to Paris, on the conditions that the *Magenta* or *Solferino* should be allowed to fire four or five shots at the stranger, and that the latter should be permitted to return one.

I was surprised to see so few wounded men in the streets—indeed, I am not sure that I saw any. The only thing that reminded me of the many wounded who, after the late war, must be scattered over the country, was the large number of advertisements of good wooden legs and arms. Very few soldiers, however, were to be seen in the streets, and one met only every now and then spare men, with shaven and strongly-marked jaw, and short moustache, whose French *képi* and long grey-blue coat, exactly the colour of our hospital uniform, and often very old and shabby, told that they were soldiers. Compared with European troops they looked very untidy. The officers, however, had a better appearance.

The Germans are in great force in New York. Their names are widely sprinkled over the shop doors; and squat German figures, with their usual lank hair, swarm in the streets, the *Lager-Bier* saloons, and the *Restaurants*. At a German barber's one day I heard the most violent abuse of England, the reason for this outburst of temper being the arrival of a shipload of immigrants at Halifax with cholera on board. Though the ship had sailed from Liverpool, most of the immigrants came from Germany, of which fact I ventured to remind the angry barbers, who nevertheless cried out against the dirtiness of Englishmen, to which they chose to attribute the outbreak of the disease. The arrival of this pest-ship threw the Americans into a perfect state of consternation, especially as the possible advent of cholera had been previously regarded with considerable alarm; and quarantine was strictly enforced all along the Gulf ports on vessels from the West Indies.

We set off on the 10th April for Boston. Our first experience of American railway travelling was very pleasant and entertaining after all the accounts we had read of its discomforts and bothers. We started early in the morning, not under the most propitious auspices, for at first the journey seemed likely to be comfortless enough. The first car we tried to get a seat in was perfectly crammed with people, and we walked up and down between the thickly-packed rows of passengers without finding so much as a square inch on which to sit. The conductor, however, at last took pity on us, and we were allowed to go into another of the long travelling corridors, which was only beginning to be filled. The passengers looked most respectable people, and I saw as little spitting, or anything unusual and disagreeable in their behaviour, as one would in similar society in England. One has heard so much of American peculiarities from writers who like to harp upon every little angularity they may either have seen or imagined they have seen, that one is surprised to observe how much the Americans resemble other folks.

The seats, on each of which there is room for two persons, are arranged like pews in a church, one close behind another, with a passage down the middle. There is less noise than on English railways, owing, I suppose, to there being fewer wheels; each of these big cars, holding fifty or sixty people, having only four wheels, two quite in front, and the others at the other end. In the interior are a stove and good lamps; and boys go about with newspapers, apples, oranges, and books, the latter generally novels by English authors, reprinted, magazine shape, in America, with paper cover and double columns. Mrs. H. Wood's novels seem very popular, but all the latest English works of fiction are to be had. The newspapers have a great trade, particularly the *New York Herald*, which unfortunately appears to be the most read. Other journals, however, are gaining ground, such as Raymond's paper, the *New York Times*. Raymond was a helper of Greeley in the *Tribune*, but has since set up for himself. An article in the *North American Review* refers the popularity of the *Herald* entirely to the pains that paper takes in getting news, and to the sensational manner in which it parades them. Every circumstance of interest regarding the Fenian movement is daily chronicled in long columns, headed in capitals very black and thick. If a British vessel is fitting out to be sent to the fishery banks, the *Herald* has an article headed, probably, "The American fishermen to be kept out by force;" "British men-of-war preparing." Men talk of their contempt for the paper, but at the next station they buy it.

The cars are taken by horses along the streets till outside of the town, where an engine, with wide-shaped funnel, and grating to clear the line in front, is hitched on, and goes tearing away at from thirty to forty miles an hour. The city stretches over an immense space of ground. All around the suburbs rise the wooden shanties and hovels of the poor Irish, the "mean whites" of the North. Detached buildings, generally of wood, dot the country, which looked bare and naked. There were no leaves or even buds on the trees, and but for the stunted growth of birch and hemlock spruce in many places, the land looked as bare as when the glaciers left it. Their marks are everywhere. In and about New York each rock is scraped by ice. Huge boulders and little boulders lie scattered confusedly over every brown ridge. The blocks near the wayside about the towns have been appropriated by quack doctors, and there is hardly a rounded rock near the railway that has not "plantation bitters," or the name of some other pleasant drink, inscribed upon it in great white letters. I observed few enclosures; but such as I saw consisted generally of a stout timber fence or stone dyke that ran by the side of a ploughed ridge or hollow. The soil generally appeared far from rich. We saw no high hills, but we crossed several great rivers.

We did not stop often. At Hartford, famous for its revolvers, and Springfield for its rifles, we were allowed time to get refreshments and look about a little. Bricks vanish in these small towns, and timber is used in all the houses. Such elaborate wooden buildings we know nothing of. They are warm and comfortable, it is said, even in the coldest weather. They look very neat, the closely-lapping boards being painted white. The windows have all green jalousie shutters, as on the continent of Europe. The edifices themselves are often much spoiled by a pretentious Greek portico, all of wood, with little wooden Doric pillars, that are anything but what Doric pillars should be. The streets are adorned with rows of trees. There is no railing or obstruction of any kind to prevent children being run over by passing trains. Perhaps the noise the engine bell and the whistle make is enough to scare them; but one cannot help feeling that accidents would be daily occurrences if trains rushed suddenly through English villages, and that infant schools would be cut to pieces.

I was tired enough of the uninteresting country by the time we arrived at Boston. Massachusetts is not a garden, and it is perhaps owing to the poverty of the soil that its men have been so hard-working, and have obtained so much influence throughout the States.

I was surprised to find Boston so large a town. It has grown greatly during the last thirty years. The Fremont Hotel, at which we established ourselves, is a rambling, huge establishment, where one must, as usual in American hotels, run half a mile to get what one wants.

Early on the morning after my arrival, Mr. Palfrey came to see me. I am afraid he had to wait ten minutes before I came down, as I was very sleepy after the journey. I found him down-stairs with Everett. He asked me to breakfast with him at the club, and was most cordial in his greeting and welcome to America, inquiring much about all whom he knew in England. He was busy getting ready and publishing a short digest of his great "History of New England." He did not stay long, and we went with E. to the Union Club to have our names written down in the books. This makes one a member for a short space of time. It is a delightful "institooshun," this, of letting strangers be members of clubs for a short time.

The Union Club has five hundred members, and very pleasant rooms for reading and dining. There is another, the Somerset, to which we were also admitted—an old Conservative club, too democratic for some of the hot Republicans of Boston, who, rather in antagonism to the Somerset, formed the Union Club when the war broke out. The English papers and magazines are to be had at both clubs, and they seemed to be quite as eagerly read as the American papers.

We took the street cars to Cambridge, passing over the Charles river by the Longfellow bridge, which is not the picturesque old timber structure that illustrators of Longfellow suppose it to be. Indeed, the only thing that reminds one of the poem by the great American bard in which it is alluded to is the odour of brine from the ocean, which is very perceptible while crossing it. It is a broad roadway, about a quarter of a mile in length, supported on piles, lighted with gas, and with the tramway cars constantly hurrying over it. It is a great, unpicturesque bridge, and none but Longfellow could have struck poetry out of anything so prosaic to ordinary mortals. At high tide the water is deep beneath it, but at ebb a muddy flat is exposed to the eye of the gazer.

The red-brick blocks of Boston rise on each side of the broad river, as if resting on it. There is no crowd of shipping as at New York, and the view of the houses and streets is unobstructed. A tall grey shaft marks Bunker's Hill.

On the other side we passed through long streets of wooden houses. The road was invariably lined with trees, mostly plane or American elm. Each tree had lately been painted round with a belt of tar a few feet from the ground, in the hope of preventing the canker-worm, as they call a small green caterpillar, from climbing up it, and committing great ravages amongst its foliage. These insects have been quite a plague during the last few years; and the tar belts, it is certain, can only prove a partial remedy, for as the males can fly, it will be impossible to keep them from the trees, though the wingless females, it is to be hoped, may be detained below.

In a short time the car stopped, and we found ourselves in a more open part of the town, near several brick barrack-like houses, three or four of which were detached, and all half hidden by the trees. Opposite to us was a chapel built of stone, and on our left was another stone building of greater pretension, which we found to be the museum. "We'll see the dons afterwards, but I'll show you some of the men's rooms first," Everett said; and he ran up several flights of rickety wooden stairs, only to find them spotted with the name of the occupant on a card outside. A student we met, after some time, told us that the Yale University musical people had come down to meet the Harvard Musical Club, and that they were singing in a house close by. Everett went in, but soon re-appeared, and invited us to follow him. The room was crowded with students, who were scarcely visible through the clouds of tobacco smoke which, as they puffed away, were every moment becoming denser. On a table was a great *débris*, that showed dinner was over. Everett made a short speech, telling them we were Englishmen of Old Cambridge, an announcement which was received with much clapping of hands by way of welcome. It was, indeed, a far more cordial reception than would have been given by an old Cambridge club to any foreigner, and we acknowledged it by bowing, smiling, and endeavouring to look pleasant. Then came songs from Yale and from Cambridge, and S. was made to sing half a dozen at least, after which there were rapturous plaudits.

An adjournment was then proposed to the river, about five minutes' walk from the college, to look at the boats. There are annual races between Yale and Cambridge, and the recurrence of this anniversary forms quite as great an event on this side of the water as the Oxford and Cambridge is on ours. "We were beat this year, just as you were, you know," some one said; but I did not know, though I did not dare to confess such ignorance. They row in a six, instead of an eight-oared boat, and there is no coxswain. All the steering is done by the bow oar, who guides the boat by pulling with his feet wires connected with the rudder.

We went back with some of the senior students, and stayed for a long time with them, listening to Yankee songs, while Strutt gave them the newest English productions of the same sort. A very nice set of fellows these American students were. Several of them took us off to another club, the Powellian, of which they were members, the whole number enjoying this privilege being fourteen. They have very good rooms close to college, and an excellent library. There was much talk of the war, to which I was told one-fifth of the graduates went off when it broke out, and, during its continuance, twenty to thirty out of a hundred who had finished their classes.

Agassiz, we heard, had just come back from his Amazon expedition. The number of new fishes he had discovered was something enormous. One of his staff, Mr. Burkhardt, came home some time ago, having suffered much from fever and insects. Their worst enemies were the mosquitoes and chiguas, or "jiggers."

During my stay in Boston I went to the State

House, to hear a debate in the House of Representatives on the equalization of bounties to soldiers; the men who had enlisted first having received no bounty, while as much as three hundred and sixty dollars had been paid to volunteers during the latter years of the war. The hall was a high room, with benches arranged in the form of a horse-shoe, facing the chair or tribune of the President, much like the arrangement at Turin. All the speaking I heard was on the popular side; that is, in favour of equal payment to all. The speakers were rough-looking men, who got up with great self-possession, and delivered their speeches in a slow but fluent manner, emphasizing their words, and pronouncing each syllable with a clearness one does not hear in England.

From the balcony of the House there is a good view of a great part of the town. Boston is more like an English city than any town I have seen in America. There is not the bustle and hurry of New York, and there are more dwelling-houses than shops. The style of building is that of our sea-side towns. The houses, the material of which is brick, are often built with curving points, and have bow windows.

In the hall of the State House are the regimental colours of the Massachusetts troops, covered with the names of the great battles of the civil war, and some of them torn to shreds. A hundred and fifty regiments, each completed up to its full complement of a thousand men, were embodied out of the population of this small State alone. Massachusetts has certainly shown herself to be as ready to give the example in war as she has been capable of taking the lead in literature.

Mr. Longfellow had taken two tickets for us to hear a lecture by Emerson. We walked down with Mr. L. Many people in the streets recognised him, and bowed respectfully to him. The lecture-room was crowded, chiefly with ladies. Emerson appeared alone from a side door, and walked with head bent, and looking nervous, to the reading-desk. The audience received him without a sign of cordiality; the only feeling, if it could be so called, manifested by them being a sort of frigid expectation. The eminent lecturer's voice was very low at first, his manner was cool and passionless, and in the expression of his sentiments there was a total want of enthusiasm. The tone in which he spoke was conversational, and the matter of his discourse was unconnected. A pretty good idea of the lecture may be obtained from the fact that after it was over, S. and I had a dispute as to what it was about.

I maintained that the general subject was Thought; he said that he supposed it to be on the Advantages of Labour. He was wrong, I am sure; but that I am right I cannot with confidence assert. Something disconnected might have been expected from the beginning, for in one of the opening remarks Emerson declared that a good sentence was nowhere out of place. It seemed to me that a number of thoughts distantly and indistinctly connected with ideas on the working of the intellect had been committed to separate scraps of note paper, which had been accumulating for some time, and were now being talked off, with a little joke appended here and there. The lecturer appeared to be in favour of letting men judge from little facts, thinking that the English were too hard on people who criticised without having gone to the bottom of the matter, while they forgot that their own Newton saw at once the movement of systems from the fall of an apple. He spoke of silkworms becoming, with intellect, Lowell operatives! Emerson's lecture, as far as I understood it, might very aptly be compared to a badly-strung set of very obscure brilliants.

CHAPTER IX.

A Ride to Winchester — Moveable Family Mansion — American Robin — Snapping Turtle — Amusement at the Fremont — A Fenian Waiter — The States and their Soldiers — State of the South — Visit to Lowell — Absorption of the Military — Peaceful Tendency of the Nation — Americanisms — A Yankee Steamer — Agreeable Recollections of Boston — Political Spirit and Sentiment — Return to New York — The Theatre — Negro Minstrels — Country beyond New York and Washington — Crossing Wide Rivers with the Train — Earthworks — View of the Capitol — The Streets of Washington — Public Buildings — Conversation with a Virginian Gentleman — Effect of the passing of the Civil Rights Bill — Hopes for the Future of America — Mr. Sumner — Military Commissions and the Trial of Davis — Mr. St. Leger Grenfell — Reconstruction of the Union — Policy of the Radicals — An American Gentleman's Opinion of Affairs in Mexico.

SHORTLY after our arrival in Boston, Everett drove us out to his place at Winchester, about seven miles from the city. The road was made very disagreeable for driving by the tramways, of which there is a double set for going and coming cars. The iron rails, which are placed in the middle of the road, may be an immense convenience to the general public, but they are certainly a great nuisance to the buggy-loving section of the population. We observed, in the course of our drive, a wooden house three stories high, and of very considerable breadth, almost entirely blocking up the roadway. As we came nearer, we perceived that it was raised from the ground, its bottom timbers resting on rollers, while at the back, in the middle of the thoroughfare, we found a horse, a windlass, and a rope, by means of which the whole building was slowly drawn along. It was, in fact, "an elegant family mansion" on its way to some more fashionable quarter. No wonder that wooden houses are popular, when they are not only so cheap to build, but also so easy to move. The family, I was informed, in many cases, sleep in the upper part of the building while the removal is going quietly on. I have heard of brick houses being occasionally lifted; but such migrations as this, which I presume are not uncommon here, are quite novel to me.

Everett's house is pleasantly situated, with a pond or lake on three sides, and a picturesque bank with rocks and trees some distance behind it. There is a little property belonging to it. Land is sold in the neighbourhood for a thousand dollars an acre. Close to Boston three times as much can be got for it.

The American Robin is very common hereabouts. It is a splendid thrush, with black head, grey back, and chestnut-red breast. It is about the size of our

Missel Thrush. E. has a Snapping Turtle, a vicious-looking brute, with toad-like skin, sharp claws, and pointed head. I think of taking it to England.

My chief amusement at the Fremont was to probe the Fenianism of the waiters. As they were all in the brotherhood, any discussion, however quietly conducted, with one of their number was sure to bring a silent group of earnest listeners behind one's chair. One of them yesterday, who had observed that I was reading a Fenian column in the newspaper, bent over me, and said in a mysterious low voice—

"What think ye of the Fenians?"

I told him they seemed numerous enough, at all events, and pumped him about their objects, and the number of members here.

"Oh," he said, "they are very strong. There isn't a son of the old country in the city that does not belong to them. They are against Sweeney; but they will follow the first that means to fight."

I told him they had done nothing but talk, and probably wouldn't fight even if they had a chance. This brought him out; and when asked if he, too, was a Fenian, he drew himself up with immense satisfaction, and said that he was proud to avow that he was—a confession which he followed up with a good deal of bravado, and the accompaniment of a threat with every dish he brought me.

"Yes, we are strong; stronger than you think. What'll ye have now?"

"Roast potatoes and beefsteak."

"Ye shall have them then, sir. The old country will be a different place soon. We'll see who's the strongest. Potatoes, sir? Yes, sir;" and he laid them down with an emphatic crash, that told of awful resolution.

"Well, what rights do you wish to have?"

"Rights! why, the right to live in a free country. Look at this country. There's no arrests here."

When the beefsteak came, I told him of the harm his friends were doing in the old country, and how money was being kept away.

"Ye'll see Oirland a different place before long. It's not for the priests, and they are against it; but it's not them we'll mind. Look what they're doing at Eastport; they will be in Canada before long."

When I asked him to specify some particular grievance, he spoke in general terms of tyranny to be broken down, of the approaching termination of Ireland's oppression, and of a future of unlimited freedom; but of anything definite for which they were to fight he had not a word of explanation. The negroes of Jamaica,

I am compelled to say, showed a more intelligent appreciation of their position, and expressed more definite ideas as to the objects at which they aimed, than at least the lower class of Irish in America, judging from the remarks with which they occasionally favoured me.

The States do not appear to have been very generous to the men who have done them good service in the war. They have granted only a few pensions; and as no decorations have been distributed, a man has nothing to show that he has been in the war, except, perhaps, an empty sleeve, or the valueless title of captain or colonel, enjoyed by many an old militiaman who never saw an army in the field.

We dined with Mr. P., who had a party of officers and others to meet us. One, who had just come from Charleston, gave, I thought, a most melancholy account of the state of the South, where even now the process of rebuilding the houses goes slowly on. The owners of estates have no capital to work them, and are compelled to lease them to Northerners, who give the proprietors a share of the produce, and of the negroes who work for them. There has been as yet no great influx of Northerners, a circumstance which may, in some measure, be attributed to the feeling of the people of the South, who show little desire to mingle socially with the Northern troops or settlers. They are quiet, and willing to obey the laws, but friendly intercourse there is little or none. Men and women who, five years ago, were on the most intimate terms with friends from the Northern States, will now cut them in the street, and absolutely refuse to have anything to do with them.

We went to Lowell to see one of the largest of the factories there, over which we were conducted by the superintendent, a son of Mr. Palfrey, who has seen a good deal of military life; and having taken to this occupation only a few months ago, has hard work to get well posted up in all the details of machinery and management. It must be dull work after the exciting military life he has led. We went with him to all the factories: to places where the cotton was piled in great rooms, in its raw state, as it came from the pod; to others where it was thrashed till the air was laden with fine shreds of it, which I felt very unpleasant; and so on from room to room, witnessing the changes which it underwent in its passage through elaborate machines, first into a carpet of snow, then into yarn, and afterwards into calico, which was printed in other houses, and dried in an apartment where the thermometer stood at 230°.

The machinery used in these factories is all made in the town; and we wandered through huge workshops, where iron implements were being taken from their moulds, like fossils from a rock, to get the finishing touch from the steam plane.

General Butler, whose house is next door, is quietly doing law work at Lowell. The way in which the officers and soldiers have vanished in their military capacity, and resumed the civil employments that occupied them before the war, is, I think, the most surprising event that has happened in America. Nowhere does one hear of former soldiers rioting, or forming guerilla bands, or even allying themselves with Fenians or Mexicans, for the sake of a little more camp life and excitement. The love of plunder, so often generated in other armies, seems to have given way to the love of honest work always to be found in America, and which is the sure stepping-stone to wealth and a higher position. This is to me marvellous; but it is only a further proof of the versatility and adaptability of the American character. While the rapidity with which the immense hosts that deluged the South returned to their usual labours after the work for which they had been incorporated into armies was accomplished, is a proof of what can be done by such men when called to act under circumstances for which none of them were prepared, it shows also that the Americans are really a peace-loving people, who, in spite of the foolish brag of the more ignorant, so offensive to the delicate ear of European nations, are not inclined to war, or favourable to aggressive movements.

There is still naturally much conversation respecting the war, but the reminiscences of battle are mixed with speculations on commerce, manufactures, or law. Dollar-getting is again in the ascendant. The nation is sick of fighting, and only too glad to resume the more prosaic occupations of peace. The leaders have set the example in returning quietly to their ordinary industrial pursuits. With the solitary exception of the Fenian Sweeney, none have encouraged the war spirit, or even tried so to direct the policy of the country that they themselves might be placed in prominent positions. Yet, notwithstanding the decided manifestation of the peaceful tendency of the nation, there is no doubt that if the interests or policy of America were in any way menaced, they would be ready at a moment's notice to defend their country against any enemy who should venture to molest it.

The Americanisms of conversation have afforded

me some amusement. Many Americans maintain that these are really genuine English expressions, which have somehow fallen into disuse in the mother country. "Right away" is constantly used here for "immediately;" and P. said he thought Swift used these words in the same sense; but, on reference to the passage, we found that the expression was "to rights"—employed, as it also is here, in the same meaning: "Then they let the hull drop into the sea, which ..... sank 'to rights.'" (Swift's "Voyage to Brobdingnag," chap. viii.) Others I have noticed are, "tiresome" for "tiring." Mr. Emerson the other day, in his lecture, used "metre" several times in place of "measure." People say "mighty" when we should say "very." A picture is "mighty pretty." A "pleasant time" is a "good time." Instead of talking of meat being "under done" or "raw," as we do, they talk of meat being "rare" or "well done." "Will you have a 'rare' piece?" is a constant question from the carver of roast beef. At Lowell I observed they talked of "machinists," when we should talk of "mechanics." But a machinist is more than a mere mechanic. What made us talk of Americanisms was somebody's reading Dean Alford's book on "The Queen's English" in the railway cars.

In one passage the Dean, not content with speaking strongly enough about the American use of the English language, speaks also of the Americans' "reckless contempt of all moral obligations." This was being handed about in the cars, causing many smiles and a few frowns.

I never enjoyed a pleasanter time than the eight days I spent at Boston. The kindness we met with made me quite love the place, and I am sorry we were not able to accept invitations to country-places which Dana and Loring gave us. One feels the town to be the abode of all that are first in literature, culture, and civilization in America. My happiness was damped only by my inability to sympathize with them in their present hopes for the policy of their country. The South had been conquered in the field, but they felt that she must also be kept down; and here I differed from them so much that we could hardly speak on the subject. The bitterness against the President seems to me too unjustifiable. I am sorry that he vetoed the Civil Rights Bill; for I believe its main provisions granted no more than justice. "He is not the man we wanted as President, and we never wished him to get there; but all will come right yet," they say, with that wonderfully sanguine spirit that has been so conspicuous throughout the worst times of the last years. But what does this "coming all right" mean? As they use it, it expresses their determination that the North alone shall have absolute power in the government of the country for at least many years to come; that the South shall not be heard even in those debates that concern the whole nation; that the North shall impose law on the South.

Many, too, are still insisting that Davis shall be tried for the supposed guilt of five millions. The alienation of two peoples lately in arms against each other has surely been enough prolonged. The South is down, helpless, crushed, unable to offer the least resistance: why should the North insist on rendering its triumph so galling to the conquered party, now that they are again to live as citizens of the Union? The Radicals insist that they shall have no voice in the government of the country until "they give unmistakable proofs of loyalty"—a form of expression which may be made to cover any exaction. It would seem that the Radicals think a man's convictions can be surrendered with his sword. "Obedience to the laws is not enough. You must embrace the policy of the men against whom you fought." If such unreasonable demands be not abandoned, re-union between North and South can only be a shadow. Ten, twenty years—the lifetime of this generation will see no change in the convictions of the South. Is it to be supposed that the Radicals can keep them out of Congress for so long a time?

On April 18th I set out, on my return to New York, in an immense steamer, built in true Yankee style. A saloon ran the whole length of the ship, about two hundred and fifty feet, with galleries at the side, and other saloons below. We started from Stonington, to which place we came by the railway cars from Boston *viâ* Providence.

On the evening of the day on which, we returned to New York, we went to the theatre. Negro minstrels—bands of whites got up as negroes, like Christy's—are very popular. The large towns have often two or three sets of these minstrels. I heard of a negro who went some time ago to a place where negro songs were being sung by one of these bands. He looked on for some time, his face expressing astonishment and contempt; and then, with the exclamation, "What cussed fools dese white men do make of themselves!" went out.

From New York we went to Washington, a long day's journey. We have now rushed into spring, and corn is making its appearance, giving to the fields along the road a bright green colour. Buds are bursting forth, and many trees are almost in full leaf. The change of temperature from that of New England is about forty degrees, and the heat feels quite oppressive after the cool breezes of the North.

The country we passed over was remarkable only for its great rivers. These vast streams are truly magnificent. Over some the train runs on a low bridge of trestle-work, raised only a few feet above the yellow waters. We crossed one river in a steamboat into which the train was driven like a carriage into a ferry-boat, driving out again when the other side was reached. On the Chesapeake I saw flocks of birds, too far off to tell what they were, but I supposed them to be ducks.

We hardly stopped at Philadelphia or Baltimore. In this last town negroes began to appear in great numbers. In New York and Boston there are few. Forts were all round the town, reminding one how it was necessary, only a year or two ago, to overawe the populace. The country throughout the day was undulating, and the woods we saw were thickly grown. Trees, tall and thin, covered many slopes. Enclosures and farms were frequently seen, the fields having timber fences. The farmstead was always the wooden, white-painted house of which all the small country towns are composed.

Towards evening we passed some shanties, then a few dwellings, and noticed the tops of some of the low hills levelled smooth into green slopes and terraces, over which the stars and stripes waved. These were earthworks. Looking out of the window, I saw, close by, a towering white dome, round the base of which was a ring of pillars with long rows of colonnades and windows beneath. This was the Capitol. We come upon it without any warning that we are approaching a great city, and it rises so finely over the poor-looking houses around it that its effect is very grand.

We walked down to Willard's Hotel, one of the largest along Pennsylvania Avenue. Some notion of the streets of Washington may be obtained by imagining the street from Kensington to Chiswick planted with rows of trees on each side, the houses thrown back a little, street cars running along tramways in the middle, and the *trottoir* crowded with people; adding some shops and a general bustle, but not changing the houses, which, except perhaps that they have not so many name-boards, are exactly alike. New York, packed in within its rivers, has been crowded till the houses form one tall line along the streets; but, as there is an unlimited amount of room here, the town has been allowed to straddle over all the space allotted to it.

The public buildings, however, are splendid. Looking down one of these broad avenues half planted with houses and trees, your eye is arrested by some fine Greek temple closing the view. We entered one of them to-day, which proved to be the Patent Office, where a model of every machine for which a patent has been taken out is kept. From the window of the gallery upstairs there was an extensive view over the huge collection of paltry brick and the few noble marble buildings that make up the city of "magnificent distances." In front we saw a stretch of the broad Potomac; and the gently-rising land in the distance, divided into field and wood, and crowned with flags that told of invisible cannon beneath, was the shore of Virginia. I wanted to ride over the long bridge to see a little of the "old dominion;" but rain came on heavily, and we gave it up.

I had a talk with Mr. ——, a gentleman who has been for some time connected with the American newspaper press. He had always belonged to the party that supported the cause of the Southern States; and when Virginia, his native State, seceded, he went with her. He spoke nearly to this effect when we asked him about the condition of the South :—

"You must not expect the hospitality for which the whole South, and Virginia especially, were so well known. Gentlemen I know, who lived in wealth and comfort before the war, are now not worth five hundred dollars. The country has been laid waste, and its inhabitants are ruined. It is owing to the war, and the ruthless way in which it was carried on. The system on which the Northern armies proceeded was to burn everything that conduced to the life of man, and the rules of civilized warfare were often neglected. Houses, fences, crops, agricultural implements, whether belonging to combatants or not, were utterly destroyed. The estates have been let out on leases to great extent, owing to the difficulty of getting labour. Northerners are often the men who lease the farms.

"The negroes are not in the contented state in which they were; and, in consequence of the passing of the Civil Rights Bill, there has already been a fight at Norfolk. The negroes were proceeding along the streets, many with guns in their hands, when a young man came across their way. Shots were fired at him; he fell, and his body was dragged along by the mob. His brother, seeing the body, went to claim it, when he too was butchered. I do not object to that part of the bill that provides that a negro's testimony should be received in court; I have always wished that they should be heard, and it is the feeling in many States in the South. The effect of the bill may be different with different judges. Take the judge[*] across the river. That man would always be raising up antagonism between the blacks and whites; his judgment would always lean to the side of the blacks. We have a repugnance to the negro socially that we

---

[*] Underwood: the same who afterwards delivered charges full of violent language to the jury in his court at Richmond.

cannot get over. I should not object to one sitting by me in the cars; but if I had ladies with me, I should object strongly. Now this bill allows them to mix freely with us. Negroes may come and sit down at the same table with my own ladies, and we cannot prevent it. Many judges would support them in their actions, and would encourage them. There is an appeal to the Supreme Court of the United States which may reverse the decision of the local judges. The composition of this court does not make it subservient to the Government now, as it was during the war, when everything was decided according to the views of the Government. Their decisions in the cases of the military tribunals have lately been a triumph for liberty in America.

"We have hope now for the future. We have interpreted the constitution to allow of secession; we have tried the experiment, and we have failed. It was much owing to doubts raised by the wording of the constitution that the war began. You hear a man saying he is proud of being a Virginian, and a man from South Carolina boasting of being a Carolinian. You do not hear them say that they are proud of belonging to America. That is our feeling. I am glad to be under the Government, for I know it to be a strong one; but I do not care to be called an American. No; I had rather live under the Government of France or England, or even of Spain. Now that our attempt to erect a separate nationality has failed, we recognise that we must give up the idea, because we cannot do otherwise, and are helpless. There is also the conviction that the time at which we made our effort was the best for such a struggle, and we can never again have a similar chance. We recognise our position, and we wish henceforth to live as citizens of this land, rendering implicit obedience to its Government, obeying all its laws, and seeking redress for the affronts and grievances to which we are daily subjected through the medium of its courts.

"I agree with the opinions of most thoughtful men in Europe. I was in favour of the abolition of slavery; but that it should be done at one stroke, that millions should possess freedom without preparation, was not in our thoughts. I wished that the boon should be granted by instalments, and that the negroes should be prepared for their new condition. The President's policy is encouraging the men of the

South in their wish to aid the Government. It has been a surprise to us that his line of policy has been what it has. He was always a violent man; and when Lincoln was killed, we looked with horror, not only on the crime, but on the probable consequences to our people from the accession of the new President.

"I have hopes, too, on other grounds. I have watched the elections that have taken place lately in the North; and in almost all of them—in Ohio, Michigan, Missouri, and others—a spirit of conciliation to the South, and opposition to the views of the Radicals, has been shown. I believe that it will not be long before the States lately fighting against the Government shall be again represented in Congress. Indeed, I look to their being represented in the next Congress."

These are the views of an able Southerner. About the Norfolk riot he spoke a little at random. Accounts agree that the negro procession was taunted by the crowd. The blacks had arms in their hands, and, backed as they were by the Federals, they were quite inclined to assert their position. All is quiet at Norfolk at the present moment; but it may be because troops occupy the town.

I heard to-day sentiments of a very opposite character from those to which I listened yesterday; to-day's came from a member of the *extreme* " Republican" party— that party which is now distinguished by most men under the name of " Radical." Johnson is their *bête noire ;* and it was when his name was mentioned that Yankee politics began to be discussed. His veto was blamed, and the reason given by him (that there was danger in consolidating or centralizing the powers of Government) was set down as of no account. "They say that Mr. Sumner wants to centralize the power here. Now, you know the system of France, by which one man can set the whole machinery of state in motion from Paris. Mr. Sumner would be the last man to introduce such a system into this country; but when the power is only for good—when a great moral cause is at stake—when the question is if black men shall have the right of suing, of holding land, of appearing in the law courts—then no machinery put in motion for such a purpose can be too strong; nor could any organization created for this purpose be turned to other ends. The South would not allow negroes, if they could help it, to give testimony in the courts. They are all against it. Things are, as yet, unsettled in the South. It was only lately I heard from a man who had recently arrived from Florida, that it was dangerous for any one, even now, to proclaim his Northern sympathies in that State. He could see no protection unless the negroes got the right of voting. It has come to this: negro suffrage is a necessity to counterbalance the rebel votes. There is nothing that can prevent the South from having their own way but that measure, and it must in time be carried. It was thought at first that a reading-and-writing qualification might be required from the blacks before they should be enfranchised; but the testimony of this gentleman from Florida, who had lived in the South, and knew well the state of feeling existing there, makes one wish to see the blacks allowed to vote at once. Southern doctrines will still reign supreme if manhood suffrage, without distinction of colour, be the law. It would be a great matter if a beginning could be made in the district of Columbia. The President would probably veto an attempt to get even this done. He is utterly wrong-headed."

It was said that Davis might have been tried at first by a military commission, but that it is too late for that now, more especially as the Supreme

Court has decided that military commissions are illegal. Great objections are urged against these military commissions, which are not courts-martial, but military courts, on which generals and officers are placed by the Government, and who often convict on evidence that would be rejected by any civil court. Just sentences are scarcely to be expected from them. The men to be judged have been, at a very recent period, in arms against their judges. It is hoped that Sir F. Bruce, now our minister here, may be able to do something for an Englishman, Mr. St. Leger Grenfell, who fought for the Confederates, and being afterwards taken, was tried and convicted, on very insufficient evidence, for complicity in the design to burn Chicago. He was sentenced by one of the commissions to be shot, a sentence which has been commuted to one of penal servitude for life, and he is now at the Dry Tortugas.

We do not think that the Southern States can be kept out of Congress much longer. The West will take their part, and all except New England will insist upon their re-admission. There might be war, in course of time, if they were too long kept out. The whole work of the reconstruction of the Union has been undertaken by the President without help. He might have called Congress together, but he did not; and though there were eleven States to be dealt with, he undertook the task single-handed. It is a most curious peculiarity in this country that a man should be able, on such a question—a question that in England could not be dealt with except in Parliament—to work alone.

The line taken by the Radicals, also, is so peculiar as to require some remark. When they thought that the President's policy would suit their tastes, they were in no hurry to call Congress together; but now that Johnson's policy has turned out adverse to their views, they loudly blame him for not having called Congress to deliberate upon the question.

I met a gentleman who had just returned from Mexico. He gave a rather rose-coloured view of the prospects of the Emperor Maximilian's Government after the withdrawal of the French. He believed it was quite strong enough to maintain its position, more especially if Maximilian won to his side the monarchical party. Political relations were, to be sure, not so pleasant as they are here. The rise and fall of parties were settled, not by "the speech," but by the bullet. The Empress was charming, and the Emperor, who had much *bonhomie*, was doing his best to conciliate his reluctant subjects. Unless the Americans interfered, it was quite possible that things might be so settled that it would be in their power to remain.

CHAPTER X.

White Labour in the South—Dying out of the Negroes—Would the South have armed the Slaves?—Confederate Forces at the End of the War—Davis's Flight from Richmond—The Capitol—Admission of Colorado into the Union—Committee of Reconstruction—Conduct of Business in the Senate—House of Representatives—Energy of the Speakers—Feeling in Congress against the President—Federal and State Authority—Southern Representatives—The Treasury—Ride into Virginia—National Monument—The Long Bridge—Vestiges of the War—General Lee's House—Interview with the President—The White House—Mortality among the Blacks in the South—Navy Yard—Monitors—French Occupation of Mexico—Visit to Mr. Seward—The Attack made on him last Year—Attack on Frederick Seward.

MR. W., who breakfasted with us to-day, thinks that white labour is quite possible in the South, and that it is not necessary, even in the cotton districts of South Carolina, to have negroes to work the plantations. At New Orleans the work done by the white porters, who are Irish, and stand the climate well, is as hard as any done by the negroes in the South. White labour and Northern capital are what it would be desirable to see introduced into the South just now. If you go to men who have plantations, and are working them with the negroes they can hire, they will tell you that So-and-so is getting on very well. If you ask them if as much work is being done as before, they will reply, "Well, I reckon that I get two-thirds of the labour I got before; but as, in hoeing and picking time, I want more than that —as much as I had before, in fact—I put on a hundred instead of fifty hands."

"Then," said Mr. W., "if you pay the same price for labour as before, that is losing fifty per cent.; and with such a loss the plan cannot answer."

We asked him about the chances of the negroes dying out, as some say they will.

"Well," said he, "that opinion you will find men holding according to the side they're on. Now what we say is this: After the emancipation was declared, the negroes showed, and have since shown, a great disposition to flock into the towns. They leave the estates where they were, in general, well fed and cared for, to stream by hundreds into Richmond, Charleston, and other Southern towns. In Richmond ladies can always find servants, while in the country it is now a common complaint that servants are not to be got. These crowds in the towns have no occupation, and loaf about in a state of poverty, living in an unhealthy way, crowded and dirty. Many die, owing to this cause; and if an epidemic should come, the loss of life among them must be enormous. The Freedmen's Bureau is giving them farms of five acres; but a man cannot live on that. Ten acres is the minimum on which he can support himself, and the cultivation of that amount requires a good deal of work."

I asked him whether, if war had continued, the Confederates would have freed and armed their slaves.

"Well, sir, the President, Mr. Davis, was in favour of doing so. He considered it to be necessary; and if it had been left to him, it would have been done. I was in favour of it, but many of our best statesmen were against it; and the reasons they had for opposing it were good. Suppose freedom given to the men, and that they were placed in line of battle against the Yankees, what reason would most of them have for staying with us? We could give them no gay uniforms like those with which the Yankees equipped their soldiers. With us they might go shoeless, and with little food, while the Yankees could give them all they wanted. With the inducements the Yankees could offer, splendid music, fine clothes, and good food, there were too many reasons to fear that the negroes would desert their colours. It was better, therefore, that they should be employed as they had hitherto been, as teamsters, and in throwing up fortifications— work in which they could be made exceedingly useful. I should set down our forces during the last few days at only forty-three thousand, opposed to one hundred and ten thousand of the enemy. We could keep the line we had fortified, which was thirty miles in length, but had no force to oppose to Sheridan. When we had to hold the lines, in case of an attack in front, he swept round our right. I knew some time beforehand that the end of our war must come shortly, but did not dare to express my sentiments to anybody. I was sent, when our lines were driven in, to tell the President, and found him coming from church. The Government left the town at once, and it was a question, at one part of the railway line along which we went, whether the enemy would not get before us. The rails had been spoilt by constant use, and we went along at the rate of eight or ten miles only, and this was considered good work.

"Most of the escort left Mr. Davis at Greensboro'. His journey was no flight. No man thought for a moment that there was any doubt about his personal safety till that point was reached. Even there nobody ventured to tell him there was danger; and I remember trying to persuade some of the staff to speak to him of his personal peril, but was not able to prevail upon them to do so. At Greensboro' many of the officials who had gone with them left, considering themselves *functus officio*. There is no truth whatever in the spiteful story got up in the North, that before he was taken he had disguised himself as a woman. An officer whom I know well, who was with him to the end, denies that Mr. Davis ever disguised himself in such a way. As he issued from his tent he cast around him a plaid which he used to wear at Richmond, and it was the only concealment he made use of."

The Capitol is a splendid building. Most of the front is of fine marble, and the staircase in the interior is of a very beautiful dappled brown. At the time of my visit the Senate was occupied with the question of the admission of Colorado into the Union; the representatives of that territory having petitioned that they might be received into it. Mr. Sumner spoke against it in a speech which was thus criticised by one who took a different view of the question:—

"You see in this oration he declares that the population is, so to speak, a fluid one, always running in at one side of the State, but moving through it and out of it westwards. Mr. Sumner has now been minifying every prospect the territory has of becoming respectable and important enough for admission to equality with the States. Her people, he says, are few in number. Her mineral wealth is insignificant, and the gold reputed to have been found in such quantities does, in reality, only exist to a small extent. This is throwing gold dust into the eyes of his audience; for the sole reason that Mr. S. wants to exclude Colorado from the Union is because, in the constitution of that territory, the black has no vote. Impartial suffrage is what the Radicals now want, and they are unwilling that any fresh territory, hostile to this policy, should be admitted as a State."

One of Mr. Sumner's opponents, in a clever speech, called him "the giant of the Senate," a name to which he is well entitled. One hears on all sides, even from the President's friends, regrets that the Civil Rights Bill should have been vetoed.

One senator expressed curious views about the conduct of the Southern States. He thinks that the men sent to Congress (supposing that men should be sent soon from the South) would very likely be extreme Union men, either owing to a reaction, or to the fact that those who would get office would be the Unionists of the South, who could at once take the test oath.

The elections to take place in the fall are looked forward to as likely to settle the question of Southern re-admission one way or the other.

The Committee of Reconstruction is now sitting, and has been examining prominent Southerners. There are several Radicals on the committee, and their report, which is anxiously looked for, is not likely to be too favourable to the Southerners.

Business in the Senate is conducted in a quiet and dignified manner. Each senator has a comfortable desk and arm-chair, and all sit in a semi-circle facing the Vice-President's tribune. The silence during a speech is almost as awful as that which prevails in the House of Lords.

The House of Representatives is very different in respect of noise. If I may use such an expression, the state of that assembly is one of chronic row. The poor Speaker has his work well cut out for him, and his voice and hammer are heard perpetually. While some debates are in progress, one might fancy one's self at a noisy auction rather than at a deliberation of a legislative body. One always knows exactly, however, what progress the business of the day is making. The Speaker's rapid announcement that a bill is before

the House, his request that contents should say
"Ay," non-contents "No," and his final declaration as to how the vote has gone, and whether or
not the bill has passed, are all uttered and over in
a moment, unless discussion should occasion any
delay. The amount of business thus got through
seems enormous.

The habit of spitting, which has often been alluded
to, is still as prevalent as ever. Each arm-chair and
desk is flanked by a spittoon, which makes itself the
more conspicuous because there is no smoking to
account for its presence. The energy of the speakers
is, to an Englishman, remarkable. Gentlemen rise
leisurely and begin quietly, but in ten minutes the
arms are sawing the air like windmill sails, while the
hard voice is ringing in loud and louder tones above the
buzz of conversation and the crinkling of newspapers.
The orator's body is raised on tiptoe, and let down
violently again on its heels; and every now and then,
when legs as well as arms must find freer play, a short
walk is taken. Sometimes, in the *abandon* of his
enthusiasm, the excited orator advances almost to the
tribune, and the Speaker must submit to being "jawed
at" by the fiery representative.

Sometimes the speaker advances to the gentleman whose arguments he is more immediately refuting, and bringing his hand down on his desk, thumps continuously on it, staring all the time into his enemy's face. I heard a motion brought forward about the trial of Davis, involving a resolution that if found guilty he should be executed. The affair, however, was "laid over;" that is, indefinitely postponed.

There is much feeling against the President among the ruling party in Congress, who speak of him with no small asperity. "He is leaning to the Democrats," they say, "to catch their vote. He, Grant, and Seward will all be candidates for the next presidency, and the first two are bent upon having the Southerners on their side. They know the Democratic vote must be looked to. It will be cast in a lump."

One thing seems clear—namely, that the war has not decided, as it was supposed to have done, how far Federal extends over State authority. Everywhere one hears of doubts on this point. It is doubted if Congress has power to declare a black franchise for the Southern States. I have heard one senator affirm that Congress has the power, and another, five minutes afterwards, declare that it has not, and that all internal affairs must be left to the Sovereign State Governments.

Southern representative men still talk much as they talked before the war about the indestructible rights given the States by the constitution. It is the old story, and parties will still be divided on that question, as they were before the breaking out of the war. "The contest will be continued with the ballot-box, instead of with the bayonet," openly say many. "The constitution was not explicit enough on the subject of Federal power. Since the belief in State sovereignty arose, it has taken too firm a hold upon the people for the war to have shaken it to any great degree. The only right that the war took from the States was the right of separation."

The Treasury is a fine building, and contains the offices of most of the cabinet ministers. They can always be found there; and a visitor fortunate enough to have introductions has only to walk down a corridor, and throwing open successive doors on either hand, he finds each member of the Government in his own peculiar pigeon-hole. Of the men who are now in office Mr. M'Culloch ought to esteem himself one of the happiest. His management of the Treasury has been most fortunate, and he has now successfully imposed taxes by which a revenue is raised, with which it will be possible to liquidate, in the lifetime of this generation, the entire debt contracted during the war.

I procured a horse one day to go over into Virginia. The long bridge being open for the passage of vessels, we crossed at Ferrytown, considerably higher up the stream. On our way we met trains of waggons, with their teams of six mules driven by negro teamsters, bringing in shot and shell from the forts on the other side of the river. The fortifications guarding the city are being dismantled.

We could not have had a finer day for our first ride into the old dominion. The air was beautifully clear, and as we cantered up the slopes on the other side of the river, the view back on the city was beautiful. The great dome of the Capitol, looking in shade like a black tiara, in sunlight shining with a dazzling whiteness, was the object that first caught the eye. Along the banks of the Potomac the houses spread, terminating on the left at Georgetown, where the river is narrow and the banks steep, and on the right dotting the lower and more distant shore, where the stream rapidly widened. Just opposite to us was the uncom-

pleted national monument, begun long ago, but only
half finished. For my part I am not sorry that it
remains imperfect, as the gigantic proportions of the
obelisk, which is not of a graceful shape, would, from
this point of view, dwarf even the Capitol.

Spanning the mile-wide water to our right was the
long bridge, with its low trestle structure. Immediately round us, on the Virginia side, was a wilderness of charred tree-stumps, that stuck out of the
ground to the height of a foot or two. Look where
you would, the same desolation met the eye. The
woods have been cut down everywhere, to give the
guns of the earthworks that crown every little hill a
full sweep. As we rode on we visited one fort after
another, there being one every few hundred yards; and
from the rising grounds one could see that the whole
country was warted with them. Taken singly, they
are not very formidable-looking; the ditch not being
very deep, nor the ramparts very high. An abatis is
formed by the branches of young fir-trees, stripped of
their needles, and with their ends sharpened, laid down,
stem inwards, just outside the ditch. Each of these
works is in such a position that it can cross its fire
with that of others; and, as the forest is down, there

is nothing to impede the view of an advancing enemy.

At one stockaded fort we found a negro, whom we asked where we were.

"Dis is Arlington Heights," he replied, "and dat house dere—dat ole Lee's house."

"What! General Lee's?"

"Yes, massa, Gen'ral Lee's. I was with his army one time. I was servant to young Massa Winston. Den I came North, and was teamster in Northern army."

The trees about Arlington House are still allowed to stand. A party of men were moving about inside a strong paling that enclosed the place. Long rows of little white boards dotted the ground around them. The negro was asked what these were.

"Oh, dem's the dead."

The party were employed in making gravel walks, and in sodding the cemetery. Five thousand dead lie there, each with his little slip of white-painted board at his head—men who have died in hospital from wounds or sickness.

The confiscation of Arlington for the dead is certainly an effectual method of preventing the General from ever wishing for his own again.

To Mr. Seward, who was most kind to us, we were indebted for an interview with the President, who received us cordially, though evidently tired with a hard morning's work of seeing people. The lobbies of the White House were crowded with men and women who wished to speak to him. A few days ago the President addressed a number of coloured men, who came in procession to serenade him. The speech has been much abused, as attributing unworthy motives to the Radicals. The President is not a man to listen quietly to abuse of himself, and he has been too deeply stung by recent attacks to let them pass by without a reply. He did not mean, however, to make any answer to what was said on this occasion; but when he got down to the portico, and found it and the space beyond filled with expectant black faces, he was almost obliged to say something, and he spoke bitterly of those who had represented him as an enemy of the coloured race.

We afterwards went over the house. In the great reception-room most of the chairs were covered with satin, very much worn. The Secretary pointed them out, and, in explanation of the condition in which we saw them, said that they had been left unrepaired since President Lincoln's death. Congress each year votes a certain amount for the repair of the furniture of the White House. Congress had voted no money for repairs this year, and the chairs had been left as they were.

We dined with our minister, who had a reception after dinner of governors of lunatic asylums. The accounts of the mortality among the blacks of the South are deplorable. More infants, it is said, died under the age of five years in 1866 than the total number of deaths registered in 1865—a mortality owing chiefly to the flocking into the towns.

On a visit to Navy Yard we saw several monitors in the river, moored in a row. One of them, the *Montauk*, had been under a heavy fire at Charleston. The shape of these vessels is now very well known. So little of the hull is seen, that it looks like a mere line just above the water. The turret is round, and the sides perpendicular, so that the vessel is like a pill-box on a raft. The walls of the turret are eleven inches thick; eleven plates, each an inch thick, being riveted together. At the base of the turret this thickness is increased, to prevent a shot jamming the turn-table machinery on which the turret revolves. Two immense guns, placed side by side in the turret, peer out of the little twin oblong port-holes, which

are closed by a folding block of iron the instant that
the guns are discharged and run back for re-loading.
They take up all the space, being sixteen-inch Rodman guns, throwing a ball of 450 lbs. The Rodman
is a smooth bore, the same in principle as the Dahlgren gun. An eleven-inch Dahlgren, throwing a
166-lb. ball, is also in great favour; and the next size
much used is the nine-inch, capable of discharging a
98-lb. ball. Parrot guns have gone out of fashion, and
not many rifled guns are used. The hulls of these
iron-clads are covered with five inches of iron again, in
plates of one inch, with a backing of four feet of
timber. The deck is also plated with inch or inch-
and-a-half plates.

The armour had been much pounded, but no ball
had made a dent of more than three or four inches in
depth. The plates, laminated as they are, were in no
instance the least cracked, nor had the rivets started.
There were marks which the officers said had been
made by Whitworth bolts fired at a short range of
three hundred yards. One shot had struck fair on
the top of the vessel's side, bending back the five-inch
plate, but no harm had been done. In other places,
long grooves of no depth gave the only trace of the

concussion of the projectiles. This monitor drew only nine feet of water.

Mr. R., with whom I dined, spoke with much feeling against the French occupation of Mexico. Nothing can exceed the jealousy with which the Americans have seen the French put foot upon that soil. Madame Juarez has been here lately, and is much praised for amiability and intelligence. They could not say much in praise of her husband, who is quite an Indian. The American Government talk of sending a minister to Juarez, and the recognition of the Mexican empire is looked on as an impossibility.

On a visit which I paid to Secretary Seward I asked him about the attack made on him last year. He was so good as to show us the room in which he was assailed, and gave us an account of all he remembered of the attack made upon him. The house is not a large one. The dining-room fronts the road below, the drawing-room is just above, and over it is Mr. Seward's bed-room. On reaching the landing at the top of the stairs on the second floor, there are two doors immediately facing you—one that of the bed-room the assassin entered, the other that of Mr. Frederic Seward's room. On the right and left are two other doors, leading into the rooms of Mr.

Seward's daughter and eldest son. The assault was made at half-past ten at night, an hour when all was quiet. A gas jet was burning on the stair-landing; but the room where Mr. Seward lay, weak from a fall from his carriage, was almost completely darkened. His eye had been hurt, and a very little light was painful to him. His daughter sat in a corner of the room, not far from the foot of the bed, which was placed sideways to the door, and between it and the window. Mr. Seward had a sort of frame placed over his jaw; and fancying, in his weak state, that if he slept the upper muscles of the jaw by contracting, and the broken bone by falling, might cause lock-jaw, he determined not to sleep. That he might the better carry out this resolution, he lay close to the edge of the bed, that if he should fall asleep he might also fall out of the bed and be awakened. The side of the bed on which he lay was the one furthest from the door, which was open, letting in some light from the gas jet on the landing.

While he was lying in a lethargic state a man came to the house door below, rang the bell, and when a coloured servant opened it, told him that he came from the doctor with medicines. The name of the doctor he mentioned, however, was not that of the one attending Mr. Seward at the time. The boy wanted to take the medicines, but the man said he must deliver them himself, and pressed on up the stairs. The boy went before him, remonstrating; but when on the flight of stairs near the sick-room, he thought he might be blamed for not letting the man pass up, and went down-stairs again. Frederic Seward, sleeping in the room next his father's, had heard the discussion between the man and boy; and, on coming out to learn the cause, found the man just at the top of the stairs, and asked him what he wanted, on which he repeated the same story about the doctor and the medicines. Frederic Seward said he would take these in himself, and told the man that he could not enter Mr. Seward's room. The messenger insisted he must; and Frederic, attributing his obstinacy merely to insolence, told him shortly he could not, on which he said, if that were so, he would take back the medicines, and being told he might do so, he turned to go. After proceeding down a few steps, however, as he afterwards said, remembering his oath not to fail, he faced about, sprang up to the landing, and drawing a revolver, presented it at the son's head. The first cap snapped, and the trigger being again pulled, the same happened with another. Then using the pistol as a club, the desperado struck Frederick Seward such a blow on the head with the butt end that his skull was broken. Drawing a knife, he then rushed past into the bedroom, making a cut on the door-post as he entered, and was at the bed in a moment.

Meanwhile the daughter, hearing her brother's fall just outside, and seeing the assassin enter, stood up and cried out, "Oh, he is going to kill my father. Do not let him kill my father." Mr. Seward, partly roused, heard the words, and saw his daughter standing, her eyes fixed upon something apparently at his side, and just above him. He had long thought that something of the sort might happen, and knowing himself to be utterly helpless, he thought that his hour was come. Turning his eyes upwards he remembered seeing above him a hand and coat-sleeve, the appearance of which, strangely enough at such a time, made such an impression on him that he distinctly remembered it, and was able to give a description of it afterwards.

"The sleeve," he said, "was of fine grey cloth mixture, and my first thought was of that cloth. I looked further up and saw the chest and chin of a handsome, strongly made man. I next felt a quick gush of warm rain on my cheek—then another—and, in a moment, another, this time on the other side. The thought passed through my brain that this warm rain came from myself, and that it was blood. I had hauled myself gradually away, and now fell over the bedside. The man who, in these three strokes, had cut down to my throat on two sides with two stabs, and with the third had left one of my cheeks hanging down in a flap, now moved round the foot of the bed to get at me on this side. He was met by the soldier nurse, and they had a tussle on the floor. Payne, the assassin, was breathless and tired with the excitement, and with the violence of his attack upon me, and the soldier, though wounded, was enabled to drive him to the door. All this had happened in so short a time, and had made so little noise, that my other son knew nothing of what was going on, but entering, when Payne had been driven to the door, he helped to drag him to the stairs, down which he dashed, and mounting a horse, got away."

From the lively and graphic way in which Mr. Seward told the story, it was hardly possible to believe that it related to himself, and that this diabolical attempt upon his life had been made only a year before.

The first thing the Secretary remembered after tumbling on to the floor, was that as in a dream he felt two hands under his arms, while a voice said, "He is not dead;" to which remark he was able to reply, faintly, "I am not dead—not dead." Then he was put into bed again. The doctor ordered him a little tea, which revived him so much that he was able to ask for the slate on which he had been in the habit of writing since his jaw had been broken, and was able to trace a few words.

The would-be assassin, though he wounded all in the room except the girl, had inflicted a fatal injury on no one.

CHAPTER XI.

Conversation with a Supporter of the President—A Freedmen's Village—White Labour in the South—Education of the People—Negro Enfranchisement—Feeling against the President—Politicians in Social Life—The proposed Paris Exhibition——Indian Troubles—Grant's Respect for Lee—State Rights and the Union—General Grant on some of the Operations of the War—Sherman and Hood—Education of the Negroes—Cultivation of Land by the Blacks—Negro Village at Arlington—Good done by the Freedmen's Bureau—Intelligence of the Negroes — Gradual Disappearance of the Antipathy between White and Black—Military Courts—Report of the Reconstruction Committee—Journey to Richmond—Banks of the Potomac—Acquia Creek—Fredericksburg—Richmond—State of Feeling among the Inhabitants — State Sovereignty — White and Coloured—Communicativeness of the Negroes—Devotion to Kind Masters manifested by them.

I HAD a conversation one afternoon with Mr. ——, who is a supporter of the President. I asked about a Freedmen's village of which I had heard on the other side of the river. "That," he said, "was a place established by us during the war. Freedmen cultivate the land you saw advertised as Government farms just below Lee's house. I went there some time ago, and walked through the little town of negroes' cottages. The people came out in great crowds, not knowing me; but hearing that I was an official, they quite looked upon me as the Government, and crowded round me with great curiosity. And what I'll relate to you will show you how ignorant and superstitious the negroes are.

"When I left the gates the crowd that had closely followed us hitherto would go no further, being afraid that if they left the neighbourhood of their houses some harm might come to them, and that, by some trick or other, they might be carried back into slavery. They trusted no one. I do not think that these people, or those in the South generally, will ever become owners of land to any great extent. They usually become barbers in the towns. A man who is well off sometimes takes a livery stable. They do not buy land.

"The excessive flocking to the towns is now over. They ran to them at first to get safety, and to be with others in their own position. They are now returning to the country, to the estates of their former masters. I believe that white labour can in time be got in the South, and that white men will be able to work in that climate without experiencing any bad effects. The negro will have to stand white labour competition, and I am sure I do not know how he will be able to do so. His future is a very doubtful one, and I never like to look forward to it. As for their education, there must be time. It may take a generation or longer—no one knows how long. The schools have been planted by the Freedmen's Bureau; but that Bureau cannot last. The States must look to the education of their people. The Government at Washington has never interfered with the States in anything regarding education. That must be left to the people, and they cannot be helped or guided. It is not the business of the Federal Government.

"It is probable that the State Governments will support the schools, for it is their interest to do so, and to raise the standard of intelligence among the people. The whites must have the land; they will buy it; the nigger wont. In Jamaica the state of things was different. There were not enough whites to buy the lands, and the nigger could get his plot and squat on it. Here the white men have the capital, and will use it for the purchase of land. Even now there is a constant influx of them, and it will in time become greater. The stream of emigration flows generally to the West, but native Americans are going South.

"We must avoid creating any fresh antagonism between the whites and the blacks. If the suffrage were given to the coloured men, they would send representatives to Congress who would demand things it would be impossible to grant them. The anger of the whites against them would thus be raised, and there would be a war of races most disastrous to the black. If the negroes got the franchise here, in this district of Columbia around Washington, it would have no further effect, because the event would have no influence beyond the district in which it occurred, and it would do no harm.

"Mr. Sumner has found himself to-day in a minority upon this Colorado question. He wanted to keep out a new State on account of its not letting a coloured man vote. The West is showing its feeling, and the extremists can go no further. These Radicals will not be able to carry their views further with regard to the Southern States. The men elected there for governorships and other appointments will be men of compromise; and that is what is best. It is what is seen after all the revolutions that history tells us of. Extremes tone down on either side, and moderate men are elected. It is of the first importance that Southern States should come in and be represented in Congress — the sooner the better."

I spoke of the feeling in New England against the President. "Yes," he said, "you observed that tone? Well, the President is a firm man, who has taken his line and will go on upon it. The minds of vulgar men are always full of notions that this or that is done by men in public positions only with a view to the next elections, and not for the benefit of the country. I do not suppose the President gives a thought to such things. I do not believe that he will even be a candidate for the next Presidency. No, he wants North and South again to join and be one. This is as necessary to the nation as the proper joining of the bones of a broken leg is for a man to walk. Painful though the process may be, both parts must be made to join."

The warm party zeal that is displayed in America does not prevent politicians of opposite principles from meeting in social life. When I dined at Senator Sprague's, it was striking to meet at the same table men of such opposite politics as Reverdy Johnson and

Thaddeus Stevens. The senator had been so good as to ask us on an evening when many distinguished men were his guests. Among those present were General Grant, the Speaker, Generals Schenk and Howard, Mr. Colfax, Mr. Chase, the Chief Justice, and Senators Wilson, Sumner, and Sherman. General Howard, is chief of the Freedmen's Bureau. He commanded one of the wings of Sherman's army.

Conversation turned once upon the proposed exhibition in the Champ de Mars at Paris, and General Grant seized the occasion to express those sentiments respecting the French occupation of Mexico which he takes no pains to conceal. His face flushed as he said—

"Well, there's one thing I want done about that Paris Exposition: I want none of our people to send a single article there unless every French soldier has first been withdrawn by that time from Mexico."

"Well, general, they are to go by instalments, you know," some one said.

"Not a bit of it," replied Grant, angrily; "they wont go till they are obliged to go. Infantry and artillery are the only things that will make them quit hold."

Should the general ever be President, no European

emperor in Mexico will be long without a war on his hands.

The Indian troubles that the United States have had at intervals, the general thought, were entirely owing to the bad faith kept towards the Indians by the white settlers and hunters in the West. "I have seen an Englishman," he said, "who belonged to the Hudson's Bay Company, just able to mount his horse, ride right away among the tribes most hostile to us, just because the Indians know that the English have always kept faith with them."

Of Lee, Grant spoke with great respect, saying that he liked him, and that he was a gentleman. Lee had told him that he was not for secession, and had never considered it necessary, but he had thought it his duty to go when his State went.

"I never took that view," Grant said, "as to State rights; and I remember, years ago, when there was some talk of such a thing in Missouri, that I resolved, come what would, that I should stick to the Union. I looked upon it as showing the demoralization of the time that such talk should be possible; that men should think in that way."

Of Joe Johnstone he said that he was "as good a general as Lee, if not better. Lee's army, just before the taking of Richmond, I should set down at eighty thousand men. I had one hundred and thirty thousand, all told. We had the outside and he the inside, which gave him an advantage. He was able to concentrate on any given point fully as many men as I could bring to the attack. We had the advantage in resources." He set down the loss of the Confederates at the great battle of Pittsburg Landing at forty thousand men. His own army lost twelve thousand.

"Well, general," some one said, "we were pretty well whipped that first day, though we whipped them on the second."

"No, sir," said Grant, "we were not. We were always confident of beating them; they brought all their troops on the ground the first day; I had a whole fresh division coming up, and I knew we should drive them on the next day.

"The losses of troops were always very heavy when an attack failed. If we broke through their line, there was not much loss in general on our side."

"It was during a retreat—after an attack had failed —that the men got so badly cut up?"

"No, sir, we never retreated. The loss was after the failure of an attack. We never retreated," repeated the general.

The general said that he should be quite at ease were either Sherman or Sheridan placed in command of an American army for any purpose, or even if their command embraced that of several detached armies requiring united action. Sherman had been uneasy when Hood replaced Joe Johnstone in the command of the Confederate forces before Atlanta. Grant said, "I knew of Johnstone's being superseded as soon as Sherman did, for we were in constant telegraphic communication; and the view I took of the matter was opposite to that of Sherman, and I was very glad to hear of it."

A good deal was said about the Freedmen's Bureau by General Howard and others. Several thought that the Southerners would not much mind acceding to the representation of the blacks. Five negroes formerly counted as two whites in the Southern representation in Congress, but it is now hoped that the Southerners will see that black representation, without black suffrage, is no longer possible. The Freedmen's Bureau it is not thought advisable to continue very long.

"We have established a number of schools. How far the States would be inclined to support them, if we left them to their care, we do not know. Florida does support schools; she taxes the negroes for the education of their children. The planters, too, in many places have done very much in the way of helping to get the negroes taught, and many of these gentlemen seem anxious that the blacks should get educated by the State. The Church has been quite in favour of the schools, knowing that if she did not take this line she should lose in influence; for the people would find out that all the good that had come to them had come through the Yankees, and not through her. No proof has, however, yet been given that the educational establishments that were founded by the Bureau would be continued were the Bureau withdrawn."

The probability is that in future the negroes of the South will be, as heretofore, the labouring part of the population. I do not think they need fear white competition; but there will be many who will rent land, or own it themselves, and cultivate it as farmers. Lately, in one of the Gulf States, I heard of several negroes who had combined together to rent and work an estate. One who was sent as their representative to the Bureau Office made the necessary arrangements, and showed great intelligence. These men, all partners in the concern, each in general with a lot of forty acres, are now working the estate. It is not often that a negro has the capital to buy land, but he may rent it, and in many cases those who have done so are getting on very well. In the Sea Islands they have rather come to grief, but they are helped sometimes to get along.

The negro village at Lee's old place, Arlington, is inhabited chiefly by decrepit people. The farms about the village are divided into five and ten acre pieces, and the negroes cultivate them. They do not, however, show the passion for acquiring land that the Jamaica negro showed after emancipation. The mortality was necessarily great among them at first, when large numbers followed the armies, particularly during Sherman's march through from Atlanta to Savannah. They had to be herded together like cattle — in many cases getting no good food, or only the rations that could be spared by the soldiers.

The Bureau has done much good in bridging over the feeling of dislike between the white and the black, and in bringing the two races together. Even men from the South admit this. I have seen encouraging letters lately from the Southern States, describing the feeling between the two classes as good, and encouraging the hope that the same may soon be the case generally throughout the South.

It was the opinion of several gentlemen whom I met, that the South would ask to be allowed to come into Congress in less than five months, even though they should be compelled to accede to the condition that the Confederate debt should not be assumed by the Government, and that they should have no representation for negroes as long as they did not admit them to the suffrage.

One distinguished member of the Republican party I found to be quite in favour of giving the blacks all rights, including the right to vote. "It is not possible for us to give the blacks of the South the right of voting immediately, but it should be done as soon as it is possible to do it. The coloured men of Louisiana are, I think, in general the most intelligent. In the towns too they are sharp enough. It is not with them here as it was with their brethren in the West Indies. Here they have many white men from whom to learn, and hear so much talk that they know fully as well as most people what is going on. You will always find that they know their friends. The other day, in Washington, when there was that immense mass meeting of coloured men, I and others addressed them, and the applause did not come when we appeared, but at points in the speeches, the bearing of which they well knew. If the President goes against them, they know well enough what to think of him. You must remember this, that we consider their right to vote is of itself a good educator.

"We believe that the best education a man can receive is to have the privilege of a free man; he becomes a person of importance, and is held in higher estimation than if he has no vote. It is only in some plantations that the ignorance of the black is so gross as is represented. In a few States the black votes would certainly swamp the white; but I do not believe that the antagonism of whites and blacks would be increased by the measure, but, on the contrary, lessened.

"In one of the Southern States there is now a newspaper edited by a negro, who says, in the columns of his journal, that the antagonism is much increased at present by the suffrage being withheld. 'You keep us out,' he says, 'and deny us full rights; and till we get them, we shall make war upon you. It is true that power would be given to many ignorant men; but the giving of that power is the best means of dispelling their ignorance. I do not believe that they would act in a body against the whites. On the contrary, it is probable that they would split into sections, and follow the lead of the white men.'

" The military courts are still in force in the South, and you will find some sitting at Richmond. The recent decision of the Supreme Court does not affect the legality of the military tribunals where martial law exists; *i.e.*, over the whole South. North of the Ohio they were illegal, for civil law has at all times been in full force."

" Is the South, then, still entirely under martial law?"

" Yes; the Habeas Corpus Act is still suspended, and the military tribunals can be held with perfect legality. It is true that it is twelve months since the war has ceased, and there has since been no active resistance. As one of your English lawyers said after the Indian rebellion, we consider the war to be not raging, but existing—*non flagrante, sed constante*. These military tribunals are not for trial, but for condemnation. A man, if tried before them, knows he has but little chance."

"Do you say they are simply instruments of execution?"

"Yes, so they are. It is not possible to get verdicts that are just from civil tribunals, and this is our expedient."

A senator who was present spoke of the difficulties between North and South. He did not think them of such vital importance. "If we surrender our attempt to give the Southern negro the suffrage, and if they surrender their attempt to get representation for negroes, whom they don't allow to vote, the difficulty may be bridged over. It is not fair that the South should be able to get a number of members into the House as representatives of men who are not allowed to have any share in the Government. It is one of our first principles that men who have a share in the Government shall alone be represented."

Such talk will give you some idea of Washington politics. Society in this town is so limited, that politicians of opposite views meet constantly; and men who abuse each other cordially in the House, shake hands with equal cordiality the same evening.

The Report of the Reconstruction Committee is just out, and the programme they propose is, as you will see, not one calculated to heal the feelings of the

people. Those who were in favour of the "rebellion"
—*i.e.*, all, with very few exceptions—are, according
to the committee's proposal, disfranchised till 1870.

We left Washington on the 28th, at seven in the
morning, and arrived at Richmond at two the same
day. Our way lay down the Potomac to Acquia
Creek, and then along the railroad, through Fredericksburg, straight to Richmond. Confederate sentiments manifested themselves as soon as we left the
Washington wharf, in the exhibition and purchasing of
very ugly life-size portraits of "Stonewall" Jackson.

The morning was light and warm, the broad river
flowing onward without a ripple on its surface.
Flocks of canvas-backs could be seen from the deck,
but they were too wild to let the steamer get near them.
After passing Alexandria—the place where young
Ellsworth, one of the first Union officers who perished,
was shot in the beginning of the war—the banks became very pretty. Nowhere of great height, they sank
often abruptly into the water. The yellow earth on the
miniature bluffs contrasted with the fresh spring
green of the trees that grew thickly above. When
we passed Mount Vernon the ship's bell was tolled
in honour of Washington.

After about three hours' steaming the vessel

rounded in to the shore, where a bay cut deeply into the land. A stage of great extent, that had once run far out into the water, was now mostly charred and burnt. A few sheds, and an earthwork thrown up on a low hill a quarter of a mile distant, were all that remained at Acquia Creek—a place that was long the base of the Union armies in their four years' struggle to get at Richmond. It has been occupied and re-occupied by Federals, and wiped out by Confederates.

The railway cars were close down to the shore, and no time was lost in getting into them. The train goes rather slowly, and we pass through a tract of country that is characteristically American. The land is often very low and swampy, and the lean forest grows at will, uncared for and unmolested. Wherever the ground is dry there is a thick undergrowth. Older trees rise above, thin and scraggy, and the dead lie rotting on the ground, or in falling have caught in the branches of others, and remain drooping against them. The forest has in many places been cut, and the blackened stumps are left by hundreds sticking out of the ground. Wherever the land rises there are these cuttings; but sometimes the wood gives way altogether to ploughed fields.

Many marks were left of the time when camps

dotted the country between Acquia Creek and Fredericksburg.

At the stations there are small earthworks, and in places in the woods one can trace the spots where the tents of the troops were pitched.

The train soon passed the Rappahannock, and we were in Fredericksburg—a pretty little town close to the river's bank. Shot and shell have done their work here, and great ragged holes appear in the walls of many of the houses. In passing out, the passengers in the car point out the field of battle of December 13th, 1863. It is a plain behind the town, about a mile and a half in length, and commanded by hills at its edge, at the foot of which was the stone wall from behind which the Confederates poured such a tremendous fire upon the Irish brigade, of whose gallantry their enemy still speak with admiration. It is no wonder that an attack on such a position failed.

Richmond is a sad place to stay in. The buildings are ruined in many parts of the town, which has suffered so much that from almost every man and woman in it you hear the same note of misery. The people are frequently very haughty, and exhibit much hatred of the Yankees. The women are the most violent, the men being generally sullen when spoken to of their position and chances. "We are helpless, and must bear all they put upon us," is the burden of their conversation.

Black clothing—the sign of mourning for some one fallen during the recent campaigns—is the rule in Richmond. They speak with a fierce exultation of the fights in which they have been engaged, and which they have so often won. There is sometimes a painful effort at jollity; and a lady, who had lost her two brothers and several other relatives in the last year of the war, told me of "the fun" they had had at Petersburg during the shelling of the town, before its evacuation. It was only when she incidentally said, "Our best and bravest—all were engaged in our effort," that the tears rose to her eyes, and she could not conceal her wretchedness. Surely no nation, or section of a nation, has ever been so terribly punished as have these Southerners for clinging to a system that was a curse to the slave, and a double curse to the master. Their present condition is most piteous; but the old ideas of State sovereignty, for which they fought, are still expressed with as much firmness, and with as undoubted a belief in their truth, as ever.

It is the feeling of loyalty to their State that Whittier describes in "Randolf of Roanoke:"—

> "Too honest and too proud to feign
> A love he never cherished,
> Beyond Virginia's border-line
> His patriotism perished.
> While others hailed in distant skies
> Our eagle's dusky pinion,
> He only saw the mountain-bird
> Stoop o'er his 'old dominion.'"

The papers frequently contain speculations as to whether the South will accept this or that condition imposed upon them as the price of re-entering the Union. Many men look upon the conditions that the Reconstruction Committee propose as a downright insult; but they are so anxious again to enter the Union, or rather to have a voice in the management of their own affairs, that I should not wonder at their accepting, in form at least, very stringent conditions. They might even yield their assent to black suffrage; but it is very evident that it would not be wise for the Northern Congress now at Washington to push their demands too far. The feelings of the Southerners are already bitter enough, and the bitterness would be increased tenfold if the present Radical policy—such policy as is shown by Thaddeus Stevens's plan of confiscating rebels' lands for the blacks—were adopted. It would tell terribly against the negroes, by setting every white man's hand against them throughout the length and breadth of "Dixie." It would create in Congress—for into Congress the Southern representatives must soon enter—a party eternally at enmity with the North, and by no means anxious to help the negro. As the case now stands, the Southerners think of the blacks very much as some English people think of the low Irish—they are nuisances, and no one troubles himself much as to what is to become of them. The fond hope indulged in by the South with regard to the negroes is, that they will all die out. There is a very unanimous opinion on this point. Every Southerner will tell you that vice, and dirt, and laziness must carry them off. This conclusion, however, is hardly warranted by the vitality the blacks show, under certain unfavourable circumstances, in the West Indies. But the Southerners declare that the darkies here, in addition to being subject to causes which have produced so little effect upon their numbers in Hayti and Jamaica, will also be placed under the disadvantage that they cannot, as in Jamaica, fatten upon a small piece of land. I am a great believer in the vitality of the negro; but there is no doubt that for some time, at all events, there will be much mortality among them in the towns, where as many as fifteen or twenty persons pig together in one room—a state of things

which cannot be conducive to long life, if continued.
If they can be got to go back to work on the estates,
there is no reason why they should not continue to
thrive till their distant descendants become absorbed
in the white population, for that will probably be
their ultimate fate. This absorbing process is being
already rapidly carried on, and one sees in the towns
nine coloured men before one meets with one that is
a pure black.

To one coming from Jamaica, the want of a distinction between the blacks and browns is striking. Here all coloured men are niggers, even though almost white in complexion. From all the right of voting would be withheld. It would be impossible to define how much of the tar-brush touch should keep a man out of the poll. None must be admitted who have any of it, although some of those that have a little of it are superior in intelligence to many a white man in the South.

The negroes here seem to be getting on well enough, and are very communicative about their feelings. Their stories must generally be taken with a " grain of salt ;" for, as soon as one speaks to them of their condition, they conclude that one comes from the North, and say all that they think will be most pleasing to a Northern ear. I have heard them abuse their former masters, although, when asked of what they complained, they have confessed that the masters, whom they now call "rebels" with great unction, were kind, and treated them well.

I have heard of instances of great devotion to kind masters, and one gentleman told me that he knew of several men who had accompanied their masters to the very end of the last campaign, although suffering great privations, and never left them till the army of Northern Virginia surrendered. The natural enmity caused by the ill-treatment some have received is plainly enough expressed when out of hearing of any white man they think a Southerner.

"Would you have fought if your freedom had been given you by the Confederates, and if they had placed you in their army?" I asked of several.

The answer—always given under the impression I was a Yankee—was, "No, no; we would never have fought against the Northerners. I looked for them to come in long before they did. When M'Clellan came so near, I thought he would get in, but he didn't that time. No, we wouldn't fight. What for we fight?" "Dey had used us too badly," one man said. "Several of my children were sold away from me," said another. "No; we weren't going to be taken out there just to be killed. Dey only wanted us to go into fire to help them. De freedom dey promised we did not believe in. Dey would have taken it from us if they had succeeded. If dey had given freedom first, then we fight. Very few went into army—not more than a hundred or so—and dat was sham to get over to Norferners."

CHAPTER XII.

Situation of Richmond—The Capitol—Governor Pierpont—The Burnt District—The Tredegar Ironworks—The Two Prisons—Treatment of Prisoners of War—Sufferings of the Southern States—Loafing Negroes—Blacks in Mixed Uniform—Defences of Richmond—M'Clellan's Advance against Richmond—The Chickahominy—Agricultural Operations—Soldiers' Graves—Federal Cemetery—Antipathy of the South to the North—Galling Treatment of Federal Officers by Southern Ladies—View of Richmond from the James River—Butler's Lines—His Attempt to cut through the Dutch Gap—Farms on the James—City Point—Idle Negroes—Rail to Petersburg—Position of that Town—Murderous Contests in its Neighbourhood—Nothing to do with Yankees—Virginian Bitterness—The Natural Position of the African — Parallel between English and American Parties.

RICHMOND is rising faster from its ruins than any other town in the South. It is well situated on hills overlooking the James river, which, above the town, is a brawling, yellow torrent, but becomes, just below, a navigable river. On the top of the principal hill is the Capitol—a Greek temple with big portico, and surrounded with trees. The houses along the ridge are pretty closely packed, and there are several church-spires that can be seen from

M'Clellan's battle-grounds. Pierpont, the newly-appointed governor of the State, lives in a house that formerly belonged to Jefferson Davis, not far from the Capitol. This man, as a Yankee governor, is very odious to the people, who had, of course, no voice in his election, and now refuse to have anything to say to him. The Richmond ladies will not see or visit his wife—a complete avoidance that has not made him less Radical in his views.

The hotel at which we stayed—the Spotswood—was in a block between the governor's house and the river, and on the border of the "burnt district," which extends from it to the James. These houses were set fire to when the city was evacuated, and it is a wonder that the fire did not do more damage. As it was, much harm was done, as the charred brick ruins show. Yankee speculators are fast rebuilding, and before long the place will be, outwardly, as gay as ever.

Just below us, on the river's bank, are the Tredegar Ironworks, that were so useful to the Confederate Government for the founding of cannon, the renewal of railway iron, &c. They look very dirty and "played out" now, though they were in full swing, turning out guns and making rails up to the last day of the war. A heap of rails taken from the road lay near the factory. It would certainly have been difficult to drive a train fast over them. They were quite splintered and flattened by the constant use they had been put to for so long. A heap of cannon balls, fired by the Federals, and picked up as old iron, to be melted and used for other purposes, was also there. They were of all shapes and sizes, from the monster sharp conical shot to grape and canister. There were some curious bolts, with flanges like the feathers on an arrow behind the body of the projectile, and shells that had buried themselves in the ground, and had forgotten to explode.

Lower down the James, more in the suburbs of the town, are the two prisons, "Castle Thunder" and "The Libby," that we have all heard so much about. They are close together, and are now marked by a boarding on which their names are written. Castle Thunder is a plain block of brick, looking like a row of ugly lodging-houses. The windows are all securely barred. The Libby is a little further on, and across the way, close to the water. It is also a brick building, of a larger size than Castle Thunder, and apparently built for a warehouse.

TREATMENT OF PRISONERS. 271

In speaking of the prisons, statements made to me by gentlemen who were officers in the Confederate army concerning the treatment of the prisoners may here be communicated. I have asked several who were in the army of Northern Virginia about it, and they one and all declare that they do not believe that the prisoners had any hardships to bear that could have been easily prevented. Much misery undoubtedly existed.

"What could we do?" they said. "We tried over and over again to get them exchanged, but we couldn't; and there they had to remain. Our armies were suffering fearfully. Rations were often not issued to the regiments at all on certain days. The troops had sometimes to wait over twenty-four hours before they could get anything to eat. What was to be had in Richmond was given to the prisoners as well as to our troops. The men in the Libby had the same food as the men in the lines. That was often scant and poor enough.

"At Spotsylvania, for instance, just to give you an idea of our state, our wounded had to be fed for seven or eight weeks on salt junk alone. Nothing else was at hand. Of course the prisoners, crowded as they were (for we had no other place to put them in, and could spare no more men to guard them), suffered terribly. Perhaps in a place or two in the South there may have been some officer over the prison who did not do his duty; but it was the wish of the Government that all in the prisons should be well treated. At Andersonville there was, undoubtedly, much misery arising from the same causes. We had absolutely no men to spare, and the consequence was that at that place the guard was quite insufficient for the number of the prisoners. Very severe rules had, in consequence, to be adopted.

"When Sherman moved near Andersonville, a number of the prisoners were taken away to be placed in a position of greater security further in the interior. There were so few soldiers to guard this large batch, that the captive Yankees were straggling all over the country: the men could not keep them together. In collecting food for these prisoners, a number of cattle were taken, and much complaint was made. Such an act is a good proof that all the food that could be got by hook or by crook was obtained for them."

The streets of Richmond are full of negroes, who are generally busily engaged in loafing. The white men, most of whom still wear the blue grey of the Confederate uniform, with the brass buttons covered with black cloth, and the usual slouch wide-awake hat, seem fewer in number.

The uniforms of the contending armies are sometimes oddly mixed up on the persons of the blacks, particularly the boys, who may be seen with the United States blue trousers and a Confederate army jacket—a happy combination which one would gladly see realized not only in the dress, but also in those who wear it. What time must elapse before such a happy consummation shall be witnessed in these States?

On the first day of May I drove out along the Mechanicsville highway—a road leading due north of this. It is a broad sandy track, with no metal, and, till the Chickahominy is reached, almost straight. As soon as we were well clear of the outlying suburbs of the city, we passed the works belonging to the first or inner line of defence erected around Richmond.

These works are fast crumbling into ruins, little of the breastwork connecting the forts being now left. The forts themselves, which are simple enough, have no turf on their yellow-clay sides, that are thickly channelled by the rains. The country is very flat to the north, though more broken to the east and south. Woods surrounding broad spaces

T

that are sometimes under the plough, and sometimes covered with rotten stumps, are the common features of the landscape.

After passing another earthwork further on, at the edge of a copsewood, a place was pointed out as the spot across which M'Clellan's picket line passed at the time of his advance against Richmond after the peninsula had been traversed. His extreme right rested on Mechanicsville, his blue lines of battle stretching away for eighteen miles in a half circle, till his left rested on the James. A battle was fought here. Then, after seven days more of hard fighting, he drew back to his gunboats, and went down to the river.

None of the earthworks now to be seen in the neighbourhood were raised at that time. They were thrown up after his defeat. The plateau, on which we had hitherto been, here dips suddenly. A battery has been constructed on the brow, and three embrasures scowl down upon the road as it dives into the wood-covered valley of the Chickahominy. Along the crest, to the left and right, breastworks and forts are constructed.

The Chickahominy is a little stream that creeps quietly along, often flooding the low land around it.

The rough log-bridges that have been put up by the army are now much tumbled down. The timbers have rotted or fallen away, and ugly holes are left, that look as if they must break the legs of any horses that are taken over them. Both horses and drivers, however, seem quite accustomed to these rickety, unsafe structures. The former take a little jump on to the first firm log, and walk over it in the cleverest way, the carriage heaving, jolting, and banging behind them. Beyond the little river the woods become more dense, their undergrowth often spangled with the white blossoms of the dogwood. The pitch pine, a tall tree, not unlike the Scotch fir, is very common.

Around the whole of this ground there was heavy fighting, though few traces of it are now seen. Farming seems to be reviving. They are now ploughing great clearings with a machine, drawn by one horse only, that hardly does more than scratch the light soil. The negro ploughmen earn their seven or eight dollars a month, and are now preparing the land for maize.

Near another villainous log-bridge, at the bottom of a little ravine, were a few soldiers' graves and a broken mill, that marked the place of one of M'Clellan's severest fights. The graves held often more than one soldier. On one head-board the names of those lying below it were not recorded at all, but simply the number of the company, and the State from which it came. A quarter of an hour's ride brought us to the battle-field of Cold Harbour. The pines grew thickly over most of the field, and rifle-pits had been thrown up by hundreds beneath them. A little shanty, riddled with balls, stands where the fire was hottest. In front of it the woods are thinner, the lines of the Confederates crossing spaces that were quite open. Dwarf cedars grow in great numbers, most of them torn by shot. Cannon balls have taken off the tops of many, and smashed the trunks. Rifle bullets, too, have cut sharp grooves in their sides, and speckled them with small holes.

Owing to the practice of the American troops on both sides of intrenching themselves by throwing up a breastwork as soon as any ground was gained, the turns of the fight can often be traced. At one spot the hostile lines approach to within seventy yards of each other. The Federals had begun a mine which never exploded. It was on the 3rd of June, two years ago, that a furious charge by the Federals drove in, for a short distance, the troops under Breckenridge. In the end, however, Grant had again to sidle off to the left, leaving more dead on the ground than he had ever lost before in any of his assaults in the Wilderness.

A cemetery has been made by the Federals within their old lines, in which two thousand dead, or more, are buried. While the dead bodies of the Federal troops found in the woods were carried in by fatigue parties, the Confederate dead were allowed to lie where they fell under the trees—at least a more poetic resting-place than those graves ticketed off in long rows, with the monotonous lines of little white boards above, and the ugly white paling around. These cemeteries are called "national;" and yet it is only the dead from the Northern section of the nation that are laid in them. The names have often been cut on slabs above the graves in the woods, so that the bodies can be identified without much trouble. Often, too, even when there is no inscription, the clothing tells who the soldier was. Where the soil is light, these bodies are now only skeletons in uniform; but where they have been buried in clay, the flesh is still on the bones.

It was dusk as we drove back to Richmond, passing the battle-field of Fair Oaks. The country reminded me of the sand and pines of Surrey.

I went in the evening to a tea-party, at which there were several Confederate officers and some ladies — all dressed in black. One can scarcely wonder at the depth of hate with which they regard their conquerors, when one hears of their terrible losses—the ladies talking of their brothers lying mangled in the hospitals, and the men of their comrades struck down with a dull bullet thud by their sides. The treatment the Federal officers receive from the ladies must sometimes be rather galling. One of these objectionable gallants was prancing, to his own great satisfaction, up and down one of the streets on a remarkably fine horse. A group of ladies, before whom he had taken care frequently to pass, at last stopped in their walk to observe him; and one of them exclaimed, when sure their victim was well within hearing, " I wonder, now, where that horse was stolen from?"

Mr. Wyse and Mr. Fox, of the Federal navy, kindly offered to take us down the James river, on their return from Richmond to Washington—an offer which we were only too glad to accept. We started at half-past four in the morning. Fancy the Thames below Cliveden, without the islands, and with the high banks a little lowered. Put a *maison-carrée-*

like Greek temple where Cliveden House stands, with a few church-spires above the trees, and you will have an idea of the view of Richmond from the James a little below the city. The hills on which the town is built soon subside into more level ground. The river, which is excessively tortuous, takes its course through a rolling country, partly under wood, partly under cultivation, on each side. Along the banks the ground sometimes rises in low bluffs, the principal of which is Drury's Bluff, some miles down the stream. It is covered with strong batteries, that completely command the passage.

A little further down we came in sight of Butler's lines, and his "crow's nest" of observation. The attempt he made to cut through the narrow gap known as the Dutch Gap looks far less foolish than one would suppose it to be, from the amount of ridicule that has been cast on him on account of it. The river at this point makes a great loop, two miles in length, and comes flowing down again only about fifty feet from its channel above. The sand and clay bank between the two channels is about twenty feet high; and if that could have been cut through, Butler would have avoided the two miles of round-about, and all the obstructions that had been placed in the course of those two miles to prevent his gunboats getting up the river. If the narrow neck were cut through, he no doubt thought the water might easily be persuaded to flow through in sufficient volume to float his vessels. But the angle at which the cutting had been made was too much of a right angle to the course of the stream, and a dirty, long puddle was all that was made. The men had to work under fire, as the batteries above could throw shell easily into the ditch. They lived as much as possible in covers scooped for themselves in the bank, which looked as if a number of gigantic sand-martins had been burrowing in its face.

There are some fine farms along the river's banks, a few of which are getting on well. The proprietors of others say they cannot get labour enough, and hope that the whites from the North will soon supply it. Those that have enough labour are confident that the free system will pay them much better than the old one. "Yes, of course," they say, "if we can only get the men to work as much as we want, it will pay much better. We have not now to nurse and take care of the hands, as we had before, and we get ten hours of work from the men. Here, however, where corn and tobacco only are grown, we shall not get on so well this year as the cotton people will. Some one is going to try cotton near Petersburg; but the climate is too cold for much probability of success in cotton-raising."

City Point, a promontory jutting into the river, was Grant's head-quarters during much of the time he directed the operations against the army of Lee. The house he used is prettily situated near the James, which, like most American rivers, is of a dirty yellow-ochre colour. A number of young niggers were on the pier.

"What are those fellows doing?" I asked.

"Oh, just loafing about, doing nothing. Most of them are vagrants. Whenever they want anything they go to the Freedmen's Bureau, and get some help. The sooner that B'reau is done away with the better."

These fellows were all dressed in cast-off soldiers' uniforms.

The rail to Petersburg is laid over level country, and leads often through woods, and over cleared ground, where little is to be seen but the eternal breastworks as one hurries by. The town, which bears many marks of shot and shell, is like a little English town, and there seemed to be a good deal of business doing in it. I called on Captain P., nephew to Colonel P., killed at Fair Oaks, and who himself commanded in turn several of the Confederate war-vessels. Another Confederate officer to whom we were introduced was so good as to promise to ride with us, to point out the places of interest in the lines around the town.

There are several gentlemen staying in the hotel. One of them has come to town to buy some sheep. He says that he is getting on pretty well with his farming. He had a number of negroes working for him, but did not like to pay them fixed wages, as they were certain, when receiving such only, to leave the estate, should they hear of anything they supposed likely to give them a better chance. His plan was to give them one-half of the produce, but to make them work at other things besides agriculture: they were house servants as well. This "share system" had answered with him, and the negroes had shown an interest in the farm, and stuck by him. Having got three horses and a buggy, we rode out to the lines with our guide, who had exchanged his sword for the birch-rod, and given his school a short holiday in order to be able to accompany us. My horse was an immense Roman-nosed charger. S.

drove, as he cannot be persuaded to cross his legs over a horse's back unless there is a fox in prospect.

Petersburg lies rather in a hollow, the ground rising on all sides of it. A little way out there are some other hollows, that served well for the massing of troops preparatory to moving out on the bare, shot-swept plain beyond. It was a lovely day, with bright sun and pleasant wind. We could see on the horizon line, between us and Richmond, the tall crow's nest near Butler's canal, and the woods bordering the James. In our front the country was covered with pine and hard wood, but not in the vicinity of the trenches. A few minutes' gallop over sandy ploughed land, and past mouldering earthworks, brought us to the spot where Grant made his great assault in 1864, after the springing of a mine in which the Federals had managed, in spite of the counter-mining of the Confederates, to place eight tons of gunpowder. The spot was guarded by a Carolina regiment, which was blown into the air. The Federals poured in, and swept the works for a distance of two hundred yards, filling with their assaulting columns the pit made by the explosion. Confederate troops and artillery were mustered as quickly as possible on a rising ground behind, and a murderous fire of shell, grape, and canister was opened, that swept the assailants down in hundreds.

Our cicerone (who had commanded one of the batteries that played upon the spot) spoke with awful glee of the effects of his fire. " You should have seen the arms and legs fly, sir," &c. Very few of them who formed a part of these storming columns got back, and the description of the appearance the " crater" presented after the struggle was all over was truly appalling. The dead, to the number of twelve or fifteen hundred, are buried below the place, which shows only confused heaps of gravel. The rains have washed the soil away in some places, and skulls of whites and blacks grin at the skies. Canteens and single bones protrude from the ground. It is not worth while to rebury them, for they help to add interest to the place, and give a better trade to the little *Lager-Bier* shanty that has been built close by.

I was amused with some Southern gentlemen who called this morning. I mentioned our proposed ride, in which one of our visitors was to accompany us. They looked embarrassed, and at last asked if both the others who were travelling with us, and whom they had not yet seen, were Englishmen.

" Yes, they are," we answered.

"We asked," they said, "for we have nothing to do with the Yankees, and were afraid that you might perhaps have been with some Federal officers, in which case we could not have gone with you. We would not shake their hands for worlds. We owe it to our State to recognise none of those who have fought to deprive her of her rights."

One of them added, "I have a relation in the North—a Virginian born. The first thing I did after our surrender was to send him word that we could never see each other again. He would be the last man on this earth that I should like to see. A Virginian, and not to go with his State! Why, sir, I should spit in such a man's face," he said gravely. "Never again will I take the hand of a Yankee, far less that of a traitor to his State."

"Do you think such feelings as those you express will with most Southerners last long?"

"Yes, sir, they will with a certain class of our people. I do not expect such bitterness as we feel to exist with the next generation, nor, indeed, with many of this. With very many, however—with all who truly had the honour of their State at heart—that feeling will go with them to the grave. It was that feeling that made Virginians fight as they did. There is no stronger pro-slavery man than myself. I was brought up and educated among slaves, and now hold to the belief that it is the natural position for the African race to occupy, when brought into contact with one so superior as the Anglo-Saxon. But I and many others were in favour of abolishing slavery, though it was, in truth, giving up all our property, because it damaged us in the eyes of Europe, whose recognition we desired. I should always have held that slavery was right; but our property, and every social arrangement, dwindled into insignificance in our eyes, if the choice was between them and independence. We are helpless now, and I know for certain that there is no plot, or even wish, to do anything more against the Government of the United States. No, we shall live now as contentedly as we can. The President is doing all he can to help us, but the Radicals are equally zealous to undo all his work. I think the President will be supported, though I don't care a d—n what is going on there now. I have no interest in events."

He then made a comparison between the late contest and that in England between the Cavaliers and Roundheads.

"There are many points of resemblance," he said. "We had, indeed, no king like Charles to fight for; but our tone was very much that of the Cavaliers. We, like them, clung to the old order of things that existed, as we believed, by right. We had, like them, at first, success in the field. We had our Rupert and Montrose in Stewart and Jackson. We, like them, knew more of war than our opponents, but were at last borne down by superior numbers. The Roundhead cavalry, like that of the Federals, learned to fight during the continuance of war; and at last Sheridan's men, like Cromwell's Ironsides, rode down all opposed to them. The Yankee Radicals, again, were represented in your history by the fanatics who cried out for 'the higher law' against constitution and usage. But remember the reaction that they brought on, which culminated in the Restoration. History is likely to repeat herself here again. In that hope we live."

CHAPTER XIII.

Virginian Country Life—Birds of Virginia—Our Host—Conduct of his Sons in the War—Sufferings from the Presence of invading Armies—A Negro Traitor—One Generous Action of Butler's—Union as understood in the South—Objectionable Provision of the Civil Rights Bill—Farming Quarters, Clothing, and Nourishment of the Slaves—Admiration of England—Federal and Confederate Government—Names and Manners of the Darkies—Reverence for Age in the South—New York *Gamins* —A Go-ahead Youngster at the Theatre—A Freedman at Bermuda Hundred—Germans in Richmond—German Troops in the Federal Army—A Scotch Farmer—Charlotteville—Anniversary of " Stonewall " Jackson's Death—University of Virginia— A Virginian Secessionist and " Rebel "—Caution to the Radicals —A Better Time coming for South and West—Commemoration of General Jackson and the Conservative Dead—University Professors and Students in the Southern Army—Mr. Black's Schemes—Yankee Troops in the University—A Freedman's School—Passengers in the Cars to Lynchburg—Campbell Court-House—Host and Hostess at the Inn—Talk with Niggers— Lynchburg to Staunton by Canal—Recruits for England in the South—Desertions from the Confederate Army—Administration of Justice by the Agent of the Bureau.

WE were anxious to see something of Virginian country life; and as we received several kind invitations, we divided our forces, two going to an estate near the scene of the " Wilderness " battles, and the rest to one on the James river. We came down from Richmond by one of the fast river boats, which brought us the sixty miles to Bermuda Hundred—General Butler's old head-quarters—in a very short time. This estate is not far off, and after some trouble we found a negro and boat to take us over the river.

On landing we found the house was near the water, and pleasantly surrounded with trees. It must have been one of the first good houses built in the country, as it has stood there for perhaps eighty years. There is a still older building close by, that is now an ivy-covered ruin, a rare sight in America. A little further back was a pleasant garden, now out of order, as the care that had evidently once been given to it was now turned to other and more necessary things. It was still, however, full of roses, most of them in full bloom, and loud with the song of birds, the redbird, the mocking-bird, and the inevitable great thrush robin—so handsome that it is a pleasure to see him. I also saw a lovely little hawk about the size of a Merlin, but much more handsomely marked.

The old gentleman and one of his sons received us very kindly, and showed us into a room full of stiff family pictures of the time of George II. and III. In passing through, we observed that the arms of the house were emblazoned in old English style in the hall. We had a long chat before the ladies came in and dinner could be got ready. Nothing could be done without the lady, and she had gone to see a brother who lived some miles off.

This gentleman had four sons, and all had been in the war. One fell at Chancellorsville, and two were wounded. At the time of our visit all their thoughts were devoted to farming, and I was glad to see that they did not think their prospects by any means hopeless. The house, more fortunate than some of its neighbours, had escaped. The farmstead, belonging to one of the sons, and only a short distance away, was levelled to the ground. This was the case with several of the private residences in the neighbourhood; armies having been encamped three times on the estate. First came the troops under General M'Clellan; and, when he was driven back, Lee with all his forces; and finally, Butler. The crops were all destroyed, and every fence was used for firewood. The ladies must have had a terrible time of it! The sons were all in the Southern lines, and the old father alone remained in the house when Butler's forces came up the James. The Federal picket line was stretched across the country only two miles away. All communication with the Confederates and their own relatives was cut off. One of the negroes living on the estate, either from spite or a wish to curry favour with the Federals, gave Butler false information that signals were being daily made from the roof. At that time two ladies, one of whom was believed to be dying, were lying very ill in the house, in which there were also several children. Butler sent a party of a hundred men to drive out the family and destroy the house, an order which the officer in command hesitated to execute until he had represented the true state of the case to his general, who behaved very well, and sent a guard to protect the place and family; warning them, however, that if any of them were detected communicating with their friends they should be executed. The general after this became their friend, and excused Mr. —— from taking the oath of allegiance to the Union. One is glad to be able to mention anything in Butler's favour after the abuse that has, rightly or wrongly, been heaped upon him. He certainly acted well towards these people, showing every consideration for them in the hard circumstances in which they were placed. If they refused to take the oath, they generally got scant mercy from the Northerners; and if the Southern Government knew that any of their people had taken the oath, all property belonging to them within the Confederate lines was confiscated.

The feelings of this family about the war were, I believe, very generally shared by many of the leading families in Virginia. They were for the most part strongly against separation from the North—being, as they said, all " Union men"—that is, not in favour of Union in the Northern sense, not putting allegiance to the Union as a whole above allegiance to their State, but in the sense of thinking continued union with the North the best policy.

About the *right* of secession they never hesitated, and when the State did determine to go, all four sons at once joined her armies, pointing, as many others did, to the proviso that Virginia held to in 1789 when she joined the Union, to the effect that she should leave it when she chose. This, however, was not admitted in 1861, and they look upon the war as having decided, by the right of conquest, against the right of secession the State had hitherto enjoyed. That right was the only one touched by the war; and it is because they think that the Civil Rights Bill is

hostile to other State rights, that they dislike some of
its provisions. No spite is manifested against the
negro—they exhibit no wish to keep him down. On
the contrary, their desire is that he should be educated and made useful. They do not object even
to his having the franchise, provided that there
should be some education or property qualification, as
a safeguard against the negroes being used as tools
against the South by the Yankees. The Civil Rights
Bill, lately passed in opposition to the wish of the
President, gives, they say, undue privileges to the
negro. The chief among the objectionable provisions is that which gives to the black a power
still denied to the whites, to appeal from the
State Tribunals to the Federal Courts. This must
tend to throw the State Courts into discredit, and
even to influence their decisions—for the decrees or
verdicts of such a court may not only be set aside, but
the judge may be punished for giving them. They
have no objection to the law which empowers the
blacks—now that they are *freedmen*—to give testimony; but they assert that there never was in Virginia
any law prohibiting the admission of freedmen's
testimony even against whites, although by usage it
was never taken. The Freedmen's Bureau is said to

be of no more use, though they admit that when first instituted it tended to smooth difficulties between owners and former slaves. Now it only encourages idleness, for wherever the Bureau exists it is found that the blacks exhibit less disposition to labour than they ever did before.

It was pleasant to see that farming was again carried on as actively as can be expected in present circumstances. Mr. —— had formerly a hundred and fifty slaves, only one-third of whom were ever at work at one time. Their quarters, which I went to see, were very good—consisting of a row of nine or ten substantial wooden cottages, divided into numerous rooms. The clothing and nourishment as well as a good deal of the nursing were formerly attended to by the ladies, but now that the people are left to clothe themselves they appear for the most part in the old pants and jackets of the United States army, cast off clothes presented to them by the soldiers. One quarter of the land formerly under cultivation is now being worked. The sons take their share of labour in the fields, and two Yankees have taken one of the farms, working it themselves, and giving the owners one-third of the profit. The crops, which were chiefly of wheat, looked well, but it is not expected that their sale will do more than just cover the expenses of the farm this year. They do not think they get out of a man more than two-thirds of the work which was usually obtained from him under the old system. Very good wages are earned; ten dollars a month being given for good field hands.

In spite of the great kindness of our entertainer, one could not but feel alittle in the way, knowing, as they took no pains to conceal it, that they were living from hand to mouth. In such circumstances one felt as if each bottle of wine they produced might be the last in the cellar. Our dinner, which for the most part was prepared by the ladies, consisted one day of corned-beef, hominy, and a bottle of champagne. They were very hospitable and kindly, and had an admiration for England that was quite un-American. They bewailed universal suffrage, and declared that all their misgovernment was owing to it. The Federal Government they thought bad enough, but one of the sons said to me, "He guessed their own, if they had succeeded, would have been worse." Their only wonder was, how they managed to hold out so long against the superior numbers of the enemy, reckoning their own army at two hundred thousand, and the sum total of the Yankee army at one million. None knew how weak they were,

except the Confederate Government; they themselves,
who were in the army, did not. Numbers were always
exaggerated to deceive the enemy. The army of
Northern Virginia, as they suppose, never numbered
more than forty thousand combatants during the last
year of the war.

The "darkies" are more respectful in manner in
this State than in the North, though the customary
touch of the hat is, as I sometimes fancy, done with
a bad grace. They have the grandest names, and it
is rather startling to hear a lady of the house tell
Napoleon to put the kettle on, George Washington
to make tea, or Julius Cæsar to rub a horse down.
The manners of the whites are far more gentle than
in the North, and they exhibit more reverence for age,
which is not saying much, for in the North it is
sometimes difficult to discover any. In that go-ahead
region the youngsters reign paramount.

New York *gamins* are the most horrible in the
world. An elderly man told me that, as he was
walking along Broadway, New York, one day,
with a fine Havana in his mouth, a small lad, of
shabby-genteel appearance, came up to him and asked
him for a light for his pipe. The elderly gentleman
good-naturedly stopped and gave the boy his cigar for

the purpose, but it was no sooner out of his hand
than it was in the lad's mouth, who, with a loud "He-
he-hee!" scampered off at a rate that rendered pursuit
hopeless as well as ridiculous.

Children, if too "loud," are hardly ever checked, and
I was delighted to see S. snub one in New York one
day. We were sitting in the stalls at the theatre,
in places that are called reserved, but in which a very
dirty, sharp-eyed little monster had accommodated
himself next to S. on a seat he had not paid for.
The imp, who was chewing tobacco, and spitting plen-
tifully, sat quiet for some time, and then, with
something like a yawn, poked S. in the ribs. S.
took no notice till the act was repeated a second
time, when looking down he beheld a dirty but
sharp little face turned up towards his own, while
an infantile voice, with a Yankee squeak, said shortly,
"Bill!"—meaning the playbill—and when, after the
repetition of the request, no notice was taken of him,
he resumed his chewing and spitting, looking insigni-
ficantly fierce and magnificent.

On the 10th we crossed the James at Bermuda
Hundred, and came up the river to Richmond, where
we stayed a day or two, and then came on to Charlotteville. At Bermuda Hundred we waited for some

time for the steamer in the hut of one of the freedmen—an elderly coloured man, a sharp fellow who had worked for a baker at Norfolk. He had kept his master's shop while the army was on the banks of the river; but when the business was given up for want of custom on the departure the troops, to console himself, he married a pretty girl, almost white, who had been a maid in a gentleman's family in the neighbourhood, built himself a hut, and settled down for the time—getting whatever work he could. His children were at the Freedmen's school, where, however, he thought that they were not learning enough, that seminary being, in his opinion, an insufficient "institooshun!" The wife chimed in, though the children were not hers, saying, "Oh dear, yes, they learn precious little there!" and she wished she could get them better taught. They were getting, it appeared, three hours a day, and were learning reading and writing; but "pains enough were not taken to *larn* them." "There were plenty of people about," he said, "who could not get work, though they wanted to." The farmers had not been able to set their work agoing, because they were so poor. The Freedmen's Bureau was some way off, at St. Petersburg, and gave no relief to them. He did not think it encouraged the people to be idle, for too little was given for them to rely upon it alone.

He was very positive in the expression of his opinion that "the colours" would never fight for the Confederates. They might have done so, if freedom had been given during the first year of the war, but not later. If, however, freedom had been given to the blacks at that time, it is probable that when their services were no longer required it would have been again taken from them. "For," said he, availing himself of an historical allusion, "when de British, in de war of 1812, under Pakenham, attacked New Orleans, the Southerners promised the blacks freedom if they would fight for them. The blacks did fight with this promise to encourage them. The British were beaten, and afterwards the blacks were put back into slavery."

At Richmond I went to a German concert, where, however, there were very few of that nation, and only one or two Southerners, who yawned and went out before the songs were half through. There are already six thousand Germans in the town, most of whom have come back to it since the war. Hardly any Germans served with the Confederates, who, I hear, made great fun of Siegel's and Blenker's German troops in the

Federal army. The Southerners declare that many of these troopers were strapped on to their horses, to prevent their falling off. The Germans here, who are mostly small shopkeepers, complain much of the laziness of those around them, and the difficulty of getting anything in the South.

Mr. Black, a Scotchman, who had found farming in the Lothians too expensive for him, came out to settle here. After having travelled about a good deal to find the best place to pitch his tent, he rented or bought in this State more than eight thousand five hundred acres of arable land, and is now busy working them. He is anxious to get emigrants out, who may be either renters of Southern farms, or get land for themselves. He himself expects to be able to employ many as labourers, and has a cargo of three hundred and sixty coming out to help him now. These people do not object to work with the negro, so that Mr. Black is able to employ mixed labour, which no Southern or Northern speculator has been able to procure to any very large extent. He gives his labourers from eight to ten dollars a month, and leases the farms he takes for ten years. He thinks that much more of the Scotch emigrant stream may now flow into Virginia, and that they, together with the Americans and the French (who will employ their own labourers to some extent on a canal about to be made between the James and the Central rivers of the continent), will drive the negro gradually Southward. White labour, in his opinion, is impossible in the Mississippi Valley and on the south-eastern seaboard; but along the central strips of country between the sea edge of the Carolinas, Georgia, and Florida, and the river edge of the Mississippi, it may be advantageously employed. But all this must be proved by experiment, for none know how it will turn out.

At Charlotteville we are among the hills once more. The country between this and Richmond is of the usual rolling character and covered with forest. The hills that flank the blue ridge of the Shenandoah begin here. On one of them, a mile from the town, is the University of Virginia. All the shops both here and at Richmond were closed on the anniversary of "Stonewall" Jackson's death. The Richmond papers came out with a black border, and with long accounts of scenes in his short but wonderful war career.

The University of Virginia was founded by Jefferson, who took much pains with it. The arrangement of the building is peculiar. Two long, parallel cloistered ranges are separated from each other by fifty yards of lawn. These ranges have several uniform porticoed edifices along their line. At one end the cloisters are united by a small imitation of the Parthenon. The other end is open, leaving a view of woods and hills.

Mr. ——, an authority in the place, and a shrewd little man, told us much about the part members of the University had taken in the recent struggle. Like many in Virginia, he called himself not only a Secessionist but a rebel, rapping out his sentences with sharp taps of a key on the book-laden table in front of him. He said he had been most earnest for the Union, hoping against hope that Virginia might find it possible to stay in it. But on the appearance of the President's proclamation of the 15th of April, 1861, he had changed his mind, and had ever since been a rebel. All thinking men in the State, however anxious they might have been to remain in the Union, said after that proclamation had appeared, that resistance was necessary. It could no longer be avoided. Constitutional principles had been infringed, and they were resolved that they should be maintained. One day was sufficient to unite the people in their determination. They had resisted most nobly, and now they knew that further resistance was hopeless. They honestly admitted to themselves that they were beaten, and wished to give all support to the Federal Government, which was now their Government. They think this to be as much a duty now as they thought resistance to be before. And it is the men who formerly considered resistance their duty that are now most anxious to prove themselves good citizens. It is the army of the Confederate States, perhaps, more than the rest of the community, who have brought about so desirable a state of things. No better feeling can be expected to exist at such a time. The Radicals had better beware lest they push these men, who are so anxious for peace and quiet, too far. There may yet come a day, even should it be twenty or thirty years hence, when the South, united with the West, indignant at the overbearing conduct of New England, will drive it forcibly from all share in the government of the country. These Radicals are here now defeating their own views. They profess anxiety for the black, and are even now doing their best to excite a war of races in the South. None could doubt the issue of such a conflict. The days of the existence of the negro could be easily numbered.

Mr. —— lived in a little room opening on to one

of the cloistered passages—a lodging that would scarcely satisfy our university professors. He invited us to go with him to see the procession to the cemetery, which was not far distant. We had noticed, in coming along the road to the university, that there were groups of people in front of the houses, and that a service was going on in one of the churches at Charlotteville, as a commemoration of "Stonewall" Jackson and the Confederate dead, whose graves were to be decorated. We went out, and found the procession coming slowly up the hill, without flags or show of any kind. Men, many of whom were now students, though they had formerly served in the army, and now wore their Confederate uniform, went first in twos and threes, followed by women and children, generally in mourning. All had wreaths and flowers in their hands as they advanced to the burial-place, on a rising ground overgrown with tall wood. It had formerly belonged to the university, and was used exclusively for the students and others connected with the place; but during the war more than a thousand soldiers who had died in field and hospital were laid there. The graves were marked only by a little piece of wood, generally unpainted, and with no name upon it, unless it happened to be that of some distinguished officer. The red mould looked still fresh upon many of them.

The people very silently, and with their heads bare, spread themselves over the place, covering with roses, lilacs, and peonies every grave beneath the trees. Then, standing in a deep ring around, they sang hymns as a requiem for their dead, and again went quietly home. The scene was more impressive than if, as is sometimes the custom in America, eulogies and long-winded speeches had been delivered in remembrance.

On the way back we met Professor G., who had entered the army, and had gone through two campaigns, from which he returned badly wounded. Another professor was a member of a crack Southern regiment —the Washington artillery—and was killed.

Out of six hundred and sixty students, fully six hundred went off at once to the armies when the State seceded.

Before the war this university was attended by more students than any other college in America, except Harvard and Yale. The number at present is about two hundred and fifty; but many more are expected next year, as Northerners who used to send their sons have not done so of late, not knowing how they would be treated. There are, however, some already. Very few Southern boys went to Northern colleges, according to these gentlemen, during the few years immediately preceding the war. "The feeling against Northerners never shows itself actively now. Throughout the country, although Yankees are not received socially, they are let alone; and every one is civil to them." The stories of outrages committed on Union men were entirely misbelieved, and even laughed at.

From the top of the little Pantheon there was a fine view of forest and hill scenery. There was much ploughed land about, and conversation turned, as it always does turn hereabouts, upon the land and labour. The friendly feeling of the whites to their late slaves was very strongly insisted on, and they remarked with justice that there was at present no reason for any grudge against them. It was only when they were incited to be bumptious by the Yankees that the negroes made themselves at all obnoxious. The way in which they behaved during the four years' contest, when they never lifted a hand against their masters, but helped them to build fortifications, and allowed themselves to be made generally useful without an attempt to rebel, had produced a strong feeling in their favour. They were now working surprisingly well, though fear was expressed that their energy would not last, and that the late Vice-President Stephens's idea, that their zeal for labour would fall off, might be realized. There was little hope of a good rice or wheat crop this year.

Mr. Black's emigrant and farming prospects were spoken of favourably, although one gentleman blamed his schemes, as involving an unnecessarily early attempt at inducing what must, indeed, come sooner or later—namely, the breaking up of the large plantations into small farms. It was very sad that the old country life should be broken up. It was a pleasant thing in old times to spend Christmas at a plantation, when money was plenty and acres broad. There was one good thing, at all events, about Mr. Black's doings. The increase of white labour might be promoted by it, and the negro would be slowly driven off. "Down South the blacks could live on a very small scratching;" and that was what they would do if they were not prevented. The Bureau was a nuisance, and the sooner it was gone, the happier every one would be.

To the question, if the schools were likely to be kept up, supposing the Bureau were withdrawn, very doubtful answers were given. Negroes might be taxed for their education, but they thought that the State would not keep up schools gratis for blacks. There were plenty of whites that were almost as ignorant, and yet the State never helped them. On the contrary, it was quite against all existing ideas that there should be State Government education. All that the State gave even to this university—Jefferson's pet institution—was 3000*l.* a year. Salaries came from the lodging of students and lecture fees. The 3000*l.* helped to make it possible to have a few "State scholars," who paid little, and were, in fact, what in England would be called "foundationers," and answer to the collegers of Eton.

We had a pleasant evening party of all the professors and several ladies. The library and all the buildings were spared by the Federals. The few remaining dons were in great trepidation when the Yankee officers clanked up the library stairs, and one pleasantly remarked, when he saw the books, that " such a collection would look well up in the North."

Before leaving Charlotteville we visited a large freedmen's school. There were many children in one room, boys and girls, from an ink-black colour to one that was nearly white, all sitting together. Spelling and reading were going on, and it seemed hard work for the teacher. He said he gave them six hours a day, and certainly showed great patience. One is generally punished for one's curiosity in visiting these schools by being requested, in the coolest manner, to " address the scholars " before leaving, which in most cases is more amusing for the children than the visitor. In another room was a class of older girls, of women, and a few men. The teacher was a clear-headed, loud-voiced, energetic New England woman, who taught capitally. One or two of the men were nearly white, and looked very sheepish when told to stand up and read. One requires to see very little of the schools to understand how much good they must be doing. I cannot feel anxious for the withdrawal of the Bureau that founded them, especially when it seems so uncertain whether the State Governments will support them.

It took a long time to get to Lynchburg, although not a very long distance. The cars are very empty on these Southern lines. Very few women travel, and the passengers are chiefly old farmers or their sons— hale and hearty fellows—or ex-Confederate soldiers, with loose grey jackets, much beard and moustache, and the shabby wide-awake hats.

Lynchburg is one of the pleasantest towns in the

States. Situated in the midst of a high rolling country, the town climbs the sides and crowns the top of several hills. The soil is as red as that of Devonshire. We took a long ride of between thirty and forty miles to Westwood, and back by a small village called Campbell Court-House, in the middle of Campbell County, pronounced here "Ca-a-a-mill Ceounty."

This village was much like many in England. There were two rustic inns, at one of which we got a capital dinner, in spite of the fact that we were looked upon with no friendly eyes by a group of young Southerners, who took us for Yankees. The innkeeper was no very ardent Secessionist. He had paid for three substitutes in succession, giving on one occasion five thousand dollars, and had managed to keep his own body in ease and comfort during all the troublous times. The landlady was a fine old woman of sixty-five, with a still older husband, who was kept in quiet order by his wife. He came up to shake hands with us; but the good dame told him he was too familiar, and shut him up by himself in a little side room, where she went to scold him every now and then. "He had been a good man to her, none better, and had behaved to her like a gentleman: not that she would take any other treatment from anybody—not she; but old men had to be kept in order. Come, now, and sit down," she shouted to her lord, who hobbled in with a thick stick. "Now you must eat that, and that, and that. Want some iced water, eh? Well, there—there. Now be quick. Where have ye come from [*to us*]? Guess you are single men? Now [*to her husband*], get up; do you hear? get up! Leave this now;" and the old man was pushed back into his little den. I asked her if he would have a cigar, but the old lady's eye sparkled at the sight of the weed, and she said, " No, no, not he—he don't smoke. I'll take it for ye— I'll take it;" and she puffed away with great satisfaction. She had never been out of Virginia.

There was much talk in the place about some oil-wells that had been set going in the neighbourhood, but there was little to be seen. A great borer, looking like a huge gimlet, had been fixed to some scaffolding; but there was nobody working, although they said that oil had been struck the day before. It was, however, believed that some person had broken a bottle of oil over a puddle hard by, and had put some also on the borer. The whole affair had only been undertaken, one man said contemptuously, because a "golgist" had said there ought to be oil underneath.

It was nearly dark before we left the red roads and green oak forest behind us, and reached the town. I talked on the way home to some niggers who were working on a neighbouring farm. Some had little huts of their own, and an acre or two of ground. Others rented the same from proprietors.

"It's mighty hard to get land. We want a good piece for ourselves, but de whites wont sell. You don't come from this part of the country?" with sudden alarm.

"No, from England."

"Yah! dat's good. Well, sir, they are screwing us down very hard. No land sold, and no hire. Farmer gives us a third of what land gives. 'Praps de Lord rise up and provide us very soon, massa," was the burden of what most of them said.

It is just as well that land should not be sold to them at present. They will do much better as labourers for a time. They get here ten to fifteen dollars a month.

We had a very lazy day's travelling in a canal boat from Lynchburg. We were far from all railways, and had to go as far as Stanton—thirty-six

miles further down the valley—before we could again
"strike the cears," as railway carriages are called
in this part of the world. The boat was to be
started, or rather towed, at half-past six from Lynchburg; but the horses that were to draw us were not
ready for some time longer, and we did not arrive at
our journey's end till ten at night. On board
our little vessel was the captain, who came and
sat down by S. to a meagre breakfast that was
sent up almost as soon as we started, and was
surprised at hearing S. say in an injured voice
(not knowing it was the captain who sat by him),
"What idiots these people are not to have something
better to eat!" The poor captain smirked, bowed,
and said we should get some eggs at the first lock.
Besides this amiable officer, there were at breakfast
several students of Virginia University, most of
them sons of Confederate generals; an old gentleman, who was proprietor of some farms near
Lynchburg; and a few other less notable "rebs."
The scenery was very pretty, and the weather such
that one could enjoy it perfectly.

The canal lay along the bank of the James, and
only left it when, by a tedious succession of locks, it
had mounted to the water-shed of the Blue Ridge.

We went at a rate of about two miles an hour, but the scenery made the pace a pleasant one. As we passed between the wooded hills the young fellows with us had many stories to tell of their campaigning in that country. They had all been in the armies, and several had served with Lee to the last, and when he surrendered had made their way south to join Johnson's army, only to be in time to be paroled by Sherman. One and all vowed that, " come what would, they would not lift a rifle again under the ' stars and stripes.' Let England only have a war with the States, and she would find plenty of recruits in the South." They confessed to the dreadful amount of desertion that took place from the Southern armies during 1864. The woods and mountains through which we were travelling had been full of the runaways. "There were pathways that had been made entirely by the deserters right across these hills. They did not blame them. They had known some of the bravest men in the army desert. Men who had been foremost in every action would get worn down by the scarcity of food and continued hardships, so that they were hardly themselves. The letters, too, they kept receiving from wife or family at home did much harm, and turned many a poor man from his duty.

Nothing else could have been expected from the misery they endured."

We had a good many songs, "Maryland, my Maryland," and the "Bonny Blue Flag" being the favourites. When tired of songs, revolvers were resorted to for amusement, and whole broadsides of pistol shots were discharged at every unfortunate big, green-headed bull-frog or water-snake that showed himself on the banks. The snakes were sometimes very large, and several shots took effect in their ugly bodies. At one of the locks there was a dam, over which the river fell in a long waterfall. A fine canal boat had been destroyed here by the Federals, who had sent it down the fall. The canal was also cut by one of the railway parties, doing much harm for the time to the Virginian army, as all the supplies came by this route from the Shenandoah Valley.

A good deal was said about the state of the country.

" Well, sir, how air you getting on?"

"Only tolerable—the crops very bad. How air yer niggers doin'?"

"Well, they're doin' remarkable well. I never thought they'd ha' done half as well as they are."

"They're workin', are they?"

"Yes, that they are, and well too, though I don't know whether they're settled to it right yet."

"I heard there was some impudence in some parts."

"No, sir, I don't believe it; I see no difference in their manner. They are just as respectful as ever."

"Well, I think they are behaving darn well."

"Yes, that they are. They have behaved, and are behaving, just as well as possible, and we owe them a great deal for it."

"Yes, sirree; the people of the South will not forget their conduct. They owe them a deep debt of gratitude."

The remark was heartily acquiesced in by several present with the words: "Yes, that's so." "'Tis so." "You're right there; we owe them gratitude."

The old gentleman, whose property was near Richmond, gave good accounts of his workpeople; but all agreed that white labour was the thing that was desirable, and that the negro could not stand that competition if it should come. He said that the Civil Rights Bill had hardly been felt yet. The negroes in most parts of the country had no clear notion of what it meant, and very few cases had come up under it. The Bureau he disliked, and thought it unnecessary, as he was perfectly sure that the judges would at all times see justice done. As it was, these Southerners were always able to outvote the Federal agent of the Bureau, if they chose to do so. The agent sat to hear cases; but with him were associated a white belonging to the district, chosen by the blacks, and another white gentleman chosen by the citizens of the district. If these two local representatives disagreed with the agent, "he was nowhere."

" In my court we often outvote the Yankee."

" Does he always go for the nigger?"

" Yes, most always; but the man the blacks choose, and I, always see that justice is done to whites as well as blacks. I have as much authority, or more, in the court as the agent, though he ain't a bad man either."

The Bureau unsettled the labourers, and made them think they would get remedy and redress for fancied grievances they would never have given a moment's thought to before. The schools were all very well, as long as the school-mistresses did not teach the children anti-Southern and Yankee songs, as they often did.

The narrow passes through which we had been drawn became, on the western slope of the mountains, broad valleys, often with rich land along the levels. There were bad accounts of the tobacco crops on these lands. All the tobacco raised here is used, not for smoking, but for chewing, which does not tend greatly, as one may imagine, to the cleanliness of the floors of rooms or decks of steamers. On one of the fields a man recognised by the passengers as Colonel Sambody, the chief of artillery, was busy digging potatoes and sowing corn. A good deal of a coarse sort of sugar-cane has been raised during the last few years. Good molasses was unattainable, and they used to make a coarse treacle, called sorghum, as a substitute.

CHAPTER XIV.

Lexington—Cadets of the Military College—Virginian Scenery—
Natural Bridge—White and Coloured Men on Farms—Negroes
eager to visit England—Education—Confederate Officers—
Parties in the South and North—Injurious Effect of the Course
pursued by the Radicals—Language of Thaddeus Stephens in
the House of Representatives—Weakness of State Governments
—Discomfort suffered by Ladies travelling in America—Mode
of serving up Dinner—A German Innkeeper—Remarkable Cave
—Curious Bill—The Affairs of Virginia—Working of the
Freedmen's Bureau—False Prognostications of the Southerners
—Mixed Labour—Derision of Northern Fears—Baltimore—
Enthusiasm excited by Confederate War Songs—Coloured Men
in the Railway Cars—Action of the Civil Rights Bill—Decisions
of the Judges respecting the State Courts—Niagara in a Mist—
Night View of the Falls—Toronto—Sensible Irishmen—Kingston—Ottawa—Canadian Houses of Parliament—The Ottawa
—Inconvenient Position of the new Canadian Capital—The
Sawmills — The Fenian Invasion — Reports at Kingston—
Skirmish at Fort Erie—Conduct of the American Government
—American Sympathy with Fenianism.

IT was quite dark by the time we got to Lexington. Our friends were met by a crowd of cadets belonging to the Military College—neat-looking, strapping lads, dressed in grey uniform. There are only about fifty of them at the college. Formerly there were over two hundred and fifty, but the fine buildings and lecture-rooms were burnt by the Federals. It was the Southern West Point. When the State seceded, the cadets were called up to Richmond, and were engaged in drilling the troops. At the battle of Newmarket, when Breckenridge was hard pressed, he sent for the young fellows composing this school; and well they justified the trust put in them, standing as firm as the oldest troops, and losing several of their number.

A fine horse was offered to me to ride over here from Lexington; S. got another; and we left the little town, whose inhabitants were pouring out of their houses to the church, where there was to be a funeral service preparatory to the reburial in the cemetery of the cadets whose graves had hitherto been where they had fallen at Newmarket. One felt sick of all this burying, and of the sight of cemeteries, and I did not care to see another. The open country was pleasanter.

There is a good deal of sameness about Virginian scenery, but it is a very pretty sameness. You meet with the same rolling land, of which forest and farm hold about equal possession. In this part of the valley of Virginia the swells of the land are higher, and the hollows give little level space. The red-soiled fields are well fenced off from each other by tall "snake" or "worm" fences, that zigzag along the sides of the roads, having a very make-shift look about them, and requiring a large amount of timber in this country, and room, both of which are not much thought of. Here and there a good wooden house with brick chimney is seen, the residence of a planter who may, perhaps, be cultivating, after his manner, his six or seven hundred acres, with the help of only ten or twelve "hands." The shanty of the poorer white is more often seen. Logs roughly fashioned with the axe, and well dovetailed, with the chinks or gaps filled in with stucco, make a comfortable cabin. One meets few travellers. A man or a woman may pass at rare intervals, generally on horseback, and always nodding their "good morning" or "evening."

The birds of Virginia are beautiful. There is a Woodpecker whose bright scarlet head is in fine contrast with the well-massed black and white of his body. It is as common as the Thrush in an English wood. There are numberless small birds, many of them with a great deal of yellow in their plumage. A very pretty species of Turtle-dove is common. These birds are so tame that they allow one's horse to approach quite close to their perch upon the fences. There is a large species of starling with a saffron breast, and a partridge that they call a quail, with the same black necklace that the French partridge wears. There is another starling, whose black uniform is set off by scarlet epaulets, that is to be seen in every meadow, and several species of the heron. The people have a pretty habit of setting up near their houses a small cot on a pole for the swallows, which take to it very well, and are to be seen every evening twittering and crowding round the little pigeon-holes prepared for them.

The natural bridge is close to this house, and we have spent a long time admiring it to-day. We scrambled for some distance down a steep path leading through thickets of juniper cedar, and found ourselves by the side of a burn that tumbled along the bottom of a deep gorge. The stream occupied nearly the whole of the space below, preventing the trees that grew thickly on both banks from shutting out from our view the limestone that rose, streaked with rusty red, on each side of the water, to a height of two hundred and fifty feet without a ledge to break its steepness. At a great height, an immense mass, one with the rock, stretched across the gorge, uniting its crags. The arch thus formed is surprisingly regular in shape, and very impressive in its grandeur. The beauty of the heights above and below this rock-marvel makes them well worth a journey.

The man who keeps this hotel farms also a good deal of the land around. His views are very different from those of his neighbours. He himself has several white labourers, who get on very well with the blacks employed at the same work. We had our tea with the whites; the blacks, or rather coloured men (for none of them were pure-blooded Africans), having their meals separately. This is universally the case in America. However humble the position of a white, he will never sit down at the same table with a coloured man. The Farmer said that in his case all were working well together. Many complain, he added, that the whites, if set to work with negroes, fall into their bad habits of laziness. They both get very much the same pay. The white man works as well as he can at first; but seeing that the black gets on as well without exerting himself so much, he becomes " demoralized," and falls off in zeal. This is the principal objection; but, by good management, continued the Farmer, he thought the evil could be mitigated. He pooh-poohed the notion as to the probability of the negroes dying out. The servants he now had were hired. The half of the money due to them was always kept to the end of the year. If given when due, the men made away with it at once by buying anything that took their fancy, though it might be perfectly useless to them. He directed them what to get, and found they were anxious for the advice. Some of his men had left him, and had come back again, after finding that they could not better their position by working in the town. The Bureau, he thought, tended to unsettle them. One of his "hands" was a clever mulatto, who had been raised in Georgia, and had had 25,00 dollars (according to his own account) paid for his services in old times.

We took another look at the bridge before we left Lexington. The gorge was bathed in sunlight, and the rock mass suspended above it threw its great shadow across the precipices below. I should have liked to stay another day to explore the glen, but our time was short, and we were obliged to be pressing northward. The hotels were here, as usual, full of black and coloured waiters. One or two of them showed great anxiety to come with us to England, our Jamaica servant having told them of his luck. One of them presented a character which, I observed had the same name for signature that he himself bore. He had come to town from the plantation where he had been raised, and worked to better his position. He would not go back, he said; for he was in a good place here, and got schooling. He had had none before, but went now regularly to the evening freedmen's school. The boys and girls were taught in the morning. His brother, who was also a waiter in the hotel, gave lessons to all who wanted to read and write, and had daily classes in one of the rooms below. This brother had had more time than most to give to his own education. He spoke against the Southerners, although he admitted that they did not harm the blacks. All the damage he had seen done to them during the last year was the breaking of a schoolroom window by a stone some one had thrown. The Yankee influence was very perceptible in this man, as it is in most who live in the towns, where are the schools; but such seed must have fallen into very ready soil.

One of our principal objects in riding to Lexington was to see some distinguished Confederate officers who were then staying there. The chief of these, a gallant old gentleman, received us with great courtesy. They were all dressed in their grey uniforms. Few men wear anything else, and a black coat is seldom seen. One hardly liked to talk to these men of the war, much less of its latter days, which were so full of sadness for them; but the chief himself mentioned the poverty of the country, and the helplessness of its people. He spoke quietly, and with no ill-feeling, of the leaders who had desolated the Shenandoah Valley. "The crops this year are bad," he said, "and I am afraid it will be long before there is any improvement in the condition of the people."

He asked where we had been, and our answer led to conversation about the feeling shown by the different parties in the North towards the Southerners. I asked if he had read the last debate in Congress upon the Reconstruction Committee's report.

"No," he said sorrowfully; "debates in Congress are not for us to read now. I never look at what they have been saying there. President Johnson has been doing much to strengthen the feeling for the Union in the South; but this Radical party is, I fear, doing much harm. I wish they would let a little of that feeling remain that used to exist in former times between the whites and the blacks; but while they wish to give help to the blacks, they are doing them harm. They are raising up feelings of race; and if a feeling of ill-will is excited, in consequence of the Radical legislation, against the weaker party, it must yield. The whites are so much stronger, that there is no chance for the blacks if the extreme party has its way. They are perpetuating, by their proposals in Congress, the feeling of the South against the North. Some feeling there must be after such a war, but it will rapidly subside, unless increased by further provocation. The South took up arms honestly, and it has laid them down honestly," he said, with much emphasis. "Surely it is best that the good-will of the people should be fostered, and not that they should be set against the North. To us the idea of 'Union' was absurd, when the parties that made the Union did not wish it to continue; but the North fought for the Union, and now a powerful party among them, *that seems to have its own way*, is doing its best to destroy all feelings of union. With such a policy, 'Union' can only exist in name."

I said that there was much inclination to support the President among many at present in the North.

"Yes, there is much inclination," he said, "but none seem to be bold enough to stand up and oppose the Radicals. They are doing what they choose, and no one stands fairly in their way. If the Union is worth preserving at all, let them conciliate the whole nation, and not do their worst against a large portion of it."

He was evidently thinking of the violent words of Thaddeus Stephens, who lately yelled to the House of Representatives this sentiment : " The best place for the rebels is hell, fenced in by bayonets." There is another proposal for the confiscation of all "rebel" lands, with the further idea of giving them to the blacks, and the disfranchising clause for the people of the South, in the Reconstruction Committee's proposal.*

General —— spoke also of the weakening of the State Governments, and of his wish to see them supported. Little is known on our side of the water of the vast disparity of the forces engaged in the American conflict. " At Sharpsburg," he said, " we had only thirty-five thousand troops opposed to the enemy's one hundred and twenty thousand." "Sharpsburg" is the battle that is known in the North as that of " Antietam ;" the Northerners taking the name of the river near the battle-field, and the Southerners that of the town in whose defence the action was fought. " At Chancellorsville we had

* Not carried through Congress.

forty-five thousand, all told, against a number equal to that the enemy brought against us at Sharpsburg."

He never spoke with bitterness, and even when he mentioned the Radicals his voice expressed only sorrow.

I am afraid one cannot advise ladies to travel for pleasure in America. There is such a want of privacy at the hotels and in the cars, and so little real comfort, except in private houses, that the annoyance and fatigue encountered would be triple that of a journey in England. Posting may be a pleasure for some time along good roads; but to a lady not "raised" in the country, and unaccustomed to be jolted over logs and rocks, or entangled in deep ruts, it can only bring headache and partial insanity. Even S. was loud in his complaints. The tiny oval dishes, on which dinner was often brought up in a condition that made one believe it must have been an hour since it had seen the fire, particularly exasperated him. These little dishes were always set in a half-moon around our plate, one holding, perhaps, a Brussels sprout, another an asparagus head, and a third a speck of blood and gristle supposed to represent a beefsteak. Eggs were always plentiful. There was nothing to be said against the drinks, and there was abundance of milk.

At our noon-day halt we found a German innkeeper and farmer, who came many years ago from the Rhine Phalte, and who croaked in ugly German for half an hour of his experiences. He had been quite cleaned out by the war, but was in great hopes of getting on well again, and was entertaining himself with golden visions of a future vineyard, in which there should be only Rhine grapes, that must thrive amazingly on the low hills around his house. He had lived so long in the State that, although a European, as he said proudly, and therefore having a European's dislike of slavery, he had kept a few slaves. This luxury was indulged in, not so much for himself, he assured me, as for the sake of his wife. He had served in the Confederate hospitals. General Lee had been very fond of him, and had given him his comforter as a present. He loved the general, and went for "Staats-Recht," though not in favour of disunion at first. His slaves had disappeared, but some had come back and died there. A girl had gone down on her knees, and begged to be allowed to work again with him. He now had a few blacks and a few whites working together, and well, upon his farm. He hoped Germans would now come southward. Their great hatred of slavery was what sent them so quickly, upon landing, to the west. Very few of his compatriots had gone with the South, but they would now take to farming.

We drove down the valley eastwards towards Harrisonburg to see a very remarkable cavern, or series of caverns, in the limestone rock of a spur of the Blue Ridge. The air was very clear, and from the rising grounds one could see far over the rolling woodlands and broad fields that once made the Shenandoah Valley famous for its beauty and fertility. The mountain range stretched away on our right till lost to view in the direction of Winchester. All the mills have been burnt by Sheridan's forces. This was a purely military measure, as the corn from the valley supplied Lee's army. The houses of the people were burned when the owners fled, but were unmolested when they remained. The man on whose farm the cave is showed us through it. The entrance is very narrow, and in the side of a hill. A series of halls are passed through, till one has gone for half a mile underground. The stalactites are most wonderful and beautiful, though their effect is rather spoilt by a coating of yellow that has formed where the drip has not been enough to prevent it. The forms are those taken by icicles, but are often far more grotesque and extraordinary.

The following is a bill that was presented to us after our visit to the cave, from which it will be seen that the people still talk of shillings and pence, though the sums understood by those terms are not what they used to be; a shilling with them being the sixth part of a dollar. The way in which they put down the sums in both coinages is curious.

2 Visits to Cave, each 9s.	$3	00
2 Dinners, each 4s. 6d.	1	50
	$4	50
Coloured Man Visit Cave, 9s.	1	50
,, ,, 2 horses, 2s. 3d.	0	75
,, ,, Dinner, 4s. 6d.	0	75
	$3	00

The tone of the men of Virginia at this time was as good as any one could possibly expect. There was no violence, and law seemed to be as much respected as before the war. There was no thought of any further resistance; they knew it would be useless if attempted, and no man was mad enough to think of it or wish for it.

I have heard the extremists of the North spoken of with scorn, but never with the fury that, if one believed Northern papers, one would suppose the Southerners habitually give vent to. Dislike was expressed towards the North, but no scorn; that the war has effaced. I have heard their military efforts laughed at, and their generals derided for incapacity, in not having mastered the South, "as they ought to have done," in one year instead of in four; but most of the Southern soldiers look with respect upon the Northern troops. Considering the hatred that they believe to be shown towards them by the Radicals, the "obnoxious" measures these have already succeeded in carrying into law, and the yet more "intolerable" ones proposed to the legislature by the same men, the wish of the Southerners to live honestly as citizens, and to obey the laws, is far more than one could have hoped for.

It is the greatest misfortune that the party in the North who are aware of this, and would, if they were allowed, do their best to promote friendly feeling, is so weak. There is much gratitude in the South to those who, like the President, have stood firm against the extremists; but it is observed with alarm that, though to all appearance numerically strong, they make little headway. If they could only gain ground, their success would do more for a real union between the divided States than one hundred years of such rule as would be exercised by the Radicals. The policy of Stephens and his party is most unfortunate in the feeling it is creating; and it is likely to be unfortunate also in defeating its own object, the welfare of the blacks.

The Virginians, I am confident, might now, after the passage of the Civil Rights Bill, be left with safety to take care of the negroes. I believe that they would get justice in the courts of the State, and that no measures such as the immediate giving of the franchise, far less the grant of confiscated lands to the blacks, are necessary for their comfort. The last would breed a jealousy that has as yet been happily not aroused against them, or any of the whites. The Freedmen's Bureau has not been looked upon with favour by the whites of late, but they know it is not to last very much longer; and it has neither created any feeling against the negroes, nor has it incited them to presumption. Some of its agents have behaved badly, as is proved by the report of two officers, Generals Steadman and Fullerton, who were recently sent on a tour of inspection; but as a whole the system has worked remarkably well, and the agents have been, in the main, honest. The power of having one of their own citizens to represent themselves, and another to represent the negroes at the Bureau Courts, has given the whites confidence that the interests of the blacks will not alone be looked to. The schools that have been established are excellent, and it is only the roughs of a few towns that have shown much dislike to them. The more intelligent object to the schools only on the ground that when the State does so little for white education, it ought not to do so much for the blacks. They are anxious the black should learn; but they think that he will be able to do so easily from those around him, now that there is no power to prevent him. Some will set up schools, say the Southerners; and all will, in course of time, get as much training as necessary.

As is natural after such a social revolution, the South believes nothing will suit masters and servants so well as the old system, now gone for ever. All sorts of misfortunes are prophesied to the blacks, but one sees little to justify the expectation. Mixed labour is said to be impossible; but there was a good deal of it on the smaller farms before emancipation, and there is more of it now. The mortality that must carry off the black population in a few years is said to be prevailing; but one finds there is no more than might have been expected from the crowding into the towns for safety. It is only twelve months since the end of the war, and yet labour, although unsettled, is already returning to the farms, and wages of from eight to fifteen dollars are being paid for it. This does not look like speedy extermination. It is to be hoped that the expectation of the Virginians, with regard to future immigration, will be realized, though it hardly follows that until that immigration becomes great, the negro will be driven entirely southwards. The west holds out such attractions, that the emigrant stream can, for some time, only eddy southwards, though, now that slavery is gone, there will be no great cause, as there has been hitherto, to keep it away. When it does come, there is reason to believe that mixed labour will be possible; and, according to all appearance, it will be very long before the negro is forced, by competition, to abandon the soil on which he now promises to be a tolerably steady labourer.

If the majority of the people do not feel gratitude to the blacks, there is at least an absence of that spite which showed itself among the whites on the abolition of slavery in Jamaica. The wish to get the old servants back to their work again, and the willingness to give them fair wages, is universal. They do not wish them to possess land, and they will not sell it to them, unless they cannot help it, for they think that the blacks would be bad neighbours and bad cultivators, and that it is best that they should, for the present at least, become a steady labouring population. There is also a great wish not to sell land to Northerners, though this, of course, yields to large sums offered to empty pockets. When it is possible, they would rather lease the land, and many are doing so. There is no social intercourse with Northerners, but they are not disturbed, so long as they behave themselves decently. The idea that they are ill-treated is heartily laughed at. A Northerner lately sent to ask a professor of Virginia University if it would be safe for his son to go there and enter as a student. The professor sent back word that they would not do more to him than take off one leg. This is the tone of derision in which the Southerners speak of Northern fears. They do not care for their society, but they are happy to get their capital. The wish for intercourse extends only to the transactions of business.

z

We went north by Washington. The most extravagant stories were told to credulous Radicals of the treatment of Unionists in Virginia. Several Virginian Unionists had called on one gentleman in the space of a few hours, saying that they could not remain in their State unless stringent measures were adopted for their protection. I can well believe, from what I have heard from Southerners, that men belonging to the State who had gone against it in the war, have no pleasant berth, though I never heard of any being personally maltreated. The chief complaints are that obstacles are thrown in the way of their settling or trafficking, to such an extent that it is not worth their while to undergo the nuisance.

The President's course in showing leniency to the South was even in the early part of the present year exciting the violent dislike of the Radical party, now, through the fall elections, in supreme power. Proposals for his impeachment were even then canvassed, and if it had been possible at that time to get the necessary two-thirds majority in both houses, there were men who would at once have brought them forward. The hesitation they showed was only owing to the doubt that such a measure would be rejected by the Senate, and to the knowledge that the step would again wrap the country in the flames of civil war. It was because the chief magistrate was in favour of a policy of reconciliation, and not of revenge, that they so hated him; and for his protégés, the Southerners, nothing could be too severe. "Why should we show them favour?" they said. "If we persecute them to the death, they cannot hate us more than they do at present. Davis must be hanged, and the rebels punished." Surely, in thus speaking, these men took no account of time, and the influence it must have in obliterating hatred, unless it be used for its perpetuation.

On the way to Canada, whither we next proceeded, we spent some pleasant days in the Secesh society of Baltimore. Only one of the gentlemen, whose acquaintance we made in that city, was a Unionist, and he had a Southern wife, whilst of five sons three were officers in Lee's army. One was prevented from going through a lady's influence, and the youngest boy had succeeded in exacting a promise from his parents that he too should join the Confederate army if it were still in existence in the fall of 1866. The parties in Baltimore, we found, usually began at half-past nine, and lasted till midnight, at which time each girl was convoyed to her home by one of the gentlemen. We had no want of singing in the evenings. English, Italian, and German songs were sung at parties with the usual cold and courteous growl of "beautiful" from the company, when each was finished. But there would sometimes come a change; for a tall Southern officer would step up to the piano, and sing to a lady's fierce banging a Confederate cavalry war song. Every eye brightened and every cheek flushed at this, and shouts of delight were heard from all when the performance was over.

"By Jove, sir," one gentleman said; "we only want another chance to be up again."

"Ah, if you had but helped us," said another.

"How long is it since you have been able to sing these songs?"

"Not long, I can tell you. We were kept down pretty tightly. Not long ago a man who had sung a song like that would have been arrested instantly."

"Maryland, my Maryland"—sounded almost like a mockery.

> "Hurrah, she spurns the Northern scum,
> She breathes, she burns, she'll come, she'll come,
> Maryland, my Maryland."

"Ah, and yet she did not come," said one poor fellow.

"Because she couldn't," fiercely replied his neighbour.

Cases were coming before the courts in consequence of the Civil Rights Bill. Coloured men are to be met with in every car between Baltimore and Philadelphia. Gentlemen who have not ladies with them are not usually allowed to enter the ladies' car. A coloured man lately insisted that he should be allowed to enter one of these. The guard refused permission, and the man brought his case before the United States courts, averring that he had, when he wanted to go "on board" the car, a lady with him. The guard said "no, he hadn't;" and the Court gave decision against the coloured man, saying that the railway companies could make what arrangements they chose for the convenience of their passengers.

The lawyers in Maryland maintain that the State courts are not affected by the Civil Rights Bill, and that the State laws of Maryland, prohibiting coloured people from giving evidence against whites of the same State, are still in force, although negro evidence is admitted by the new bill in the United States courts.

The same question was, in Virginia, decided against a coloured man, by a judge who tried a recent case. In the court sitting at Alexandria, Virginia, May 25th, when the case of a white man charged with felony was being tried, the Commonwealth's attorney asked permission to introduce negro witnesses to testify, claiming the right under the Civil Rights Bill. Judge Thomas declined permission, on the ground that his was a State court, and he was acting under the laws of the State of Virginia, which forbade that black evidence should be received against a white, "except where the case arises out of an injury done, attempted, or threatened to the person, property, or rights of a coloured person, or Indian, or when the offence is committed by a white person in conjunction with a coloured person or Indian." The judge stated that it was his determination to execute the laws of the State until ordered to do otherwise. It is difficult to see why the State legislators should still be anxious to keep up a law always most unjust, and now without excuse, since the slaves, with regard to whom the provision was framed, exist as slaves no longer. It is, however, I believe, not owing to a dislike for the privileges of the freedmen that such questions are still argued by the Southern lawyers, but from a desire to resist any attempt at consolidating the power of the Executive; and from a determination to support the State Governments, by which alone, it is thought, such questions can be constitutionally decided. Should they decide in favour of admitting the testimony of the blacks in State courts, few would be against it. The decision, however, must come from the State legislatures; not from Washington. The Sovereign States must legislate for those within their borders.

In thus acting, they do all they can, as it seems to me, to keep their vast country as one nation. They are working for a unity they themselves have attempted to destroy; for it is impossible to conceive that so large a territory as that possessed by the United States, with such difference of geographical interests and of feeling between the inhabitants of many of its parts, can always hold together, unless wide range be given to local power.

Passing through Philadelphia, we made our way rapidly to Niagara by Harrisonburg, skirting for some distance the noble Susquehanna river, on two bridges of which, that had not yet been repaired, General Early had left his mark.

At Niagara we had very bad luck as far as weather was concerned. The Falls were perpetually enveloped in mist, and I suppose it was owing to this that S. and I agreed that they were exactly what we expected. One feels that one is not deprived of the power of appreciating smaller waterfalls, any more than one is rendered incapable of admiring a picturesque irregularly built cottage, after looking at the formal lines of an Italian palace. The regularity of the American Fall rather destroys its effect, for the water comes over the even ledge with a yellow-white colour, very different from the green rush that plunges from the centre of the horse-shoe terrace forming the Canadian fall. The point from which the grandest view is to be got, was, we thought, from a walk half way down the cliff on the Canada side, where one faces the whole semicircle of the great Fall. The spray hung heavily in the damp air, and concealed much we should have liked to see.

We enjoyed much more a view the preceding night, when the rain had not yet begun, and there was a fine full moon that crested with silver the river-waves as they flashed over in long line into the darkness, only to appear again from beneath the spray-cloud that curled upward, as smoke from the mouths of cannon, pale with the foam of their struggle.

The weather at Toronto was cold, raw, and wet, and the town looked too dull for words. There is some good land about, one hears; but beyond the town, we saw only the wretched looking white pines, leaning here and there and everywhere, as if too much blown about ever to think of holding themselves straight again.

The Torontoites were all talking of the proposed North American federation; and most of them were seemingly in its favour. They flattered themselves Fenianism had exploded, in spite of Stephens's attempt to revive it. All the way up to Niagara there was no sign of Fenian movements. On the American shore I met two Irishmen, who said they would give five dollars to see the Fenian leaders hanged—a rare piece of good sense, worth mentioning. Two days afterwards the "invasion of Canada" had actually begun.

We stayed a day at Kingston—a pretty town with warm-looking stone houses, a good bay for ships, and some fortifications on the rising ground of a peninsula that runs out into Ontario and bends round so as to lie parallel with the shore of the mainland. There was little, however, to be seen in the sleepy little city, except a few companies of the Canadian rifles, and some artillery guarding the forts.

We went on by steamer down the St. Lawrence, whose course is here studded with numbers of copse-covered and rocky islets. We landed at Prescott; and after a few hours' travelling through a dreary country, with few clearings, and tangled larch and white pine forests, we arrived at Ottawa. Even at this time of the year many of the trees have only just begun to show that leaves may be expected perhaps in autumn.

The newly-built Houses of Parliament, of which the Ottawa Canadians are justly proud, for they were designed by a Montreal architect, and do him great credit, could be seen a long way over the woods. There is a high tower in the central building, with steep French roof, crowned with elaborate iron work, and many towerlets besides.

The rooms for the Upper and Lower Houses are the same in size and arrangements. The galleries are large, and encircle the chambers. As at Washington, they do not hang over the representatives' heads, but at a height of fifteen or twenty feet recede backwards, so that the chamber is larger above than below. The roof, which is of wood and glass, is supported by handsome arches, resting on pillars of grey marble. There is to be a large circular library, but it is not yet finished. The edifice is built on the verge of the cliff that overhangs the river. Immense quantities of timber that have been piloted down the shoots of the Chaudière falls, a mile higher up the stream, are collected here to be formed into large rafts and floated to the St. Lawrence. By a staircase of beautifully constructed locks a canal is led down to the level of the river, which tumbles in wild sheets of spray down the Chaudière rocks; and the broad current swirls afterwards strongly past the high cliff on which the Parliament houses and the little city behind them stand. It is a fine situation for a town; but most people belonging to the government fear that, if the new confederation of all the North American provinces is ever formed, it will be difficult to keep Ottawa as the capital of the country. The position of the town is most inconvenient, and it is never likely to gain from commerce much importance. The lumber trade is nearly all that it has, and as the country gets cleared that will become more and more insignificant.

I took a drive to a small village named Chelsea, on the other side of the river. Around the collection of wooden houses the woods had been a little cleared; but far off was a river (a tributary of the Ottawa), where some large saw-mills were at work. The logs floating in hundreds down the rapid current were guided, if near the banks, into a quiet side canal, and there drawn upon trucks that ran on a partially submerged tramway into the sheds, where several frames, each with eight or nine saws, cut the largest trunks quickly into planks. These are sent

down an aqueduct to the stacking-yards, a few miles
below. Some strong French Canadians were pushing,
with long pikes, the logs that had come into an eddy
of the river back into the main stream. They had
hard work of it, as every moment brought fresh trees
swinging in upon them, as if anxious to escape in the
eddy from the rapids below. But there they stood,
often knee-deep in the cold water, for hours, pushing,
butting, lifting, and shoving, in the most picturesque
attitudes.

At Ottawa all was excitement that evening. Telegram after telegram had arrived in rapid succession, announcing the descent of the Fenians upon Fort Erie, a little village, innocent of fortifications, at the outlet of Lake Erie. Two thousand men were asserted to have crossed, well armed with bowie-knives, revolvers, and rifles, and meaning to fight. The commander of the Federal war-steamer *Michigan*, the only vessel on the St. Lawrence, at that point, was said to be a Fenian partisan, and was reported to have subscribed a number of dollars quite lately to some Fenian folly at Buffalo. It was certain that he would allow as many more boatloads of Fenians to cross as chose to do so, and we should not drive out the invaders without bloodshed. Troops were being rapidly sent to the front, volunteer corps poured in from all the country round, and eager offers of service were made in every quarter. The place that was taken possession of was one of those most hotly contested during the last American war, and it was supposed the object of these madmen was to destroy the Welland Canal.

At night news came that the Irish force was encamped two miles below Fort Erie. It was confidently hoped that on the morrow the troops that had been sent against them would entirely demolish them. No artillery had been known to cross.

Next day, at Prescott, all were on the alert. A large force of Fenians was on the opposite shore of the river at Ogdensburg, declaring their intention to cross with the first opportunity. The United States revenue cutter had been moored, in compliance with the command of the Governor, immediately between the two towns, with her steam up and guns shotted. The steamer bound to Hamilton was full of officers going to rejoin their corps, and not knowing exactly where to find them, as so many had been ordered hastily to the front. At Broomsville, the first place we touched at, there was further news. Tiny scraps of paper, the sixth or *seventh* edition of the morning's journal, were brought on board, and eagerly read. In flaring type was printed: "The Very Latest—Battle now raging—The Queen's Own of Toronto fired the First Shot—They are driving the Fenians back—Gen. Peacock, with Regulars, coming to their Relief (?)—All behaved splendidly, and were rushing on the Retreating Fenians with Great Gallantry—Several of the Queen's Own are killed—A Great Number of Fenians are killed." Sentries guarded the quays, and groups of people talked excitedly in the streets. It was difficult to believe that a skirmish was going on, even while the absurd bulletins we received gave account of its progress on that quiet morning. In the steamer were several Toronto people whose anxiety was naturally great, since it was among the Toronto volunteers that most casualties were said to have occurred. We knew now that another fine regiment, the Royals, had been added to the force at Niagara, and every moment was bringing in fresh companies from the country.

It was some time before we got to Kingston, where, although they had no list of killed or wounded, bad reports had come in that the volunteers, being unsupported, had been obliged to fall back. They had started from the shores of Lake Erie, having gone round

there by railway, and were to have marched back upon
the Fenians, co-operating with the regular troops who
were to march from Niagara, thus enclosing the invaders between the two forces. The volunteers had
started too soon—had met the Fenians, and, without
waiting to ascertain their strength, or giving time for
the regulars to take the Fenians in rear, had commenced "driving" them back. The Fenians, who were
mostly old soldiers, commanded by an able officer,
allowed this to proceed for some time, till the Canadians suddenly found that the Irish were getting round
their flanks. An alarm was created by some one
raising the cry of "cavalry," at which there was a
somewhat disorderly movement to form squares, which
was not promptly done; and the ammunition of some
of the companies having at the same time failed, it
was found necessary to retreat. The Fenians, who
were superior to the volunteers in number, knowing
that the regulars were coming quickly down upon
them, did not pursue, but "made tracks" in the
direction of Fort Erie, dispersing at that place a small
body of volunteers that a Dr. King had very rashly
landed from a small steamer. To any one who could
have had a bird's eye view of the country at this
moment, a curious picture would have presented

itself—the red-coats moving slowly along the roads from Niagara, while their enemies the Irish, and their friends the volunteers, were both retreating in different directions.

The accounts that had reached Kingston came partly from the Americans who had crossed to see the progress of affairs and report for their newspapers. One of these was dated from the "Fenian camp," and described the approach of the British. "The road from Frenchman's creek to Waterloo (a village)," said the reporter, "was thronged with Fenians mounted on horses, two deep, moving to the front. The Fenians were said to be carrying boxes of ammunition in lumber waggons, and frantically leaping mud puddles, and shouting 'Come on.'"

Toronto and Hamilton were in a state of fever. At the latter place the wounded were being hourly expected. Crowds waited at the railway station to receive them, and notices were posted requiring the services of nurses.

A detachment of troops was quartered at the Clifton House, which was not more comfortable in consequence. A regiment, made up of ten different country volunteer companies, was drilling daily at the suspension bridge. From all parts of the frontier, from

Quebec to London, came reports that raiding expeditions were expected. There was hardly a border town in Canada that, according to these messages, was not in immediate peril. But danger had disappeared. At Erie all was again quiet, for the Irish had recrossed, taking with them every boat they could lay hold of. United States troops had been hurried up all along the line to the St. Lawrence, and the officers were strictly enjoined to see that the neutrality laws should not be violated. This was more than was expected on our side, and did the Government at Washington the greatest credit. Although the Cabinet at Washington believed that we had frequently violated neutrality by the manner in which English ships had become Confederate cruisers, and was aware that the Southern refugees had received sympathy in Canada, where plots had been organized against American towns, it never hesitated. Many an Irish vote in the approaching important elections was lost to the party then in power by its honourable conduct on this occasion. It was entirely owing to their promptitude that the Canadians had not to wage a most troublesome war against men who, however despicable in intelligence, are formidable in number.

It is noticeable how much the Canadians sympathized with the South during the American war, and how much dislike exists between the inhabitants of the opposite banks of the St. Lawrence, although many American and Canadian families have intermarried. While Dr. King's little detachment of Volunteers was being broken up and fired into by the Fenians returning from Ridgeway, the inhabitants of Buffalo crowded down to the opposite shore, and cheered the Fenians to the echo. The newspapers took their side, and it seemed as if any slaughter would be acceptable, so long as "Kanucks," as the Canadians are called, were the victims. The hated Britishers had the laugh eventually on their side. A number of the invaders had been caught by the United States gunboat *Michigan*, and were confined for some days in mid-stream on a scow or open barge. There crowded together and exposed to sun and rain, their condition was deplorable enough, and it was amusing to see the river bank lined with people who, through telescopes and opera glasses, could minutely observe all that went on amongst them.

Small parties of Fenians who were not fortunate enough to get across were captured or shot down in the woods around Fort Erie by the volunteers, who were here in great force. Every man belonging to the volunteers had joined his company, leaving business, and willing to serve for any time that might be necessary. Their loyalty was proved, if nothing else was effected by that expensive joke— Fenianism.

THE END.

LONDON:
SAVILL AND EDWARDS, PRINTERS, CHANDOS STREET,
COVENT GARDEN.

13, GREAT MARLBOROUGH STREET.

MESSRS. HURST AND BLACKETT'S
LIST OF NEW WORKS.

NEW AMERICA. By WILLIAM HEPWORTH DIXON.
SIXTH EDITION. 2 vols. demy 8vo, with Illustrations. 30s.

"The author of this very interesting book having penetrated through the plains and mountains of the Far West into the Salt Lake Valley, here gives us an excellent account of the Mormons, and some striking descriptions of the scenes which he saw, and the conversations which he held with many of the Saints during his sojourn there. For a full account of the singular sect called the Shakers, of their patient, loving industry, their admirable schools, and their perpetual intercourse with the invisible world, we must refer the reader to this work. Mr. Dixon has written thoughtfully and well, and we can recall no previous book on American travel which dwells so fully on these much vexed subjects."—*Times.*

"There are few books of this season likely to excite so much general curiosity as Mr. Dixon's very entertaining and instructive work on New America. None are more nearly interested in the growth and development of new ideas on the other side of the Atlantic than ourselves. The Mormons, the Shakers, the Bible Perfectionists, the Spiritualists, the Tunkers, the Free Lovers, &c., are most of them of English blood, though they are born on United States soil. The book is really interesting from the first page to the last, and it contains a large amount of valuable and curious information."—*Pall Mall Gazette.*

"In these very entertaining volumes Mr. Dixon touches upon many other features of American society, but it is in his sketches of Mormons, Shakers, Bible-Communists, and other kindred associations, that the reader will probably find most to interest him. We recommend every one who feels any interest in human nature to read Mr. Dixon's volumes for themselves."—*Saturday Review.*

"We have had nothing about Utah and the Mormons so genuine and satisfactory as the account now given us by Mr. Dixon, but he takes also a wider glance at the Far West, and blends with his narrative such notes of life as he thinks useful aids to a study of the newest social conditions—germs of a society of the future. There is not a chapter from which pleasant extract might not be made, not a page that does not by bright studies of humanity in unaccustomed forms keep the attention alive from the beginning to the end of the narrative."—*Examiner.*

"Intensely exciting volumes. The central interest of the book lies in Mr. Dixon's picture of Mormon society, and it is for its singular revelations respecting Brigham Young's people, and the Shakers and Bible Communists, that nine readers out of every ten will send for an early copy of this strange story. Whilst Mr. Dixon speaks frankly all that he knows and thinks, he speaks it in a fashion that will carry his volumes into the hands of every woman in England and America."—*Post.*

"A book which it is a rare pleasure to read—and which will most indubitably be read by all who care to study the newest phenomena of American life."—*Spectator.*

"We are much mistaken if both in America and England Mr. Dixon's volumes do not win for themselves the widest circulation."—*Standard.*

"Mr. Dixon's 'New America' is decidedly the cleverest and most interesting, as it has already proved the most successful book published this season."—*Star.*

"Mr. Dixon has written a book about America having the unusual merit of being at once amusing and instructive, true as well as new. Of the books published this season there will be none more cordially read."—*Macmillan's Magazine.*

"Mr. Dixon's book is a careful, wise, and graphic picture of the most prominent social phenomena which the newest phases of the New World present. The narrative is full of interest from end to end, as well as of most important subjects for consideration. No student of society, no historian of humanity, should be without it as a reliable and valuable text-book on New America."—*All the Year Round.*

"In these graphic volumes Mr. Dixon sketches American men and women, sharply, vigorously and truthfully, under every aspect. The smart Yankee, the grave politician, the senate and the stage, the pulpit and the prairie, loafers and philanthropists, crowded streets, and the howling wilderness, the saloon and boudoir, with woman everywhere at full length—all pass on before us in some of the most vivid and brilliant pages ever written."—*Dublin University Magazine.*

"Mr. Dixon's 'New America' is a book of books. He writes with vast knowledge and vigour, and no work has ever appeared which furnishes so accurate and just an appreciation of the colossal social, and religious eccentricities which flourish in the United States, and of their present and future significance. As a contribution to this end, Mr. Dixon's book is invaluable."—*Lancet.*

13, GREAT MARLBOROUGH STREET.

MESSRS. HURST AND BLACKETT'S NEW WORKS—*Continued.*

THE LIFE OF JOSIAH WEDGWOOD; From his Private Correspondence and Family Papers, in the possession of JOSEPH MAYER, Esq., F.S.A., FRANCIS WEDGWOOD, Esq., C. DARWIN, Esq., M.A., F.R.S., Miss WEDGWOOD, and other Original Sources. With an Introductory Sketch of the Art of Pottery in England. By ELIZA METEYARD. Dedicated to the Right Hon. W. E. GLADSTONE. Complete in 2 vols. 8vo, with Portraits and 300 other Beautiful Illustrations, elegantly bound, price 42s.

"This is the Life of Wedgwood to the expected appearance of which I referred at Burslem."—*Extract from a Letter to the Author by the Right Hon. W. E. Gladstone.*

"We have to congratulate the authoress on the publication of her Life of Wedgwood. We can award her the praise due to the most pains-taking and conscientious application. She has devoted her whole mind and energy to her subject, and has achieved a work not less creditable to herself than it is indispensable to all who wish to know anything about English ceramic art and its great inventor. The two volumes before us are in themselves marvels of decorative and typographical skill. More beautifully printed pages, more creamy paper, and more dainty woodcuts have seldom met our eyes. It is rarely that an author is so well seconded by his coadjutors as Miss Meteyard has been by her publishers, printers, and the staff of draughtsmen and engravers who have contributed the numerous illustrations which adorn this sumptuous book."—*Saturday Review.*

"This very beautiful book contains that Life of Wedgwood which for the last fifteen years Miss Meteyard has had in view, and to which the Wedgwood family, and all who have papers valuable in relation to its subject, have been cordially contributing. In his admirable sketch of Wedgwood, given at Burslem, it was to the publication of this biography that Mr. Gladstone looked forward with pleasure. It is a very accurate and valuable book. To give their fullest value to the engravings of works of art which largely enrich the volumes, the biography has been made by its publishers a choice specimen of their own art as bookmakers. Neither care nor cost have been grudged. The two volumes form as handsome a book as has ever been published."—*Examiner.*

"The appearance of such a work as Miss Meteyard's 'Life of Josiah Wedgwood' is an event of importance in the sister spheres of literature and art. The biographer of our great potter has more than ordinary fitness for the fulfilment of her labour of love. She is an enthusiastic admirer and a practised connoisseur of Ceramic Art, and she brings the pleasant energy of individual taste and feeling to the aid of complete, authentic, and well-arranged information, and the well-balanced style of an experienced *littérateur*. The interest of the book grows with every page. The reader will peruse the numerous interesting particulars of Wedgwood's family life and affairs with unusual satisfaction, and will lay down the work with undoubting confidence that it will rank as a classic among biographies—an exhaustive work of the first rank in its school."—*Morning Post.*

"An admirable, well-written, honourably elaborate, and most interesting book."—*Athenæum.*

"No book has come before us for some time so stored with interesting information. Miss Meteyard is a biographer distinguished by a clever and energetic style, by delicate judgment, extensive information, and a deep interest in her subject. The history of the Ceramic Art in England, and the biography of the eminent man who brought it to perfection, have evidently been to her a labour of love; and of the spirit and manner in which she has executed it we can hardly speak too highly. The splendid getting up of the work reflects much credit on the house from which it is issued."—*Dublin University Magazine.*

"In this magnificent volume we welcome one of the very noblest contributions to the history of the Ceramic art ever published. We place it at once and permanently side by side with Bernard Palissy's Memoirs and with Benvenuto Cellini's Autobiography. An abundance of rare and very precious materials is here admirably put together by the dexterous hand and exquisite taste of Miss Meteyard. A more conscientious discharge of the responsible duties devolving upon the biographer of a really great man has not been witnessed, we believe, since the days of Boswell, the greatest of all biographers."—*Sun.*

2

13, GREAT MARLBOROUGH STREET.

MESSRS. HURST AND BLACKETT'S NEW WORKS—*Continued.*

A TRIP TO THE TROPICS. By the MARQUIS OF LORNE. 1 vol. 8vo, with Illustrations. 15s.

WILD LIFE AMONG THE PACIFIC ISLANDERS. By E. H. LAMONT, ESQ. 1 vol. 8vo, with numerous Illustrations.

A BOOK ABOUT LAWYERS. By J. C. JEAFFRESON, Barrister-at-Law, author of 'A Book about Doctors,' &c. New, Revised, and Cheaper Edition. 2 vols. post 8vo. 24s.

PRINCIPAL CONTENTS:—The Great Seal, Royal Portraits, The Practice of Sealing, Lords Commissioners, On Damasking, The Rival Seals, Purses of State, A Lady Keeper, Lawyers in Arms, The Devil's Own, Lawyers on Horseback, Chancellors' Cavalcades, Ladies in Law Colleges, York House, Powis House, Lincoln's Inn Fields, The Old Law Quarter, Loves of the Lawyers, The Three Graces, Rejected Addresses, Brothers in Trouble, Fees to Counsel, Retainers Special and General, Judicial Corruption, Gifts and Sales, Judicial Salaries, Costume and Toilet, Millinery, Wigs, Bands and Collars, Bags and Gowns, The Singing Barrister, Actors at the Bar, Political Lawyers, The Peers, Lawyers in the House, Legal Education, Inns of Court and Inns of Chancery, Lawyers and Gentlemen, Law French and Law Latin, Readers and Mootmen, Pupils in Chambers, Wit of Lawyers, Humorous Stories, Wits in Silk and Punsters in Ermine, Circuiters, Witnesses, Lawyers and Saints, Lawyers in Court and Society, Attorneys at Law, Westminster Hall, Law and Literature, &c.

FROM "THE TIMES," DEC. 6.—"'A Book about Lawyers' deserves to be very popular. Mr. Jeaffreson has accomplished his work in a very creditable manner. He has taken pains to collect information from persons as well as from books, and he writes with a sense of keen enjoyment which greatly enhances the reader's pleasure. He introduces us to Lawyerdom under a variety of phases—we have lawyers in arms, lawyers on horseback, lawyers in love, and lawyers in Parliament. We are told of their salaries and fees, their wigs and gowns, their jokes and gaieties. We meet them at home and abroad, in court, in chambers, and in company. In the chapters headed 'Mirth,' the author has gathered together a choice sheaf of anecdotes from the days of More down to Erskine and Eldon."

"These volumes will afford pleasure and instruction to all who read them, and they will increase the reputation which Mr. Jeaffreson has already earned by his large industry and great ability. We are indebted to him for almost eight hundred pages, and that rare and valuable addition, a capital Index, all devoted to the history and illustration of legal men and things. It is much that we can say for a book, that there is not a superfluous page in it."—*Athenæum.*

"The success of his 'Book about Doctors' has induced Mr. Jeaffreson to write another book—about Lawyers. The subject is attractive. It is a bright string of anecdotes, skilfully put together, on legal topics of all sorts, but especially in illustration of the lives of famous lawyers. Mr. Jeaffreson has not only collected a large number of good stories, but he has grouped them pleasantly, and tells them well. We need say little to recommend a book that can speak for itself so pleasantly. No livelier reading is to be found among the new books of the season."—*Examiner.*

"This book is full of amusement. It is a mine of curious anecdote, gathered apparently from a wide extent of reading. The volumes detail the strangest of actual romances, the wildest of adventures, the drollest of humours, the brightest of witty sayings and repartees."—*London Review.*

"These two very delightful gossiping volumes contain a vast amount of pleasant anecdote and interesting information. Mr. Jeaffreson has exercised considerable industry in the collection, and has displayed both taste and judgment in the arrangement of his materials. Lawyers of every grade and every possible shade of character, from the student below the bar to the Lord Chancellor upon the woolsack, lawyers of ancient times, and lawyers of our own day, here pass under review, and are subject to the closest inspection. The anecdotes of celebrated individuals, who are scattered throughout the chapters, are most amusing. We have said enough to demonstrate the very attractive character of this Book about Lawyers, in which our readers will find ample materials for occupying many a pleasant and not unprofitable hour."—*Sun.*

13, GREAT MARLBOROUGH STREET.

MESSRS. HURST AND BLACKETT'S NEW WORKS—*Continued.*

LIFE IN A FRENCH CHATEAU. By HUBERT
E. H. JERNINGHAM, ESQ. *Second Edition.* 1 vol. post 8vo, with Illustrations. 10s. 6d. bound.

"Mr. Jerningham's attractive and amusing volume will be perused with much interest."—*Morning Post.*

"A thoroughly fresh and delightful narrative—valuable, instructive, and entertaining."—*United Service Magazine.*

"A readable, pleasant, and amusing book, in which Mr. Jerningham records his life among the denizens of the French Château, which extended its courtly hospitality to him, in a very agreeable and entertaining manner."—*Court Journal.*

A LADY'S GLIMPSE OF THE LATE WAR
IN BOHEMIA. By LIZZIE SELINA EDEN. 1 vol. post 8vo, with Illustrations. 10s. 6d.

"Miss Eden is a pleasant companion, and recounts her experiences with an earnest and womanly sincerity, which is engaging. We have read and can recommend her book with pleasure."—*Athenæum.*

"A most interesting work, full of well-told incidents. The writer has succeeded in presenting a most lively and instructive description of her experiences as an observer of the occurrences which marked the recent conflict between the Prussian and Austrian armies."—*Observer.*

NOOKS AND CORNERS OF OLD FRANCE.
By the Rev. G. M. MUSGRAVE, M.A. Oxon. 2 vols. with Illustrations. *(Just Ready).*

MY PILGRIMAGE TO EASTERN SHRINES.
By ELIZA C. BUSH. 8vo, with Illustrations. 15s.

"This work contains a great deal of interesting matter, and it will be read with pleasure by all who are interested in the country to which so many devout Christians have made their pilgrimage."—*Observer.*

THE SPORTSMAN AND NATURALIST IN
CANADA. With Notes on the Natural History of the Game, Game Birds, and Fish of that country. By MAJOR W. ROSS KING, F.R.G.S., F.S.A.S. 1 vol. super royal 8vo, Illustrated with beautiful Coloured Plates and Woodcuts. 20s. Elegantly bound.

"Truthful, simple, and extremely observant, Major King has been able to throw much light upon the habits as well as the zoological relations of the animals with which he came in collision; and his descriptions of the country, as well as of the creatures inhabiting it, are as bright and graphic as they are evidently correct."—*Athenæum.*

"In 'The Sportsman and Naturalist in Canada' we have a full, true, and comprehensive record of all the facts concerning American animals which the author was able in a three years' residence to collect. We have these facts in a goodly volume, splendidly illustrated, and with its contents so well arranged that a reference to any description of bird, beast, or fish may be made almost instantly. It is an important contribution to Natural History, and a work the intending traveller will consult once and again, since it gives him the information he most needs, and finds least generally accessible. The book will take its position in the foremost rank of works of its class. The descriptions throughout are written by one who is a master of his subject, and who writes English such as few are able to equal. Of recent British travellers few can vie with its author in close observation of nature, and in those graces of style and scholarship which make the information contained in his volume as pleasant to obtain as it is valuable to preserve. In fact, since the works of Eliot Warburton and Kinglake, no book of travels with which we are acquainted has been written in a style more clear, forcible, picturesque."—*Sunday Times.*

13, GREAT MARLBOROUGH STREET.

MESSRS. HURST AND BLACKETT'S NEW WORKS—*Continued.*

MEMOIRS AND CORRESPONDENCE OF FIELD-MARSHAL VISCOUNT COMBERMERE, G.C.B., &c.
From his Family Papers. By the Right Hon. MARY VISCOUNTESS COMBERMERE and Capt. W. W. KNOLLYS. 2 v. 8vo, with Portraits. 30s.

"The gallant Stapleton Cotton, Viscount Combermere, was one of those men who belong to two epochs. He was a soldier, actively engaged, nearly ten years before the last century came to its troubled close; and he was among us but as yesterday, a noble veteran, gloriously laden with years, laurels, and pleasant reminiscences. To the last this noble soldier and most perfect gentleman took cheerful part in the duties and pleasures of life, leaving to an only son an inheritance of a great name, and to a sorrowing widow the task of recording how the bearer of the name won for it all his greatness. This has been done, evidently as a labour of love, by Lady Combermere, and she has been efficiently assisted in the military details by Captain Knollys. Apart from the biographical and professional details, the volumes, moreover, are full of sketches of persons of importance or interest who came into connection with Lord Combermere."—*Athenæum.*

"A welcome and gracefully written memorial of one of the greatest of England's soldiers, and worthiest of her sons. It is a most interesting work."—*Morning Post.*

"This biography, abounding in letters and other unpublished materials, is all fresh and trustworthy information, as to the life of a man whose career deserved a record."—*Examiner.*

"All through the lengthened career of this grand old soldier we are enabled to follow him step by step, incident by incident, through the pages of these thoroughly readable and most entertaining volumes."—*Sun.*

THE HON. GRANTLEY BERKELEY'S LIFE AND RECOLLECTIONS.
Vols. III. and IV. completing the Work. 30s., bound.

Among the other distinguished persons mentioned in these volumes are the Emperors Alexander, Nicholas, and Napoleon III.; Kings George IV., William IV., and Leopold I.; Princes Talleyrand, Esterhazy, Napoleon, Pueckler Meskau; the Dukes of Sussex, York, Cambridge, Wellington, d'Orleans, d'Aumale, Brunswick, Manchester, Beaufort, Cleveland, Richmond, Buckingham; Lords Byron, Melbourne, Lansdowne, Holland, Brougham, Alvanley, Yarmouth, Petersham, Craven, Salisbury, Devonshire, Ducie, Glasgow, Malmesbury, Castlereagh, Breadalbane, &c. Sirs Robert Peel, T. Lawrence, W. Knighton, George Dashwood, George Warrender, Lumley Skeffington, Bulwer Lytton, Count d'Orsay, Count de Morny, the Rev. Sydney Smith, Tom Moore, Shelley, Thomas Campbell, Beau Brummell, Theodore Hook, Leigh Hunt, W. S. Landor, James and Horace Smith, Jack Musters, Assheton Smith, &c. Ladies Holland, Jersey, Londonderry, Blessington, Shelley, Lamb, Breadalbane, Morgan, Mrs. Fitzherbert, Mrs. Jordan, Miss Landon, the Countess Guiccioli, &c

"A book unrivalled in its position in the range of modern literature."—*Times.*

"It is pleasant to be told about men of note, or the various phases of high social life, in the light and sparkling manner peculiar to these memoirs. The most fastidious critic will scarcely deny that Mr. Berkeley possesses the gift of writing in an amusing strain on social, sporting, or general subjects."—*Morning Post.*

"A clever, freespoken man of the world, son of an earl with £70,000 a-year, who has lived from boyhood the life of a club-man, sportsman, and man of fashion, has thrown his best stories about himself and his friends, into an anecdotic autobiography. Of course it is eminently readable. Mr. Grantley Berkeley writes easily and well. The book is full of pleasant stories, all told as easily and clearly as if they were related at a club-window, and all with point of greater or less piquancy."—*Spectator.*

FROM CADET TO COLONEL: The Record of a Life of Active Service.
By Major-General Sir THOMAS SEATON, K.C.B. 2 vols. with Illustrations, 21s.

"It is difficult to imagine anything more interesting both to soldiers and civilians than Sir Thomas Seaton's record of his active career."—*Athenæum.*

13, GREAT MARLBOROUGH STREET.

MESSRS. HURST AND BLACKETT'S NEW WORKS—*Continued.*

TRAVELS IN FRANCE AND GERMANY IN
1865 AND 1866: Including a Steam Voyage down the Danube, and a Ride across the Mountains of European Turkey from Belgrade to Montenegro. By Captain SPENCER, author of 'Travels in Circassia,' &c. 2 vols. 21s.

"This work would at any time be read with pleasure, but at this moment it is invested with peculiar interest. It presents a clear and comprehensive view of Germany on the eve of war, and throws much light on many questions which have recently occupied, and are still destined to occupy, a considerable share of attention. It is more than a narrative of travel, although it possesses all the attractions of a well written work of that nature. There is sufficient of adventure for those who love that which is exciting; sketches of wild and beautiful scenes; glimpses of life, not only in cities, but in secluded villages, and notes and observations on the social, moral, and political condition of the countries passed through. The unity of Germany is regarded as a gain to the whole civilized world; the exclusion of Austria from Germany a gain to herself and to the magnificent countries she rules over in eastern Europe. With these countries the reader renews his acquaintance. A characteristic sketch of the present state of Hungary is given in connection with the story of a voyage down the Lower Danube. The narrative of a ride across the mountains of European Turkey is filled up with a description of the manners and customs of a people still living in a state of primitive simplicity. The author's style is lucid and anecdotal, and the range of his book gives scope for much pleasing variety as well as for much useful information."—*Post.*

ENGLISH TRAVELLERS AND ITALIAN
BRIGANDS: a Narrative of Capture and Captivity. By W. J. C. MOENS. Second Edition. Revised with Additions. 2 vols., with Portrait and other Illustrations. 21s.

"Mr. Moens had a bad time of it among the Italian Brigands. But his misfortunes are now to himself and to his friends a source of no little entertainment, and we can say for those who listen to his story that we have followed him in his adventures with pleasure. He tells his tale in a clear and simple style, and with that confident manliness which is not afraid to be natural."—*The Times.*

"Mr. Moens has had an experience and an adventure of startling magnitude in these prosaic times of ours. He has seen what no other Englishman has seen, and has done what no one else has done, and has written a bright and charming book as the result."—*All the Year Round.*

"In these volumes, the literary merits of which are numerous, we have the true story of the capture of Mr. Moens by the brigands. We have no doubt that the book will be extensively read; we are quite sure that it will do an immense amount of good. It lets in a flood of light upon the dens of these robbers."—*Daily News.*

A WINTER WITH THE SWALLOWS IN
ALGERIA. By MATILDA BETHAM EDWARDS. 8vo, with Illustrations. 15s.

"A pleasant volume; a genuine, graphic record of a time of thorough enjoyment."—*Athenæum.*

"A fresh and fascinating book, full of matter and beauty. It is one of the most instructive books of travel of the season, and one of the brightest. It would be difficult to overpraise it."—*Spectator.*

"A bright, blithe, picturesque, artistic book, full of colour and sunshine, and replete with good sense and sound observation. To the enthusiasm of the book a great portion of its beauty and its attraction are owing, but solid information and the reality of things in Algeria are never disguised in favour of the bright land to which the author followed the Swallows."—*Post.*

TRAVELS AND ADVENTURES OF AN OFFI-
CER'S WIFE IN INDIA, CHINA, AND NEW ZEALAND. By Mrs. MUTER, Wife of Lieut.-Colonel D. D. MUTER, 13th (Prince Albert's) Light Infantry. 2 vols. 21s.

6

13, Great Marlborough Street.

MESSRS. HURST AND BLACKETT'S NEW WORKS—Continued.

LADY ARABELLA STUART'S LIFE AND
LETTERS: including numerous Original and Unpublished Documents. By ELIZABETH COOPER. 2 vols., with Portrait. 21s.

"The 'Life and Letters of Lady Arabella Stuart' is an unusually good specimen of its class. Miss Cooper has really worked at her subject. She has read a good deal of MSS, and, what is better still, she has printed a good deal of what she has read. The book has a real and substantial historical value."—*Saturday Review.*

"One of the most interesting biographical works recently published. The memoirs have been arranged by Miss Cooper with much care, diligence, and judgment."—*Post.*

"Miss Cooper has laid before us a work of equal value and interest, respecting one of the most romantic and interesting passages in English history, in which the actors are living men and women, not merely historical figures."—*Globe.*

IMPRESSIONS OF LIFE AT HOME AND
ABROAD. By Lord EUSTACE CECIL, M.P. 1 vol. 8vo.

"Lord Eustace Cecil has selected from various journeys the points which most interested him, and has reported them in an unaffected style. The idea is a good one, and is carried out with success. We are grateful for a good deal of information given with unpretending good sense."—*Saturday Review.*

HISTORIC PICTURES. By A. BAILLIE COCHRANE,
M.P. 2 vols. 21s.

"Mr. Baillie Cochrane has published two entertaining volumes of studies from history. They are lively reading. 'My aim,' he says, 'has been to depict events generally known in a light and, if possible, a picturesque manner.' Mr. Cochrane has been quite successful in carrying out this intention. The work is a study of the more interesting moments of history—what, indeed, the author himself calls it, 'Historic Pictures.'"—*Times.*

COURT AND SOCIETY FROM ELIZABETH
TO ANNE, Edited from the Papers at Kimbolton, by the DUKE OF MANCHESTER. *Second Edition.* 2 vols. 8vo, with Fine Portraits.

"These volumes are sure to excite curiosity. A great deal of interesting matter is here collected, from sources which are not within everybody's reach."—*Times.*

HAUNTED LONDON. By WALTER THORNBURY.
1 vol. 8vo, with numerous Illustrations by F. W. FAIRHOLT, F.S.A.

"Mr. Thornbury points out to us the legendary houses, the great men's birth-places and tombs, the haunts of poets, the scenes of martyrdom, the battle-fields of old factions. The book overflows with anecdotical gossip. Mr. Fairholt's drawings add alike to its value and interest."—*Notes and Queries.*

PRISON CHARACTERS DRAWN FROM LIFE.
BY A PRISON MATRON, Author of 'Female Life in Prison.' 2 v. 21s.

"These volumes are interesting and suggestive."—*Athenæum.*

"A woman lodged among imprisoned women, with a kindly sympathy, a quick eye, and a mind apt to record clearly its well-directed observations, has something to tell that thousands will be glad to learn. Her quick-witted transcripts of living character are studies that nothing can make obsolete or deprive of interest for living men."—*Examiner.*

RECOLLECTIONS OF A LIFE OF ADVEN-
TURE. By WILLIAM STAMER. 2 vols. with Portrait. 21s.

"Mr. Stamer has been by turns a sailor, a soldier, a dasher in Paris, a recruit in a foreign legion, a sportsman in America. His book is a story of a wild life, not without a certain vivacity and amusement."—*Athenæum.*

13, GREAT MARLBOROUGH STREET.

MESSRS. HURST AND BLACKETT'S NEW WORKS—*Continued.*

A JOURNEY FROM LONDON TO PERSEPOLIS; including WANDERINGS IN DAGHESTAN, GEORGIA, ARMENIA, KURDISTAN, MESOPOTAMIA, AND PERSIA. By J. USSHER, Esq., F.R.G.S. Royal 8vo, with numerous beautiful Coloured Illustrations. Elegantly bound.

"This is a very interesting narrative. Mr. Ussher is one of the pleasantest companions we have met with for a long time. We have rarely read a book of travels in which so much was seen so rapidly and so easily, and in which the scenery, the antiquities, and the people impressed the author's mind with such gentlemanly satisfaction. Mr. Ussher merited his success and this splendid monument of his travels and pleasant explorations."—*Times.*

TRAVELS ON HORSEBACK IN MANTCHU TARTARY: being a Summer's Ride beyond the Great Wall of China. By GEORGE FLEMING, Military Train. 1 vol. royal 8vo, with Map and 50 Illustrations.

"Mr. Fleming's narrative is a most charming one. He has an untrodden region to tell of, and he photographs it and its people and their ways. Life-like descriptions are interspersed with personal anecdotes, local legends, and stories of adventure, some of them revealing no common artistic power."—*Spectator.*

YACHTING ROUND THE WEST OF ENGLAND. By the Rev. A. G. L'ESTRANGE, B.A., of Exeter College, Oxford, R.T.Y.C. 1 vol. 8vo, Illustrated.

"A very interesting work. We can scarcely imagine a more pleasant and romantic yachting voyage than that of the author of this volume round the rough and rugged west coast of England, which forms the coasts of Cornwall and Devonshire."—*Observer.*

SPORT AND SPORTSMEN: A Book of Recollections. By CHARLES STRETTON, Esq. 8vo, with Illustrations.

"This is an amusing book; as interesting as genuine books of sporting adventures seldom fail to be. The Highlands, Wales, the English counties, Australia, have all been visited by the writer, and we have his adventures in each."—*Globe.*

ADVENTURES AMONGST THE DYAKS OF BORNEO. By FREDERICK BOYLE, Esq., F.R.G.S. 1 vol. 8vo, with Illustrations.

"Mr. Boyle's Adventures are very pleasant reading—smart, lively, and indicative of no slight amount of bonhomie in the writer."—*Athenæum.*

A PERSONAL NARRATIVE OF THIRTEEN YEARS' SERVICE AMONGST THE WILD TRIBES OF KHONDISTAN, FOR THE SUPPRESSION OF HUMAN SACRIFICE. By Major-General JOHN CAMPBELL, C.B. 1 vol. 8vo, with Illustrations.

"Major-General Campbell's book is one of thrilling interest, and must be pronounced the most remarkable narrative of the present season."—*Athenæum.*

BRIGAND LIFE IN ITALY. By COUNT MAFFEI. 2 vols. 8vo.

"Two volumes of interesting research."—*Times.*

WILLIAM SHAKESPEARE. By CARDINAL WISEMAN. 1 vol. 8vo, 5s.

13, Great Marlborough Street.

MESSRS. HURST AND BLACKETT'S NEW WORKS—*Continued.*

THE BEAUTIFUL IN NATURE AND ART.
By Mrs. Ellis, Author of 'The Women of England,' &c. 1 vol. crown 8vo, with fine Portrait. 10s. 6d.

"With pleasure her numerous admirers will welcome a new book by the popular authoress of 'The Women of England.' A very charming volume is this new work by Mrs. Ellis. Its aim is to assist the young students of art in those studies and subjects of thought which shall enable them rightly to appreciate and realise that oft-quoted truth, 'A thing of beauty is a joy for ever.' 'The Truthfulness of Art,' 'The Love of Beauty,' 'The Love of Ornament,' 'Early dawn of Art,' and various chapters of a kindred nature, are followed by others descriptive of 'Learning to Draw,' 'Imitation,' 'Light and Shadow,' 'Form,' 'Colour,' 'Lady's Work,' &c. The work will interest many fair readers. It deserves a welcome and very cordial commendation."—*Sun.*

GARIBALDI AT HOME: Notes of a Visit to
Caprera. By Sir Charles R. McGrigor, Bart. 8vo, with Illustrations. 15s.

LIFE IN JAVA; WITH SKETCHES OF THE
JAVANESE. By William Barrington D'Almeida. 2 vols. post 8vo, with Illustrations.

ADVENTURES AND RESEARCHES among the
ANDAMAN ISLANDERS. By Dr. Mouat, F.R.G.S., &c. 1 vol. demy 8vo, with Illustrations.

MEMOIRS OF QUEEN HORTENSE, MOTHER
OF NAPOLEON III. Cheaper Edition, in 1 vol. 6s.

"A biography of the beautiful and unhappy Queen, more satisfactory than any we have yet met with."—*Daily News.*

THE OKAVANGO RIVER: A NARRATIVE
OF TRAVEL, EXPLORATION, AND ADVENTURE. By C. J. Andersson, Author of "Lake Ngami." 1 vol. Illustrations.

TRAVELS IN THE REGIONS OF THE
AMOOR, AND THE RUSSIAN ACQUISITIONS ON THE CONFINES OF INDIA AND CHINA. By T. W. Atkinson, F.G.S., F.R.G.S., Author of "Oriental and Western Siberia." Dedicated, by permission, to Her Majesty. Royal 8vo, with Map and 83 Illustrations.

THE LIFE OF J. M. W. TURNER, R.A., from
Original Letters and Papers. By Walter Thornbury. 2 vols. 8vo, with Portraits and other Illustrations.

LIGHTS AND SHADOWS OF LONDON LIFE.
By the author of 'Mirk Abbey,' 'Lost Sir Massingberd.' 2 vols. 21s.

"'Lights and Shades of London Life,' is a collection of sketches from the pen of an author whose facility for placing the realities of existence in various forms—the pathetic, the solemn, the picturesque, and the humorous—before his readers, is as remarkable as his talent for fiction. Good-sense, good-feeling, and good-humour, characterise these 'Lights and Shadows' as strongly as shrewdness, observation, drollery, and originality mark them. Most people have seen the sights which these sketches describe, or remember the occasions which they record; but each is put in a new point of view, invested with a fresh interest, and impressed upon the mind of the reader by some happy illustration."—*Star.*

THE NEW AND POPULAR NOVELS,
PUBLISHED BY HURST & BLACKETT.

TWO MARRIAGES. By the Author of 'John Halifax, Gentleman,' 'A Noble Life,' 'Christian's Mistake,' &c. 2 vols. 21s.

"This work is marked by all that fertility of description, and high moral tone for which the authoress has so much distinguished herself. It will in no degree detract from her reputation as a writer whose productions may be read with interest by everybody."—*Star*.

"A new novel by the author of 'John Halifax' is always welcome to many readers, and the work now brought forward by that popular author will in no wise disappoint the expectations of her many admirers. The 'Two Marriages' is a very interesting and effective work."—*Sun*.

SYBIL'S SECOND LOVE. By JULIA KAVANAGH, Author of 'Nathalie,' 'Adele,' &c. 3 vols.

"A clever, interesting, and eminently readable novel. The plot is intricate and well worked out. The characters are excellently drawn."—*Globe*.

"A clever novel. The story is keenly interesting, thoroughly pure in tone, full of good, pointed dialogue and admirable descriptive writing, and has a well-conceived plot, most skilfully worked out."—*Star*.

OFF THE LINE. By LADY CHARLES THYNNE. 2 v.

MY SON'S WIFE. By the Author of 'Caste,' 'Mr. Arle,' &c. 3 vols.

MADONNA MARY. By Mrs. OLIPHANT, Author of 'Agnes,' &c. 3 vols.

"From first to last 'Madonna Mary' is written with evenness and vigour, and overflows with the best qualities of its writer's fancy and humour. The story is thoroughly original, as far as its plot and leading incidents are concerned; and the strength of the narrative is such that we question if any reader will lay it aside, notwithstanding the fulness in his throat, and the constriction of his heart, until he has shared in the happiness which is liberally assigned to the actors of the drama before the falling of the green curtain. But the principal charms of the work are subtle humour, fineness of touch, and seeming ease with which Mrs. Oliphant delineates and contrasts her numerous characters."—*Athenæum*.

"A book of great power and beauty—a perfect work of its kind."—*Morning Post*.

CHRISTIE'S FAITH. By the Author of 'No Church,' 'Owen,' 'Mattie,' &c. 3 vols.

"This book deserves to be singled out from the ordinary run of novels on more than one account. The design and execution are both good. The characters are original, clearly conceived, and finely as well as strongly delineated. Christie herself is a delightful sketch."—*Pall Mall Gazette*.

LEYTON HALL, AND OTHER TALES. By MARK LEMON, Author of 'Falkner Lyle,' &c. 3 vols.

"We can heartily recommend these spirited tales to all who are in search of pleasing reading."—*Athenæum*.

"These volumes are full of interest, humour, and pathos. They are sure to be popular."—*Star*.

ST. ALICE. By EDWARD CAMPBELL TAINSH. 3 vols.

"An entertaining, readable book. That Mr. Tainsh can think like a gentleman, and write like a man of cultivated taste, 'Saint Alice' affords ample proof."—*Athenæum*.

A WOMAN'S CONFESSION. By LADY CAMPBELL. 3 vols.

"'A Woman's Confession' deserves to be a successful novel."—*Post*.

THE NEW AND POPULAR NOVELS,
PUBLISHED BY HURST & BLACKETT.

ANNALS OF A QUIET NEIGHBOURHOOD.
By GEORGE MAC DONALD, M.A., Author of 'Alec Forbes,' 'David Elginbrod,' &c. 3 vols.

"Mr. Mac Donald is a true poet. The 'Annals of a Quiet Neighbourhood' are as full of music as was Prospero's island; rich in strains that take the ear captive when they are first heard, and afterwards linger long upon it."—*Saturday Review.*

"The charms and value of Mr. Mac Donald's work need not be sought—they present themselves unasked for, in the tender beauty of his descriptions, whether of nature, or of life and character; in his almost supernatural insight into the workings of the human heart, and in his unceasing fertility of thought and happy exactitude of illustration. Whoever reads the book once will read it many times."—*Pall Mall Gazette.*

A NOBLE LIFE. By the Author of 'John Halifax, Gentleman,' &c. 2 vols. 21s.

"This is another of those pleasant tales in which the author of 'John Halifax' speaks, out of a generous heart, the purest truths of life."—*Examiner.*

"'A Noble Life' is remarkable for the high types of character it presents, and the skill with which they are made to work out a story of powerful and pathetic interest."—*Daily News.*

CHEAP EDITION OF CHRISTIAN'S MISTAKE.
By the Author of 'John Halifax,' &c. Illustrated by Sandys. Price 5s. bound. Forming the New Volume of 'Hurst and Blackett's Standard Library of Cheap Editions of Popular Modern Works.'

"A more charming story, to our taste, has rarely been written. Within the compass of a single volume the writer has hit off a circle of varied characters all true to nature—some true to the highest nature—and she has entangled them in a story which keeps us in suspense till its knot is happily and gracefully resolved; while, at the same time, a pathetic interest is sustained by an art of which it would be difficult to analyse the secret. It is a choice gift to be able thus to render human nature so truly, to penetrate its depths with such a searching sagacity, and to illuminate them with a radiance so eminently the writer's own. Even if tried by the standard of the Archbishop of York, we should expect that even he would pronounce 'Christian's Mistake' a novel without a fault."—*Times.*

MAIDENHOOD. By MRS. SARA ANNA MARSH.
Author of "Chronicles of Dartmoor." 3 vols.

KINGSFORD. By the author of 'Son and Heir.' 2 v.

"'Kingsford' is one of the most interesting stories we have read this season, and we are sure our readers will thank us for recommending to them a work so attractive and enthralling. The plot is of a very interesting character, and there is powerful ability displayed in the creation of the characters."—*Sun.*

RACHEL'S SECRET. By the Author of 'The Master of Marton.' 3 vols.

"'Rachel's Secret,' is a deeply interesting and affecting story, artistically and powerfully wrought."—*Post.*

LORDS AND LADIES. By the Author of 'Margaret and her Bridesmaids,' &c. 3 vols.

"'Lords and Ladies' is one of the most charming books with which the literature of fiction has been enriched this season. The truth and value of the moral of the story will recommend it as highly as the vivacity and humour of its style and the ingenuity of its construction."—*Post.*

THE WILD FLOWER OF RAVENSWORTH.
By the Author of 'John and I,' 'Doctor Jacob,' &c. 3 vols.

"A beautiful tale, written with deep feeling."—*Illustrated News.*

Under the Especial Patronage of Her Majesty.

Published annually, in One Vol., royal 8vo, with the Arms beautifully engraved, handsomely bound, with gilt edges, price 31s. 6d.

LODGE'S PEERAGE
AND BARONETAGE,
CORRECTED BY THE NOBILITY.

THE THIRTY-SIXTH EDITION FOR 1867 IS NOW READY.

LODGE'S PEERAGE AND BARONETAGE is acknowledged to be the most complete, as well as the most elegant, work of the kind. As an established and authentic authority on all questions respecting the family histories, honours, and connections of the titled aristocracy, no work has ever stood so high. It is published under the especial patronage of Her Majesty, and is annually corrected throughout, from the personal communications of the Nobility. It is the only work of its class in which, *the type being kept constantly standing*, every correction is made in its proper place to the date of publication, an advantage which gives it supremacy over all its competitors. Independently of its full and authentic information respecting the existing Peers and Baronets of the realm, the most sedulous attention is given in its pages to the collateral branches of the various noble families, and the names of many thousand individuals are introduced, which do not appear in other records of the titled classes. For its authority, correctness, and facility of arrangement, and the beauty of its typography and binding, the work is justly entitled to the place it occupies on the tables of Her Majesty and the Nobility.

LIST OF THE PRINCIPAL CONTENTS.

Historical View of the Peerage.
Parliamentary Roll of the House of Lords.
English, Scotch, and Irish Peers, in their orders of Precedence.
Alphabetical List of Peers of Great Britain and the United Kingdom, holding superior rank in the Scotch or Irish Peerage.
Alphabetical list of Scotch and Irish Peers, holding superior titles in the Peerage of Great Britain and the United Kingdom.
A Collective list of Peers, in their order of Precedence.
Table of Precedency among Men.
Table of Precedency among Women.
The Queen and the Royal Family.
Peers of the Blood Royal.
The Peerage, alphabetically arranged.
Families of such Extinct Peers as have left Widows or Issue.
Alphabetical List of the Surnames of all the Peers.

The Archbishops and Bishops of England, Ireland, and the Colonies.
The Baronetage alphabetically arranged.
Alphabetical List of Surnames assumed by members of Noble Families.
Alphabetical List of the Second Titles of Peers, usually borne by their Eldest Sons.
Alphabetical Index to the Daughters of Dukes, Marquises, and Earls, who, having married Commoners, retain the title of Lady before their own Christian and their Husband's Surnames.
Alphabetical Index to the Daughters of Viscounts and Barons, who, having married Commoners, are styled Honourable Mrs.; and, in case of the husband being a Baronet or Knight, Honourable Lady.
Mottos alphabetically arranged and translated.

"Lodge's Peerage must supersede all other works of the kind, for two reasons; first, it is on a better plan; and secondly, it is better executed. We can safely pronounce it to be the readiest, the most useful, and exactest of modern works on the subject."—*Spectator*.

"A work which corrects all errors of former works. It is a most useful publication."—*Times*.

"A work of great value. It is the most faithful record we possess of the aristocracy of the day."—*Post*.

"The best existing, and, we believe, the best possible peerage. It is the standard authority on the subject."—*Herald*.

NOW IN COURSE OF PUBLICATION,

HURST AND BLACKETT'S STANDARD LIBRARY
OF CHEAP EDITIONS OF
POPULAR MODERN WORKS,
ILLUSTRATED BY MILLAIS, HOLMAN HUNT, LEECH, BIRKET FOSTER, JOHN GILBERT, TENNIEL, &c.

Each in a single volume, elegantly printed, bound, and illustrated, price 5s.

VOL. I.—SAM SLICK'S NATURE AND HUMAN NATURE.

"The first volume of Messrs Hurst and Blackett's Standard Library of Cheap Editions forms a very good beginning to what will doubtless be a very successful undertaking. 'Nature and Human Nature' is one of the best of Sam Slick's witty and humorous productions, and well entitled to the large circulation which it cannot fail to obtain in its present convenient and cheap shape. The volume combines with the great recommendations of a clear, bold type, and good paper, the lesser, but attractive merits, of being well illustrated and elegantly bound."—*Post.*

VOL. II.—JOHN HALIFAX, GENTLEMAN.

"This is a very good and a very interesting work. It is designed to trace the career from boyhood to age of a perfect man—a Christian gentleman, and it abounds in incident both well and highly wrought. Throughout it is conceived in a high spirit, and written with great ability. This cheap and handsome new edition is worthy to pass freely from hand to hand as a gift book in many households."—*Examiner.*

"The new and cheaper edition of this interesting work will doubtless meet with great success. John Halifax, the hero of this most beautiful story, is no ordinary hero, and this his history is no ordinary book. It is a full-length portrait of a true gentleman, one of nature's own nobility. It is also the history of a home, and a thoroughly English one. The work abounds in incident, and is full of graphic power and true pathos. It is a book that few will read without becoming wiser and better."—*Scotsman.*

VOL. III.—THE CRESCENT AND THE CROSS.
BY ELIOT WARBURTON.

"Independent of its value as an original narrative, and its useful and interesting information, this work is remarkable for the colouring power and play of fancy with which its descriptions are enlivened. Among its greatest and most lasting charms is its reverent and serious spirit."—*Quarterly Review.*

"A book calculated to prove more practically useful was never penned than 'The Crescent and the Cross'—a work which surpasses all others in its homage for the sublime and its love for the beautiful in those famous regions consecrated to everlasting immortality in the annals of the prophets, and which no other writer has ever depicted with a pencil at once so reverent and so picturesque."—*Sun.*

VOL. IV.—NATHALIE. BY JULIA KAVANAGH.

"'Nathalie' is Miss Kavanagh's best imaginative effort. Its manner is gracious and attractive. Its matter is good. A sentiment, a tenderness, are commanded by her which are as individual as they are elegant."—*Athenæum.*

VOL. V.—A WOMAN'S THOUGHTS ABOUT WOMEN.
BY THE AUTHOR OF "JOHN HALIFAX, GENTLEMAN."

"A book of sound counsel. It is one of the most sensible works of its kind, well-written, true-hearted, and altogether practical. Whoever wishes to give advice to a young lady may thank the author for means of doing so."—*Examiner.*

[CONTINUED ON THE FOLLOWING PAGES.]

HURST AND BLACKETT'S STANDARD LIBRARY
(CONTINUED).

VOL. VI.—ADAM GRAEME. BY MRS OLIPHANT.

"'Adam Graeme' is a story awakening genuine emotions of interest and delight by its admirable pictures of Scottish life and scenery. The eloquent author sets before us the essential attributes of Christian virtue, their deep and silent workings in the heart, and their beautiful manifestations in life, with a delicacy, a power, and a truth which can hardly be surpassed."—*Post.*

VOL. VII.—SAM SLICK'S WISE SAWS AND MODERN INSTANCES.

"We have not the slightest intention to criticise this book. Its reputation is made, and will stand as long as that of Scott's or Bulwer's Novels. The remarkable originality of its purpose, and the happy description it affords of American life and manners, still continue the subject of universal admiration. To say thus much is to say enough, though we must just mention that the new edition forms a part of Messrs Hurst and Blackett's Cheap Standard Library, which has included some of the very best specimens of light literature that ever have been written."—*Messenger.*

VOL. VIII.—CARDINAL WISEMAN'S RECOLLECTIONS OF THE LAST FOUR POPES.

"A picturesque book on Rome and its ecclesiastical sovereigns, by an eloquent Roman Catholic. Cardinal Wiseman has treated a special subject with so much geniality, that his recollections will excite no ill-feeling in those who are most conscientiously opposed to every idea of human infallibility represented in Papal domination."—*Athenæum.*

VOL. IX.—A LIFE FOR A LIFE.
BY THE AUTHOR OF "JOHN HALIFAX, GENTLEMAN."

"We are always glad to welcome Miss Mulock. She writes from her own convictions, and she has the power not only to conceive clearly what it is that she wishes to say, but to express it in language effective and vigorous. In 'A Life for a Life' she is fortunate in a good subject, and has produced a work of strong effect."—*Athenæum.*

VOL. X.—THE OLD COURT SUBURB. BY LEIGH HUNT.

"A delightful book, that will be welcome to all readers, and most welcome to those who have a love for the best kinds of reading."—*Examiner.*
"A more agreeable and entertaining book has not been published since Boswell produced his reminiscences of Johnson."—*Observer.*

VOL. XI.—MARGARET AND HER BRIDESMAIDS.

"We recommend all who are in search of a fascinating novel to read this work for themselves. They will find it well worth their while. There are a freshness and originality about it quite charming."—*Athenæum.*

VOL. XII.—THE OLD JUDGE. BY SAM SLICK.

"The publications included in this Library have all been of good quality; many give information while they entertain, and of that class the book before us is a specimen. The manner in which the Cheap Editions forming the series is produced deserves especial mention. The paper and print are unexceptionable; there is a steel engraving in each volume, and the outsides of them will satisfy the purchaser who likes to see books in handsome uniform."—*Examiner.*

VOL. XIII.—DARIEN. BY ELIOT WARBURTON.

"This last production of the author of 'The Crescent and the Cross' has the same elements of a very wide popularity. It will please its thousands."—*Globe.*

HURST AND BLACKETT'S STANDARD LIBRARY
(CONTINUED).

VOL. XIV.—FAMILY ROMANCE; OR, DOMESTIC ANNALS OF THE ARISTOCRACY.
BY SIR BERNARD BURKE, ULSTER KING OF ARMS.

"It were impossible to praise too highly this most interesting book. It ought to be found on every drawing-room table. Here you have nearly fifty captivating romances with the pith of all their interest preserved in undiminished poignancy, and any one may be read in half an hour."—*Standard.*

VOL. XV.—THE LAIRD OF NORLAW.
BY THE AUTHOR OF "MRS MARGARET MAITLAND."

"The Laird of Norlaw fully sustains the author's high reputation."—*Sunday Times.*

VOL. XVI.—THE ENGLISHWOMAN IN ITALY.

"We can praise Mrs Gretton's book as interesting, unexaggerated, and full of opportune instruction."—*The Times.*

VOL. XVII.—NOTHING NEW.
BY THE AUTHOR OF "JOHN HALIFAX, GENTLEMAN."

"'Nothing New' displays all those superior merits which have made 'John Halifax' one of the most popular works of the day."—*Post.*

VOL. XVIII.—FREER'S LIFE OF JEANNE D'ALBRET.

"Nothing can be more interesting than Miss Freer's story of the life of Jeanne D'Albret, and the narrative is as trustworthy as it is attractive."—*Post.*

VOL. XIX.—THE VALLEY OF A HUNDRED FIRES.
BY THE AUTHOR OF "MARGARET AND HER BRIDESMAIDS."

"We know no novel of the last three or four years to equal this latest production of the popular authoress of 'Margaret and her Bridesmaids.' If asked to classify it, we should give it a place between 'John Halifax' and 'The Caxtons.'"—*Herald.*

VOL. XX.—THE ROMANCE OF THE FORUM.
BY PETER BURKE, SERJEANT AT LAW.

"A work of singular interest, which can never fail to charm. The present cheap and elegant edition includes the true story of the Colleen Bawn."—*Illustrated News.*

VOL. XXI.—ADELE. BY JULIA KAVANAGH.

"'Adèle' is the best work we have read by Miss Kavanagh; it is a charming story full of delicate character painting."—*Athenæum.*

VOL. XXII.—STUDIES FROM LIFE.
BY THE AUTHOR OF "JOHN HALIFAX, GENTLEMAN."

"These 'Studies from Life' are remarkable for graphic power and observation. The book will not diminish the reputation of the accomplished author."—*Saturday Review.*

VOL. XXIII.—GRANDMOTHER'S MONEY.

"We commend 'Grandmother's Money' to readers in search of a good novel. The characters are true to human nature, the story is interesting, and there is throughout a healthy tone of morality."—*Athenæum.*

VOL. XXIV.—A BOOK ABOUT DOCTORS.
BY J. C. JEAFFRESON, ESQ.

"A delightful book."—*Athenæum.* "A book to be read and re-read; fit for the study as well as the drawing-room table and the circulating library."—*Lancet.*

HURST AND BLACKETT'S STANDARD LIBRARY
(CONTINUED).

VOL. XXV.—NO CHURCH.
"We advise all who have the opportunity to read this book. It is well worth the study."—*Athenæum*.

VOL. XXVI.—MISTRESS AND MAID.
BY THE AUTHOR OF "JOHN HALIFAX, GENTLEMAN."

"A good wholesome book, gracefully written, and as pleasant to read as it is instructive."—*Athenæum*. "A charming tale charmingly told. All the characters are drawn with life-like naturalness."—*Herald*. "The spirit of the whole book is excellent. It is written with the same true-hearted earnestness as 'John Halifax.'"—*Examiner*.

VOL. XXVII.—LOST AND SAVED.
BY THE HON. MRS NORTON.

"'Lost and Saved' will be read with eager interest. It is a vigorous novel."—*Times*. "A novel of rare excellence; fresh in its thought, and with a brave soul speaking through it. It is Mrs Norton's best prose work."—*Examiner*.

VOL. XXVIII.—LES MISERABLES. BY VICTOR HUGO.
AUTHORISED COPYRIGHT ENGLISH TRANSLATION.

"The merits of 'Les Misérables' do not merely consist in the conception of it as a whole; it abounds, page after page, with details of unequalled beauty. In dealing with all the emotions, doubts, fears, which go to make up our common humanity, M. Victor Hugo has stamped upon every page the hall-mark of genius."—*Quarterly Review*.

VOL. XXIX.—BARBARA'S HISTORY.
BY AMELIA B. EDWARDS.

"It is not often that we light upon a novel of so much merit and interest as 'Barbara's History.' It is a work conspicuous for taste and literary culture. It is a very graceful and charming book, with a well-managed story, clearly-cut characters, and sentiments expressed with an exquisite elocution. The dialogues especially sparkle with repartee. It is a book which the world will like. This is high praise of a work of art, and so we intend it."—*Times*.

VOL. XXX.—LIFE OF THE REV. EDWARD IRVING.
BY MRS OLIPHANT.

"A good book on a most interesting theme."—*Times*.
"A truly interesting and most affecting memoir. Irving's Life ought to have a niche in every gallery of religious biography. There are few lives that will be fuller of instruction, interest, and consolation."—*Saturday Review*.
"Mrs Oliphant's Life of Irving supplies a long-felt desideratum. It is copious, earnest, and eloquent. Irving, as a man and as a pastor, is exhibited with many broad, powerful, and life-like touches, which leave a strong impression."—*Edinburgh Review*.

VOL. XXXI.—ST OLAVE'S.
"This charming novel is the work of one who possesses a great talent for writing, as well as experience and knowledge of the world. 'St Olave's' is the work of an artist. The whole book is worth reading."—*Athenæum*.

VOL. XXXII.—SAM SLICK'S TRAITS OF AMERICAN HUMOUR.
"Dip where you will into this lottery of fun, you are sure to draw out a prize. These racy 'Traits' exhibit most successfully the broad national features of American humour."—*Post*.

www.ingramcontent.com/pod-product-compliance
Lightning Source LLC
Chambersburg PA
CBHW032026220426
43664CB00006B/384